THE LOST SHIP
SS WARATAH

Best wishes
to

Derek

BLUE ANCHOR LINE,
T.S.S. "WARATAH."

THE LOST SHIP SS WARATAH

SEARCHING FOR THE TITANIC OF THE SOUTH

P. J. SMITH

Frontispiece: A painting of the *Waratah*, showing the waratah flower after which she was named. (Courtesy of Andy Lee)

Cover images: Courtesy of B. Putt, Emlyn Brown, Andy Lee and P&O Dubai.

First published 2009

The History Press
The Mill, Brimscombe Port
Stroud, Gloucestershire, GL5 2QG
www.thehistorypress.co.uk

British Library Cataloguing in Publication Data.
A catalogue record for this book is available from the British Library.

ISBN 978 0 7524 5157 2

Typesetting and origination by The History Press
Printed in Great Britain

CONTENTS

The waratah flower. Photograph taken by Margaret Bradhurst and reproduced with kind permission. (Thanks also to Sutherland Group of the Australian Plant Society)

ACKNOWLEDGEMENTS

My thanks of course go to my editor for her patience with me as this project grew and grew and deadlines came and went. She understood its potential straightaway and has been supportive. Thank you Amy Rigg and crew at The History Press.

The inimitable Clive Cussler, who has for generations written breathtakingly about adventures at sea and whose interest in the SS *Waratah* is more than a passing curiosity, as his support for the dives to the bottom of the treacherous South African coast prove. His comments are most appreciated as is his contribution to the ongoing awakening of people's interest in this oft-forgotten part of maritime history.

Thanks to Bryan Putt for generously lending his grandfather's precious diary (Captain Putt of the SS *Wakefield*) and for lending Lieutenant Seymour's account, yet another primary source. He was also kind enough to lend me photographs. We are about equal in our ability to bore on the subject!

Thanks to Vincent Owen, who was contacted via Willa Owen by Greenwich Maritime Museum and kindly provided pictures and information relating to Captain Stanley Owen (captain of the SS *Sabine*), whose journal had been donated to Greenwich by his family. Owen was a fascinating character and I am grateful for both the pictures and anecdotes.

Emlyn Brown represents the modern-day search, using advanced equipment for detecting wreckage beneath the sea and backed by an equally dedicated team as they manoeuvred submersibles in the treacherous currents off the coast. Emlyn's passion remains intact and he is still dedicated to the *Waratah* and finding the missing pieces to the puzzle. His generosity in supplying photographs is very much appreciated.

I have been blessed with the most tenacious and experienced genealogist. I have known her for many years as a dear friend and she was the one I turned to for expert research. Thank you, Jean Elmer Gaisford, for burning the midnight oil, scouring every source and leaving no stone unturned to breathe life into these people, giving us an idea of who was travelling where and with whom. These stories include the axemen from Tasmania heading across the seas to perform their feats for the King and Queen of England, and the fascinating anecdote from a relative of one of the passengrs lost on board, who recounted that his great-grandmother had been planning to travel with a child whose life was saved, literally at the last minute, by his fearful mother who decided she would rather keep him with her. Interestingly, Jean herself had a relative who was a *Titanic* survivor. A friend of her grandmother's was not so lucky and he went down with the ship. Jean may be contacted at jeangaisford@sswaratah.com.

A big thank you also to Micheal Gaisford, Jean's husband, for his help and support.

Sir Robin Knox-Johnston, who was for a short time cadet on board my uncle's ship, was kind enough to allow me to use his quotes about Captain 'Dick' Smith's lifeboat adaptations. Sir Robin is a rare breed of true adventurer and one who commands respect naturally. Sir Robin, I thank you.

To Greenwich Museum, the UK Hydrography Department and friends at the Australian and South African Museums I say great 'thank you's. Your patience and kindness were beyond the call of duty! Your knowledge and willingness to help find the items required were just marvellous.

Thanks to Susie Cox at P&O Dubai for the pictures and directions to information.

Thanks to Andy Lee for his generous donations of information and pictures – Andy your time was about sharing and I am so grateful. Thanks to Jean and puppy Poppy for loaning you! Andy kindly supplied pictures of items in his private collection for this book; he may be contacted at trans.atlantique@virgin.net and is an extremely knowledgeable contact for those interested in this subject.

Thanks to Hans Helfenbein for his interesting information about Kerguelen Island, one of the most remote islands and one visited by the search party in 1910. His recent photographs are a bonus. To Anthony Hemy and the Hemy family, whose haunting paintings stir the emotions.

To David Hyatt of the Cusslermen for taking time and effort.

To Dr Stuart Kinsella, Research Advisor, Christ Church Cathedral, Dublin, for his kind help and interest; Mike Scott-Williams in South Africa and his excellent site Scotts End; Arthur Champkins in South Africa for his enthusiastic help; Jennifer Longstaff; Peter Searle of Canada; and J. Rose.

To Nic Klaassen, Flinders Ranges Research, South Australia, for his kind help and permission to use some information from his site, Flinders Ranges Research.

Not forgotten are the amazing friends who have had to endure my tedious deliveries on this material, and Alice and Libby for reminding me how to keep a childlike humour on it; for the patience of my dear son David who has, by now, had quite enough!

It has been my aim to put together a readable piece whilst avoiding pretence of expertise. The journals speak for themselves and are stories to relish and remember. There is so much to thank these authors for, but I particularly wish to thank them for making them so beautifully legible.

I hope you all enjoy the input from these ordinary people who found themselves in the midst of an extraordinary adventure, and that in joining them you too have a wonderful sea voyage.

INTRODUCTION

Mystery and myth are synonymous with the *Waratah* and her disappearance in 1909. She was certainly the Lost Ship but over time she was also to become the Forgotten Ship. Unlike the *Titanic*, whose disaster was to occur just three short years later and whose tragic story has long held people captivated, the *Waratah* remains a mystery very much along the lines of the *Marie Celeste*, a question mark permanently hanging over her name.

Within these pages I invite you to join the story of a ship and her 211 passengers and crew; a story of intrigue, fear, premonitions and a complete lack of substantial evidence, which left many families in a dreadful quandary wondering over the fate of their loved ones. Obviously thoughts of a quick and merciful end were preferable to those anxiously awaiting news, and yet there was hope the *Waratah* might be drifting and the searches at the time spent many months optimistically searching uninhabited islands in the belief there was a chance of finding her.

For many, the name *Waratah* itself means little, and yet at the time, July 1909, she was the daily subject of newspaper articles as three continents held their breath waiting for some news of their families aboard this beautiful cruise liner. In what was to be the longest continuous search for a missing ship, hope was held that she would be found. The previous disappearance of another ship and subsequent discovery in an almost identical position provided the template for the search teams and they were to venture way outside the shipping routes at that time, far south into the ice, finding uncharted reefs and graves of shipwrecked mariners, their memories recorded in journals which are both compelling and fascinating to read whilst also heartwrenchingly sad.

This book is the definitive guide to the three main searches for the *Waratah*, both on and beneath the waves. It offers the chance to read first-hand accounts of the two main sea searches by the SS *Sabine* and SS *Wakefield* a century ago as well as Emlyn Brown's modern account of his highly skilled underwater wreck searches, with the help of world-famous nautical adventure author Clive Cussler. All the accounts show a remarkable dedication and passion for their individual searches. The names of their authors are linked absolutely with the search for the liner and no story involving the *Waratah* would be complete without them.

⟹·◈·⟸

A thoroughly British ship, built in Glasgow, the *Waratah* – named after an Australian flower, the emblem of New South Wales – was on her second voyage on the run between England and Australia via South Africa, her maiden voyage having passed without major incident and her Lloyd's rating of 100 A1 being presumably well earned. Later, of course,

SS *Waratah*. (Courtesy of P&O Dubai)

her superiority was to be questioned, but for now all seemed well set for the future of the flagship of the Blue Anchor Line in the expanding and lucrative emigrant trade. On her second run she saw passengers embark at Sydney, Melbourne and Adelaide and also took on much cargo, as was the norm at that time. Trading was vital and an opportunity to bring cargo to South Africa and England from the land of plenty, Australia, was certainly a great run for the ship. These were not the dedicated cruise ships of today, rather dual-purpose cruise liners whose designs were perfectly suited to the trades they operated in. After filling the holds with goods, and boarding passengers and crew, she made the journey as far as Durban and then, between Durban and Cape Town, she vanished.

What could have happened? A freak wave? An underwater earthquake? Piracy? Speculation was rife as to what had befallen her and here the theories are examined. Bafflingly nothing has ever been positively and absolutely identified as originating from the *Waratah*, which in itself is remarkable, only one lifebuoy which popped up on a beach in New Zealand – in itself inconclusive as she certainly left nearby Australia – and which cannot be taken as wreckage at all.

At the time the world sat up shocked and stunned as no clues emerged and there was nothing to indicate the events of that night in 1909. There was even a rumour that Sir Arthur Conan Doyle held a séance in an attempt to assist in the search for the missing people. Certainly that particular coast is notoriously treacherous and it was said that no captain could take a ship around there without some misgivings. However, the *Waratah* had watertight compartments, splendid lines and the Blue Anchor Line's Commodore of the Fleet, one Josiah E. Ilbery, the most experienced man on the run to Australia in the world at that time, so it was assumed her safety would be assured.

Despite this, other ships – arguably far less stable ships – made it through the storms that night, hobbling into port little the worse for wear. When it finally dawned on the world that the ship and her passengers were not just caught up in stormy weather and were not about to arrive at Cape Town a little late, as others had that night, tugs were firstly sent out to see if she was within reach before being joined by the British Navy vessels HMS *Pandora*, HMS *Forte* and, later, HMS *Hermes*. They were sent off to track a possible drift had she been disabled in some way and swept away by the notorious current. It is a busy shipping area and yet no trace was found by anyone. Reports of bodies in the water were thoroughly investigated but eventually dismissed. Due to few ships having radio on board at the time, ships in the area were notified whilst in port or by signals to keep a lookout.

Eventually, of course, the British Navy ships had to return to their naval duties and it became apparent that far more extensive searches were required, so it was that two merchant ships, the SS *Sabine* and the SS *Wakefield*, were chartered by the Search Committee to visit the wildest seas in search of the lost ship and affect a possible rescue mission. They were to carry their own crew but be joined by a five-man Royal Naval contingent who would man the specially fitted searchlight and the primitive barrel tied to the mast as a makeshift crow's-nest for daylight hours' lookout. They were to be the landing party when arriving at remote islands.

——————◆——————

My interest was ignited in this project when I decided it was time to address a task which I had managed to ignore for many years: to sort and transcribe the family documents which had been kept by my father. He died in 1994 and in 2006 I started to catalogue and read the letters and reports of pilots on lost ships in 1806 and still more from 1854.

I discovered that a relative, Walter C. Smith, was aboard HMS *Hermes*, returning from Beira, when she joined HMS *Forte* and HMS *Pandora* ordered out to search. He was furthermore seconded to *both* subsequent searches. The eventual transcribing of his journal a few years ago was to spark an incredible passion about the subject for me. I was horrified that I had not even heard about the *Waratah* beyond family and even then very little – I had certainly never read about it. The story then grew beyond my wildest imagination as the material I had access to went from one journal to an incredible four! I had both ships' captain's journals and also that of the lieutenant from the SS *Wakefield*. As with any diary or personal account, each unique perspective and observation of the same event is wonderfully diverse and provides us with a rounded view of the unfolding story.

Walter's journal was written on flimsy Naval Signal paper on pitching ships but had stood the test of time and, in true Victorian style, the writing was beautiful. It reads with a desire to involve his family in his experience as though chatting over a pint of beer. It is an informal yet essential guide to the conditions they were enduring. He kept a wry view on it all, always looking for the humour in what must have been a gruelling experience.

——————◆——————

The investigation into the disappearance of the *Waratah* turned up many twists, turns and unexpected outcomes. The searches alone changed the face of charts at the time. Expert genealogist, Jean Gaisford, has unearthed some spellbinding histories and backgrounds about some forty of those on board, enabling us to build up something of a

SS *Waratah*. (Courtesy of P&O Dubai)

tableau of what it may have been like on the ship. Passengers hailed from Australia, South Africa and Great Britain; even in those days some passengers had property in two countries and would make regular trips between the two.

Known as the '*Titanic* of the South' or sometimes the 'Southern *Titanic*', the *Waratah*'s mystery is resurrected here. My aim is to bring her back into public awareness and ignite a renewed passion for her enigmatic story. Journey with the tenacious characters who risked everything attempting to track her down and bring peace to the minds of those who truly longed for it. It is thus only fitting that the *Waratah* now takes centre stage with all her opulence, magnificent elegance and dark secrets.

CHAPTER 1

THE BACKGROUND
TO A DISASTER

When the *Waratah* disappeared in 1909 the world was in the grip of massive changes, socially and economically. With greater need for change came greater inventions and minds to fill the gaps. With increased industrialisation in Europe there sprang up large cities and with them severe problems for those whose work was still in agriculture. The large cities were not the safe havens it had been hoped they would be, and as families packed up and moved to the cities it was often to a harsh and underpaid welcome where reality did not deliver the promise.

The notion of 'Health and Safety' was a long way in the future and many people were employed using dangerous equipment, working long, unhealthy hours at a time when complaint would not be well received – someone else would always be ready to take your job if you dared complain. The cities had expanded after the rapid growth in machinery, heralding the manufacturing era when items could be made en masse and the textiles industry offerred huge manufacturing potential for those with the means to set up the businesses.

The development of the bus and the train had changed the lives of people all over the world, offering greater choices and flinging people together whether they liked it or not. It was not until the invention of the motor car by Henry Ford that individual transport free of unsavoury company could be enjoyed.

Each country had their own requirement and solution to a greater or lesser extent, but the steam train rapidly become one of the greatest worldwide phenomenon; to this day trains transport vast amounts of people in a fast and direct fashion. Many found the speed of the first trains terrifying as they had no bends or hills to slow them down, initially a strange concept to grapple. Steam was the driving force behind this, also changing forever the face of the shipping industry. Steam had been utilised in shipping in various forms for some time by 1909.

The finding of natural deposits had a way of enforcing change. Australia had deposits of iron ore and gold and was racing ahead in an economical boom as a result, which in turn attracted immigrants to her shores. Iron ore was in massive demand for the manufacture of steel and iron, building bridges and for other industrial purposes, and of course gold was desired by everyone. These mining areas welcomed all workers, the towns constantly growing around the resources and the miners and their families in turn in need of all the usual merchants. The space and the associated health benefits promised by this new way of life were a magnet to people dissatisfied with their lot elsewhere and many took a leap in the dark, packing up to start a new life on the other side of the world, where they had never visited and almost certainly knew no one else

The tea clipper *Thermopylae*. (Courtesy of Greenwich Maritime Museum)

who had. Liverpool docks alone saw the mass of emigrants reach nine million; that represented a huge percentage of the population. Change was swift.

These people were risking everything, as emigration was by no means an easy option. The journey alone was one which all too often ended in death as ordinary emigrants were loaded into dormitories and left there for the duration of the crossing. When the journey was taken by sailing ship it would have been most uncomfortable as the ships were rarely upright and the crew more interested in getting there fast and being a good advertisement for their owners than worrying about the comfort of the passengers. Often the crew themselves were living in equally harsh conditions so would not have been overly sympathetic.

America and New Zealand were also favoured places for the Victorians and Edwardians looking to migrate. The towns there had similarly grown around gold and America was in her Progressive Period, heralding new cities around the gold resources alongside a still-prevalent agrarian society somewhat at odds with it all. This led to political unrest at a time when America was trying to put its past internal conflicts behind it and create stability and growth in order to establish a power base in the world.

Europe had also been in the midst of political uprisings, and in some cases rebellion. It was obvious that the paradigm had well and truly shifted and the changes were to have an effect on everyone.

It is a true statement that necessity is the mother of invention and certainly with the production of steam engines came greater manufacture. The huge iron bridges for the trains and the steam ships completely revolutionised the world's trading markets.

Sailing ships had been trading goods since before records began and the ancients had a marvellous system of boats, each area producing craft which fitted their exact requirements, as the schooners would do much later on. The trade would naturally dictate the type of ship needed, as would the waters they were crossing to trade.

Certainly one of the most romantic of the sailing ships is the magnificent clipper ship, combining speed and power with grace. It is said they were named thus as their aim was to clip time off the run home with the much-anticipated cargo. The clipper ship contests began in earnest when the Navigation Laws were repealed and this opened the way for other countries to have a share in the most renowned run of all for these beauties: the tea run from China. These tea ships were nicknamed the 'China birds' and they do carry a look of lightness about them. Competition was serious and ferocious. It was imperative that the goods were in the best condition when received and that they were unpacked quickly, but it went deeper than that. The owners wanted their ships to be the fastest and the crews were urged to bring them home with the utmost haste. This was in all probability quite enjoyed by some of the crews, who would wager with crews on competing ships on the outcome of the races. Other terms are used to describe these ships and whilst clipper ships mainly refer to the brief yet supreme reign of those racing ships with their cargo of tea, many others fall into different categories, such as tall ships, ships, brigs, brigantines, barques and barquentines.

Some of the clipper officers were less than kind and many earned themselves the name 'Bully' as prefix instead of Captain. One of these was so extreme he had two suicides on one trip. Crews could be beaten with sticks with nails in and frequently suffered ongoing cruelty; these were known as 'Hell Ships' and they were run by thuggish behaviour rather than a desire to teach seamanship.

Conversely there were the captains who took great pride in their ships and crew and in educating the youngsters on board on all things seamanlike. Some, such as the *Brenda* under Captain Learmont and the *Cimba* with Captain Holmes, would even take their wives and families along. Captain Shakespeare reputedly held birthday parties for the crew and allowed other apprentices on board the ship when in port. The captain's children would run around the deck and create a surrogate family for those who were far from home and often not prepared for the shock of a life at sea having come straight from family life. These ships were rare but at least they existed and would have been a wonderful experience. Men would take a job dockside just so that they could be first in the queue when these enlightened captains were signing on for their next voyages.

Clipper ships were running until around the 1930s and so would have been a common sight to those at sea in 1909. Steam ships, however, became more popular due to their constant speed and ability to provide a more elegant living space due to their demure, upright setting. Yet even they would have been thrown about in the treacherous waters off the Cape, where many a ship made its final voyage. However, the change was to herald a new era of shipping and the *Waratah*, one of the first of that class of new ship, offered much opulence and luxury for the few who could afford it. With the advent of the steam ship came the need for less hands, as the sailing ships needed many men to trim sails, be active on deck at all times ready to bring sails down, and be up the masts (and there would often be four or more masts to keep juggled). Of course on the liners there would be a demand for more cooks, stewards and pursers, so the shape of shipping with passengers was changing fast.

With the advent and rise of the long-distance steamer, the square riggers had to compete and to this end often had to remove some of the square sails, replacing them with the barque design, which held a few square sails and mizzen masts which were easier to manage and therefore required fewer men. Technically the purists would not call these barques but still define them as a 'ship' rig; nonetheless, generally they would be identified as a barque.

At the time of the searches for the *Waratah*, the horizons would have been a backdrop to a great variety of splendid ships all plying their trade in a colourful display. Work in port was hard and dangerous; the *Wakefield* captain reported a dock worker killed and another seriously injured as cargo fell when he was unloading just prior to her prolonged search. Sadly these types of incidents were not uncommon at the time due to a combination of lack of equipment and long hours, with ships often being delayed. Certainly on this occasion Captain Putt revealed that they had been working through the night offloading. There were never enough wagons to take the cargo, so valuable time was wasted creating dangerous conditions.

A couple of his crew also had to be left at the hospital with malaria, although we do not learn of their fate and it is to be hoped they recovered and signed on another ship. It was a tough life.

At the time of the *Waratah* searches P&O were not yet in the emigration business, but all that was to change when they took over the Lund Line's Blue Anchor fleet in the aftermath of the *Waratah*'s loss. P&O were rapidly expanding and had taken over the mail contract out to Australia following pressure from that quarter for mail deliveries to those now residing there, and this contract enabled their ships to use the Suez Canal, although this was an expensive route and most ships still went around via the Cape.

Schooners were still much in evidence and they have a special place in terms of ship design as they were built for their trade purpose and consequently vary greatly in their style; there is no one schooner design. Schooners were possibly named from the word 'schoon' or 'scoon'which means to move smoothly and quickly. Other definitions of schooners include topsail schooners, ketches, yawls, cutters, sloops and two-masted brigs as well.

The author Basil Greenhill quotes Joseph Conrad in *The Mirror of the Sea* as a perfect observation of the schooner and their rig:

The schooner *Robert Ingle Carter*. (Courtesy of Greenwich Maritime Museum)

A fleet of fore-and-afters at anchor has its own slender graciousness. The setting of their sails resembles more than anything else the unfolding of a bird's wings; the facility of their evolutions is a pleasure to the eye. They are birds of the sea, whose swimming is like flying, and resembles more a natural function than the handling of man-invented appliances. The fore-and-aft rig in its simplicity and the beauty of its aspect under every angle of vision is, I believe, unapproachable. A schooner, yawl or cutter in charge of a capable man seems to handle herself as if endowed with the power of reasoning and the gift of sweet execution. One laughs with sheer pleasure at a smart piece of manoeuvring, as at a manifestation of a living creature's quick wit and graceful precision.

The comparison of ships being likened to birds in flight, along the lines of the China birds, is a convincing one, as the sailing ships will silently glide by whereas there is little bird-like about a steam ship thundering away, belching out the smoke onto the horizon! They had a different glamour but less of the natural grace required in using the elements to transport around the globe.

Schooners were still in production as late as the 1920s and held their own niche markets as often their size and depth gave them a distinct advantage over even small steam ships in some areas. It is noted by Basil Greenhill that in the UK the three ships *Kathleen*, *May* and *Irene* were fully rigged three-masted schooners in business and trading until 1960. Schooners had to suit their trade, so for example there would have been fruit schooners and fish schooners, and they all had to adapt to the ports they traded in. With these trades the time spent in loading and unloading was key to the state of the cargo on arrival and therefore having a fast loading and small cargo was essential to keeping the goods fresh. More ships employed with smaller loads made viable trade.

For a point of interest, there are some beautiful pictures of these and other sailing ships on classic sailing websites and they truly highlight the magnificence of these great beauties. In fact there are still square rigged ships around today, used mainly as training ships for groups, but some run races where they may be observed in all their glory.

One of the most remarkable examples was the American *Wyoming*, carrying six identical-sized masts with the classic schooner rig. Sadly she ran ashore in 1924. So successful was the schooner rig that *Wyoming* was built in the same year the *Waratah* disappeared, despite the increased interest in highly developed ship designs in 1909. These ships would have been very busy yet, somewhat unbelievably, an enormous ship such as this would have a complement of just twelve hands.

Two-masted ships tended to be referred to as 'brigs' and another small schooner with a slightly altered rig was a 'snow'. 'Topsail' schooners were identified by their square topsail as an addition to the schooner rig.

So at this time a vast array of vessels were busy with their trades, cutting through the seas to and from exotic lands and quite often bringing treasures back with them, so many items we take for granted now.

Walter Smith would have found it a challenge moving from the flagship HMS *Hermes* to a merchant ship with a small crew battling the elements. It was to be a mercy mission, of course, and so the appalling conditions were not uppermost in their minds; discovering the whereabouts of the ship with her crew and passengers – hopefully safe – was the crew's driving force. Their story unfolds…

Chapter 2

SS Waratah

SS *Waratah* was built for the Blue Anchor Line by one of Scotland's most prolific ship-builders, Messrs Barclay, Curle & Co., responsible for some of the most inspiring commissions of the time. The company started with John Barclay in 1818 and was later run by his sons, Thomas and Robert Barclay. In 1844 two new partners joined – Robert Curle and James Hamilton – and the company evolved into Robert Barclay & Curle, moving to Whiteinch Yard in 1855. In 1863 the ship-builders was renamed to become the company that was to be synonymous with fine ships, Barclay, Curle & Co.

This ship-building firm had already built two ships previously for Blue Anchor, the *Commonwealth* in 1902 and *Geelong* in 1904, bringing the fleet – including *Waratah* – up to six altogether, with *Waratah* the twentieth ship owned by Blue Anchor. It is noteworthy that the quotation from Barclay, Curle & Co. was not the cheapest they considered, illustrating that Blue Anchor did not cut corners.

The *Waratah* was launched in 1908. She was an impressive 9,339-ton, twin-screw, coal-fired ship which Lloyd's had passed with flying colours, pronouncing her 100A1 – absolutely the finest rating a ship could have bestowed upon her, such was the confidence in her design and build. In fact, she was constructed to a similar plan as that for her sister-ship *Geelong*, which had proved highly successful; built in 1904, *Geelong* was nearly 8,000 tons with a speed of around 12 knots.

Waratah was to be the flagship of the Blue Anchor Line and her future was assured; she had been specifically designed for the popular dual-purpose travel requirements, comprising an outward journey carrying emigrant passengers and a return journey holding cargo including skins, iron ore and all the goods which Australia had in abundance. Huge amounts of meat and butter were also loaded as she was a refrigerated cargo ship and took fresh produce, so unlike the present passenger ships dedicated purely to the transportation service or recreation; these ships were an essential resource for world trade.

She was built to appease the ever-increasing demand for emigrant travel, which had been an expanding trade for some time. The clipper ships had transported many to the favoured countries of Australia, America, Canada and South Africa, often in appalling conditions frequently resulting in higher numbers of deaths than occurred among the convicts who were transported before them.

Waratah was to carry passengers from London out to Australia via South Africa, calling at Adelaide, Melbourne and Sydney, load on cargo and coal at those ports, and then return with far fewer passengers but thousands of tons of cargo. Along with meat and butter, she also carried tallow, skins and far more which we will detail later. It was stated that she had capacity for nearly 15,000 tons of coal and cargo. She was 500ft long, 59ft broad (beam), with a depth of 38ft and a speed of around 13 knots. That is not significantly fast compared to say the clipper ships, which were known to notch up around 18

Waratah. (Courtesy of P&O Dubai)

Luxurious drawing room. (Courtesy of Emlyn Brown)

Third class dining room. (Courtesy of Emlyn Brown)

Third class smoke room. (Courtesy of Emlyn Brown)

knots, but the fact was that she could sustain that speed relentlessly, whereas the clippers were dependent on the prevailing elements.

Waratah had sufficient lifeboats and rafts to rescue 921 people, should there have been the time to launch them. In this she differed dramatically from the *Titanic*, which famously had far too few lifeboats, a major factor in the terrible events that followed. However, *Waratah* was built with watertight compartments (something she did share with *Titanic*), which supposedly rendered her 'unsinkable', and confidence in her was high. A few 'firsts' were introduced in the *Waratah* design, including the first ocean-travel nursery – a room dedicated to the needs of the many children who would find themselves on board for weeks, clearly a popular move forward. She also had high promenade decks and covered deck areas which allowed the passengers protection whilst they enjoyed the sea air.

Ships of the standard of *Waratah* offered a vastly improved service even for the emigrant passengers, who were, however, still crammed into dormitory accommodation. Her maiden voyage saw her carrying a record number of emigrant passengers, nearing 700. Their dormitory accommodation was lower down in the ship, leaving the above decks for the first class passengers who enjoyed well-appointed cabins and saloons which were plush and expensively fitted out. There were smoking rooms and ladies' rooms, all of these public areas hives of activity providing the opportunity for company and entertainment.

There was no second class on the *Waratah*, and third class rooms were rather more austere. Nonetheless, the third class smoke room was certainly far from primitive and would have been a place to meet and compare stories on the unusual behaviour of the ship. There were fated to be many such conversations in the social rooms of the *Waratah*.

Another result from the events surrounding the *Waratah* was the inspiration for the British Government's initiative to have all passenger and large cargo vessels fitted with wireless equipment, as the ability to send a distress call could have made all the difference that night. Had she drifted, of course, then the wireless would have been her lifeline, and in fact she was scheduled to be fitted with wireless in London upon her return. It was to be the 1930s before this finally became law after resistance from many shipping quarters, presumably due to the cost. The legislation is often attributed to the *Titanic* but of course she was fitted with Marconi wireless equipment and it has been well documented that she was in busy communication on her fateful night.

Captain Ilbery was the Line's most experienced captain, as befitted the demands of the *Waratah*'s route plan and the leading design of the ship, and in fact he was very much involved in running the Lund Line, to which Blue Anchor belonged. There was great mutual professional respect between the Lund family and their leading captain. Ilbery was the most seasoned captain of the time with the widest knowledge of Australian crossings. He was also recognised by the US government for the rescue of the *Grace Clifton* and later he rescued the crew of the *SS Koning der Nederlanden*, so he earned himself quite a reputation. Born Josiah Edward Ilbery in the British port of Liverpool in 1840, in 1857 he was indentured to Liverpool company Prowse & Co. and apprenticed to Captain John Fowler on board the sailing ship *Joshua*. Their alliance was to withstand a change of ship when they both transferred to the *Nourmahal* in 1862, still with the same company. That ship was to see him elevated to the rank of mate within a short time – it was a sign of his skill and learning that he had risen so quickly and would have been in no small way thanks to his commander. He first commanded the *Mikado* in 1868 for Walker & Co., having also supervised the building of his new ship. This experience was to lead to him being respon-

Captain Ilbery, Commodore of the Blue Anchor fleet and captain of the SS *Waratah*. (Courtesy of Greenwich Maritime Museum)

sible for new ships and taking their maiden voyages, and he was in the perfect position to then notice any imperfections or subtle issues which could later become more pronounced.

Lund brought *Mikado* from Walker & Co. and Lund and Ilbery were to start a professional alliance which was to last for forty years and see Ilbery become as much a manager of the shipping company as he was a commander. Ilbery was to command several ships of the sailing fleet, after which he oversaw the building of *Delcomyn*, Lund's first steamer. In order to acquire the vast number of necessary skills for the transition from sail to steam, Ilbery was seconded to *Ocean King*, a steamer belonging to W. Ross & Co., where he quickly mastered the qualities needed and went on to take ships for Lund on the Australian run. Lund was to choose Aboriginal names for these ships and even *Commonwealth* was named for Australia; the ships comprised *Yeoman, Hubbuck, Woolloomooloo, Warrambool, Narrung, Wilcannia, Commonwealth, Geelong* and *Waratah*.

Lund had other ships in his fleet over the years, believed to include *Bungaree, Culgoa, Echuca, Murrumbidgee, Riverina, Wakool, Wallarah, Warrigal, Yarrawonga* and *Yeoman*.

Wilhelm Lund founded the company in London in 1869, quickly directing his attention on the Australian run and commissioning his first steam ship in 1890. This was to be the run which made Captain Ilbery the most experienced commander at that time, rising to Commodore of the Fleet. He was without question the most trusted captain for this run, and taking into account his vast experience in overseeing ship-building, he would have had a keen eye for any small and seemingly insignificant behaviour from any of his ships, a familiarity not often shared between ships and officers. This knowledge makes it all the more unthinkable that something might have been wrong with the *Waratah* and gone unnoticed or been ignored.

Lund was the owner of one of the most prestigious shipping companies in Britain and had proved himself aware of the changing fortunes in ocean transport when he moved from clippers to steam and Australasian destinations. He was a man of considerable standing in the merchant fleet community, a trustee with Lloyd's and, somewhat remarkably, chairman of the Bank of Adelaide. Quite a noteworthy achievement for a man who had a sail loft on the Thames – he had clearly made prudent business decisions at the crucial times.

Lund's Sailing Fleet

Talavera	1853	—
Jeddo	1865	Walker & Co., Rotherhithe
Eleanor	1867	—
Mikado	1868	Walker & Co.
Ambassador	1869	Walker & Co.
Serapis	—	Scott & Co.
Ella	1873	—
Harland	1885	—

Points of Interest on Lund's Steam Fleet – Blue Anchor Line

As noted on the previous page, Blue Anchor Line ships were many and here are a few details on just a few of them. *Narrung* was a 400ft, 5,078-ton ship with quadruple expansion engines, built by Sunderland S.B. Co. Ltd in 1896. Interestingly this ship, under the command of Captain A.W. Bond RNR, left Sydney on 20 April 1902 with excited passengers making the voyage to see the coronation of King Edward VII, a remarkable event considering Queen Victoria had ruled for sixty-four years. This was an historically momentous occasion and these people undertook a massive journey so that they could be there to savour the moment. It must, therefore, have been something of a shock when Captain Bond went to the assistance of another ship – the stricken *Boveric* – and towed her to safety to Fremantle. It would be fair to assume that Captain Bond did not find favour for his heroic deed and that he had to suffer the admonishments of his 150 disappointed passengers. As it turned out all was not lost, as King Edward suffered an illness and had to undergo surgery which set the coronation back to 9 August; Captain Bond would, I am sure, have been more than a little relieved.

Wakool was the second of the Blue Anchor ships at 5,004 tons, built in 1898 by Sunderland again. She was also 400ft in length and had triple expansion engines. An interesting anecdote regarding the *Wakool* recalls Captain Putt making mention of passing her on his way out to South Africa, completely unaware that he was about to embark upon a search for a ship within the same company. They exchanged the customary signals.

Commonwealth was the fourth ship for Blue Anchor and the first by Barclay, Curle & Co. Ltd, coming in at 6,611 tons, 450ft, triple expansion engines and the first twin screw of the fleet. She was launched in 1902. She was also to be caught up in a problem hot on the heels of sister-ship *Waratah* when she was delayed two weeks out of Sydney after a coal strike and was then held up again in Fremantle. This meant a change of schedule for Blue Anchor and another ship had to take her place during the difficult time when the *Waratah* was missing. It would have been catastrophic for the Lund family, who had put so much into their outstanding fleet of ships. *Commonwealth* made the final Blue Anchor sailing in 1910 and then sailed for P&O's newly named Branch Service, which was to be their first move into emigration travel.

Geelong was a 7,954-ton ship of 450ft length, delivered by Barclay, Curle & Co. Ltd in 1904. She was a twin screw ship with triple expansion engines.

Actually outliving her sister-ship, *Geelong* was bought by P&O for £88,426 in May 1910 from the disillusioned Lund family. She ran further trips to Australia and was converted to

Left SS *Geelong*. (Courtesy of P&O Dubai)

Below SS *Waratah*. (Courtesy of P&O Dubai)

carry 700 third class passengers only, this emigrant trade being a new departure for P&O at the time. She ended her career in the Mediterranean in January 1916 following a collision with British ship *Bonvilston* en route from Sydney to Gibraltar and London via Port Said, carrying a mixed cargo including tea and lead. Her crew were rescued. Ironically *Geelong* was intended to be known as the *Australia* but her name was changed as P&O already had a ship of that name and wanted to avoid confusion. Little did they know that P&O would own her in the future. *Geelong* and *Waratah* were named in honour of the Antipodean route they were built to serve, Geelong being a place in Australia and the waratah a flower, the emblem of New South Wales.

Waratah's maiden voyage passed without major incident, although there was a fire which took three hours to extinguish and an unscheduled coaling. *Waratah* created quite a stir with her high promenade deck and her single funnel with the distinctive angled blue anchor denoted on it. It would be interesting to see her against the vast multi-storey ships today which really do look top-heavy to the uninformed (such as the author!). She left for Australia from London on 6 November 1908 and called at St Vincent and Cape Town, finally arriving at Adelaide on 15 December. She then called at Melbourne, reaching her final Australian destination, Sydney, on Christmas Eve. One can try and imagine the excitement as families were reunited or emigrants started their new lives in unfamiliar surroundings. After so long at sea they would have taken time to adjust to land again as even hardy sailors do. The ship's load was 8,369 tons of mixed cargo and bunkers.

She left Sydney for her return journey on 9 January 1909, calling at Melbourne, Adelaide, and on this trip but not the next, Albany; she went onwards to Durban, then Cape Town, arriving at London on 7 March. She was dry-docked and given a clear survey by Lloyd's.

This trip was proof indeed that the ship was worthy of the title 'flagship' of the Blue Anchor Line and many more sucessful trips would have been anticipated.

SS *Waratah*. (Courtesy of P&O Dubai)

Her second, ill-fated journey began in London on 27 April, where she took on board nearly 200 passengers. Her ports were Adelaide, 6 June, where around forty disembarked, and then Sydney, arriving on 17 June, where the remainder left the ship. Again, no serious problems were officially identified.

On the return journey, she left Sydney on 26 June, had a longer call at Melbourne, 28 June–1 July, arriving in Adelaide on 2 July. Leaving Adelaide for Durban she had a total of eighty-two passengers and 6,665 tons of cargo. Her cargo was mixed and later the nature of her cargo was identified as a possible theory for her loss. She was carrying oats, wool, flour, skins, leather, meat, tallow, rags, furniture, sheepskins, butter, rabbit, mutton, 1,000 tons of lead concentrate, 300 tons of lead and 200 tons of timber.

Her trip to Durban was uneventful and some good weather was enjoyed by the passengers on the high promenade deck. When she arrived in Durban on Sunday 25 July she was actually a day ahead of her schedule, which would have been most exciting.

At this stage there were the rumblings of things amiss from some of the passengers and talk was growing of the ship's listing to one side or the other. Extraordinarily, one man actually left the ship claiming he had experienced a premonition so powerful he could not remain on board a moment longer. This man was Claude G. Sawyer, a seasoned traveller whose engineering work took him all over the world. It seems he was unsettled by dreams of a man brandishing a bloodied sword and calling the name *Waratah*. Some of the details change slightly at the Inquiry, but the facts remain irrefutable; he left the ship proclaiming her unsafe and she indeed disappeared.

Captain Ilbery was already sixty-nine years old at this point and it is thought that this journey was intended to be his last. He would have taken the new ship on the round trip twice and declared her safe to perform the task of safely transporting passengers and cargo across the world. Later there would be speculation about the safety of the lost ship, but I believe it would be an error to suggest that the captain would allow the passage of a ship which he found unseaworthy. Captain Ilbery was the backbone of the shipping line he loved and had devoted his career to.

The last confirmed sighting of the *Waratah* was on 27 July at around 6.00 a.m., when she was spotted by the *Clan McIntyre*. From that point onwards she can be considered missing, with the mournful ringing of the Lutine Bell at Lloyds confirming this fear on 15 December 1909.

CHAPTER 3

PASSENGERS AND CREW

It took time, patience and a lot of work by an excellent genealogist to unearth the following details on the passengers and crew of the *Waratah*. I am confident that the information that follows is the definitive research on the people who were lost aboard the ship. A full list of all passengers and crew appears at the end of this chapter.

The Passengers

BLACK, Niel Walter was forty-one years old when he boarded the ship in Melbourne. He was the son of Niel and Grace Greenshields Black, *née* Leadbetter. As there are two Niel Blacks, I have identified the gentleman who was aboard *Waratah* as Niel Walter.

His father Niel was born in Argyllshire, Scotland, in 1804 the son of Archibald, a tenant farmer to the Duke of Argyll, and Janet. Archibald was tragically killed when he fell from his horse in 1808, leaving a widow and eight young children. His mother Grace was born in Scotland in 1833, the daughter of John, a merchant, and Janet Leadbetter *née* Hutton. She married Niel Black at the end of 1856 in the County of Warwickshire, England.

Niel emigrated to Australia in 1839 and finally settled in Victoria, where he bought stock and land. He built a grand property near Lake Terang which he named Glenormiston and was said to have been the most successful stock breeder of his time. This imposing mansion is now an agricultural college. He entered political life in 1859 when elected a member for the Western Province to the Victorian Legislative Council, a position he held until his death.

The first royal visitor to Australia in 1867 was Alfred Ernest Albert, the Duke of Edinburgh, second son of Queen Victoria, and he was the guest of Niel Black and his family at Glenormiston.

Glenormiston. (Courtesy of Glenormiston College, agricultural and equine college, Australia)

Niel later moved to Mount Noorat and built another house where he died in 1880 leaving a widow and three sons, Archibald John, Stuart Gladstone and Niel Walter. A new Presbyterian church was erected in Noorat in 1883 as a memorial to Niel Black.

There is a Niel Walter Black fund and donations have been bequeathed to the University of Melbourne since his death in 1909. In 1961 a book was published called *Men of Yesterday* by Margaret Kiddle in which she tells of a settler called Niel Black.

BROWNE, Colonel Percival John was born in South Australia around 1863, the son of William James Browne and Mary *née* Nixon. William James Browne was a qualified surgeon who had studied in Paris and was an early settler arriving in Australia in 1839. The family was originally from Wiltshire, England.

William James turned to sheep farming, exporting his wool to England, and was also involved in politics, representing Flinders in the House of Assembly from 1860–62.

The family returned to England in the 1860s and in 1871 they were living in Cheltenham, Gloucestershire, with six servants in attendance. By 1881 they were living in Kensington, London, this time with ten servants.

In 1880 William James bought Buckland House, Buckland Filleigh, in Devon and this huge property employed a butler, two footmen, a coachman/groom, a cook, two housemaids, two kitchen maids, a scullery maid and a 'whipper in', the huntsman's assistant. The estate stayed in the family until 1942.

Percival John was an army man and in 1891 he was a lieutenant in the Cavalry and Artillery Barracks in Colchester, Essex. He saw action in the South African War and was mentioned in dispatches.

William James, the father of Col. Browne. (Courtesy of The State Library of Australia, Image B10844)

He married Bernarda Gracia Lees in 1892, the daughter of Thomas Evans Lees, a wealthy cotton-spinning manufacturer of Oldham. A Miss K. Lees also boarded in Adelaide with a maid, Miss L. Cook, and it is very likely that she was a relative of his wife.

He had six siblings and his younger brother, Arthur Scott Browne, was a captain in the Yeomanry Cavalry. Arthur was also deputy-lieutenant for the County of Devon.

The family retained the sheep farm in South Australia at Mount Gambier and Percival was on his way home after visiting South Australia in 1909.

A brass plaque was erected in Sherborne Abbey by the Dorset Imperial Yeomanry to the memory of Lieutenant-Colonel Browne, their former commander.

CAMPBELL, Miss Margaret was twenty-five and from Noorat, Victoria.

CARRICK, Dr J.T. boarded the ship in Durban bound for London. He was a South African mining expert.

CLARK, Alfred was twenty-eight years old and a bricklayer by trade. He boarded the ship in Melbourne bound for London. He was also a champion axeman from Tasmania

Blue Anchor advertisement. (Courtesy of Andy Lee)

and was coming to England to perform his chopping skills in front of the King and Queen. The first world wood-chopping championship was held in November 1891 at Latrobe, Tasmania, and in 1905 Alfred was the champion. The sport of wood chopping had started around 1870 and soon spread throughout Australia. Alfred must have been a big man as he had a new pair of boots made especially for the trip – he took a size 14.

CONNOLLY, Honora (Nora) *née* Power boarded the ship in Durban through to London. She was from Tipperary, Ireland, the daughter of Mary Power, and had emigrated to Australia around 1889. She married Patrick Connolly in Sydney NSW in 1892. They later went to South Africa where Patrick was killed in a mining accident in 1908. Nora was returning to Ireland with her husband's ashes accompanied by Patrick's sister Miss Connolly. Nora had sent £1,300 to her bank in London to await her arrival and her mother Mary was to be granted this sum in probate.

COOTE, William boarded the ship in Durban bound for London.
A William Coote left England aged twenty-three for Cape Town on 3 December 1902 on board the *Whatatane* listed as a clerk. Is this the same William Coote who was born in Pimlico and was a clerk in England returning home to visit his widowed mother Sarah Ann Coote? It would certainly seem likely.

DAWES, Mary Jane Elizabeth *née* Donaldson was about sixty when she boarded the ship in Durban. She was the daughter of John Malcolm Donaldson and Sarah King and the grand-daughter of Andrew (Captain) Donaldson. The Donaldson family were originally from Scotland and had settled in South Africa in the 1840s. Mary was first married to William John Terry in 1870 at Bloemfontein and they had five daughters and two sons. They divorced in 1884 and she married Edward William Dawes in 1885 in Maritzburg. Divorce in those days meant that a woman lost her children and custody went to the husband; usually the mother never saw them again.
Mary was a lifelong member of the Seventh Day Adventists.

Mary Dawes in pork pie hat. (Courtesy of
Arthur Champkins)

Mary Dawes (seated), when she was Donaldson,
with her two sisters, Henrietta and Sarah Jane.
(Courtesy of Arthur Champkins)

A child is mentioned on the passenger list with Mary but there is no conclusive proof
as to the identity of this child. A lovely story has been related by Mary's great-grandson
Arthur Champkins, describing the child as a little boy of a year old to whom Mary was
being kind by taking him to Scotland for a holiday. His mother Eva was not well and
had other children to look after and Mary thought it would help the family if the little
boy went on the trip with her. Once his mother saw him being taken up the gangway
she changed her mind and rushed to take him back from Mary's arms, sobbing that she
could not bear to be parted from him. Whilst this story cannot be proven now, it could
well be correct and if so the child listed with Mary, believed to be Malcolm Donaldson's
grandson, was saved.

DAY, Stanley was a passenger (number 3074) on the *Waratah* on her maiden voyage,
leaving for Adelaide on 5 November 1908. He was a mechanical engineer going to
Australia to start a new life. Twenty years after the loss of the *Waratah* the landlady where
Stanley Day had been boarding recalled him telling her that he had talked to the engineers on the *Waratah* and one of them had remarked that he thought the *Waratah* would
end up sinking in heavy seas, saying that she was top heavy.

DONALDSON, Malcolm was born in 1838 in Scotland the son of Andrew (Captain)
Donaldson and Elizabeth Johnston. He married Adelaide Sibthorp in Glasgow in
1875 and they had one son and two daughters. He was a cousin of Mary Dawes (*née*
Donaldson) mentioned above. Malcolm worked for the South African Government as
overseer in the Public Works Department in Natal.

The Donaldson family had already had one tragedy befall them in 1896 when Mary's brother Alexander Edward King Donaldson was a passenger on board the British steam cruise ship *Drummond Castle* which sank near Ushant off the coast of France with the loss 245 lives; only three people survived, saved by French fishermen who were rewarded with medals and money for their bravery. It is believed the ship ran into a bad storm and hit rocks, as she sank within three minutes, with no time to lower the lifeboats. Alexander Donaldson had been on his first trip to England, going with the purpose of floating a Free State gold property on his discovery in the Orange River Colony. He was engaged to marry Isabella Boyd, who later married his brother Stephen.

Unlike the *Waratah*, the wreck of the *Drummond Castle* was discovered in 1929 quite by accident by an Italian salvage crew looking for a different ship.

Malcolm Donaldson with his wife Charlotte and children Francis and Elizabeth. (Courtesy of Arthur Champkins)

Within the space of thirteen years the Donaldson family had lost three members in the same tragic circumstances.

EBSWORTH, John Frederick was forty-five when he boarded the ship in Melbourne, Australia, the son of William and Jane *née* Price. A solicitor, he married Sarah Jane Cherry in 1892 in Melbourne, where they resided. They had six children, John, born 1894, Reginald William, born 1896, Marguerite Louise, born 1899, Violet Rosina, born 1901, Alfred Colin, born 1905, and Frank Edwin, born 1907. His wife gave evidence at the Board of Trade Inquiry in London.

HAY, Agnes Grant *née* Gosse boarded the ship in Adelaide. She was born in 1837, the daughter of Dr William Gosse and Agnes *née* Grant. She had a sister Mary and brothers David Grant, William Christie, Henry and Charles, and before they left for South Australia in 1850 they resided in a house in the High Street, Hoddeson, Hertfordshire. Her brother William Christie was a surveyor and at the age of thirty he was appointed by the South Australian government to open up a route from Central Australia to Perth. In 1873 he was sent to the Northern Territory to map a route from the just completed Overland Telegraph Line at Alice Springs to Perth, and it was at this time that he discovered and named Ayres Rock, in honour of Sir Henry Ayres, the Chief Secretary of Australia. He later wrote, 'this is certainly the most wonderful natural feature I have ever seen.' In 1875 he became Deputy Surveyor General.

Agnes Grant Gosse married Alexander Hay, a widower, in 1872, and they had four children, Gertrude Agnes Gosse, born 1873, Alexander Gosse, born 1874, William Gosse, born 1875, and Helen Gertrude Gosse, born 1877.

Above Mount Breckan, the rebuilt home of Alexander and Agnes Hay. (Courtesy of Nic Klaassen, Flinders Ranges Research)

Left Agnes and Alexander Hay. (Courtesy of Nic Klaassen, Flinders Ranges Research)

Alexander Hay was born on 12 January 1820 in Dunfermline, Fife, Scotland, the son of Peter and Susan Thomson, and he had a brother Robert and sisters Helen and Susan. He left Scotland at the age of nineteen and arrived in Port Adelaide on 15 May 1839. He married Agnes Kelly in 1845 and their daughter Agnes was to marry William Christie Gosse in 1874. Alexander was widowed in 1870.

On a visit to England in the 1880s Alexander was presented to Queen Victoria and Prince Albert. He entered political life and was a member of Parliament for many years, retiring in 1890. He was a well-known and respected man and by all accounts a gener-ous one, as he offered £20,000 towards the building of a Scotch College in Adelaide.

He bought a block of land of 160 acres in Victor Harbour, South Australia, in the early 1870s and together with his second wife decided to build a house which over-looked the sea. The foundations for Mount Breckan were laid in April 1879 and in early 1881 Alexander and his famiy moved in. Alexander died in 1898.

In 1908 Mount Breckan was destroyed by fire. The property was acquired and rebuilt as the Mount Breckan Cub, a high class guesthouse. After another two ownerships the property was bought in 1996 by the Baron and Baroness of Ballintober, who have restored it to its former glory.

Helen Gertrude was travelling with her mother on that fateful voyage, and it has been said that Agnes took the family jewels with her, including a tiara. They boarded the *Waratah* in Adelaide and a Miss M. Hesketh Jones, aged twenty-five, was travelling with them as a companion. It would seem that Agnes was no stranger to the *Waratah* as she and her daughter were passengers on her maiden voyage from England in 1908. In fact they made several voyages to England, travelling on to Scotland. Agnes was well known in the Dunfermline area of her husband's birthplace. She was on board the *Geelong* (sister-ship to the *Waratah*) in 1904 bound for London and again on the *Geelong* going back to Adelaide in 1905. In April 1892 she was on board *Oceana* arriving in London with Helen and her son Alexander Gosse, who was listed as a student. Her son

William received letters from Durban in 1909 telling him how satisfactory they found the *Waratah* and they were most complimentary about the officers.

In 1899 Agnes Hay wrote the book *Footprints: A Memoir of the late Alexander Hay, one of the Fathers and Early Colonists of South Australia.*

HENDERSON, Miss boarded the ship in Sydney. She was twenty-five years old and the daughter of George Henderson of Forfar, Scotland. She had been working as a lady's maid in New Zealand and was travelling with the family back to Forfar.

HUNTER, James was forty-nine years old and boarded the ship in Sydney bound for London. He was from Troon, Ayrshire, Scotland, married with a son living in New South Wales. He was going to Australia hoping to settle there with his son and then send for his wife and family. He was a house painter/furnisher who had sold his business in Troon for his new life; unfortunately upon arriving in Australia he found that trade there was not good and he decided to return home three months later.

LASCELLES, Miss Laura E. was thirty and from Geelong, Victoria.

MURPHY, Miss Bridget was twenty-five and from Footscray, Victoria.

PAGE, Ernest B. was thirty-four, an agent from Collingwood, Victoria.

SAWYER, Claude Gustav left the ship in Durban having experienced a vivid dream of the *Waratah* going down in heavy seas. He was a seasoned traveller who obviously took this to be a premonition he could not ignore. He was to recount his dream many times and was called to give evidence at the official Board of Inquiry.

Claude was born in Vevey, Switzerland, on 14 November 1852 to George Cappalen Sawyer and Mary Rebecca *née* Wilhouse. He married Emeline Alexandrina Dickson in 1883 and a son Claude Patrick was born in 1891. Claude was a man of substance and in the 1901 census he was living in Brunswick Road, Hove, Sussex, his occupation being 'Director of Companies'. In 1891 he was listed as 'living on own means' in Howard Square, Eastbourne, Sussex, and ten years previously he lodged in Hanover Square, when his occupation was 'Gentleman'.

He eventually left Durban for Cape Town, where he took a first class passage on board the *Galician*, arriving in Southampton on 9 September 1909. His family must have been overjoyed that he had left the ship when he did.

At the Board of Inquiry he gave evidence that he had heard passengers complaining about the ship's behaviour. He told of Mrs Caywood, who fell and hurt her arms and hip and was taken off the ship in an invalid chair when they arrived at Durban. He further stated that Dr Fulford and Miss Lascelles also suffered injuries when the ship gave strange jerks even though the sea was calm.

He told several people of his intention to leave once they arrived in Durban as he was not happy with the ship – he mentioned his disturbing dream to fellow passenger John Ebsworth who thought it must be a warning, although Mr Ebsworth decided to remain on the ship. He tried to persuade Mrs Agnes Hay and her daughter Helen to leave the ship at Durban but they too chose to ignore his warnings. It is probably true to

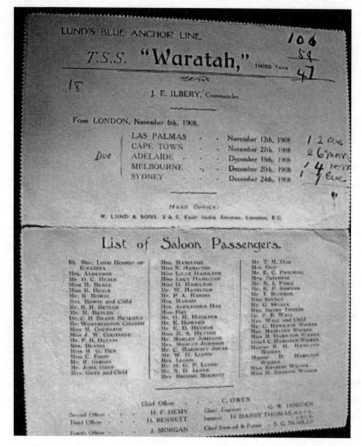

Maiden voyage
saloon class
and officer list.
(Courtesy of Andy
Lee)

say that no one believed him. Claude Gustav Sawyer was a very lucky man and lived for many years, dying in 1925. Thankfully the £1,000 life assurance he had taken with the Royal Exchange was not to be paid to his widow in 1909.

STARKE, Mrs Elizabeth Jemima *née* Mattingley was sixty years old when she boarded the *Waratah* in Melbourne. She married Dr Anthony George Hayden Starke in 1869 in Melbourne and was widowed in 1877. She was born in Berkshire, the daughter of John Thomas Mattingley, a brewer, and Elizabeth Anne. She resided in Malvern, Victoria, with her daughter Bessie Mattingley Starke, born 1872, who was accompanying her on the trip to England.

Her son Hayden Erskine Starke, born in Melbourne in 1871, was to challenge a Codicil to the Will of Maria Mattingley in the Probate Court in London some years after death his mother's death. Elizabeth Starke's spinster aunt Maria Mattingley died on 28 July 1909 in London, almost the same day that it was supposed Elizabeth Starke had died.

Mrs Starke and Dr Frederick Byran were the legatees under the will and Mrs Starke's son was disputing the codicil, as if Mrs Starke died before her aunt Maria Mattingly, Dr Bryan would inherit the legacy, but if Maria died first Elizabeth Starke would share the legacy with Dr Bryan, and any legacy left by Elizabeth Starke would then go to her children.

Frederick Bryan was born in 1862 in Melbourne, the son of Frederick and Ellen *née* Mattingley. Sadly Frederick's father died before his son was born. Frederick had been living in London since the late 1870s, where he had been a medical student. Both Dr Frederick Bryan and Hayden Starke were nephews of Maria Mattingley.

The case lasted a few days and the court took into account that Capt Ilbery, Master of the *Waratah*, had died on or since 26 July 1909, the ship having last been seen on 27 July 1909. At the close of the case it was concluded that Mrs Starke had died first and the court ruled in favour of Dr Frederick Bryan. Maria Mattingley's estate amounted to around £26,000.

Interestly both Elizabeth Starke and her daughter Bessie are noted to have died on 27 July 1909, according to their Wills listed in Victoria.

STARKE, Miss Bessie Mattingley, born in 1872, was from Malvern, Victoria, and travelling with her mother, Elizabeth Starke.

STAUNTON, ? No christian name is known for this man but investigating him reveals a strange story. He claimed to be the only survivor of the *Waratah*, said to have returned to Ireland to find his parents no longer living there, prompting him to put an advertisement in the paper asking for information on their whereabouts. Thinking his parents were dead he joined the army. His parents wrote to the address in the paper, and correspondence in 1915 from their son, then in France, informed them that he was the only survivor of the ship and would explain everything that had happened. Mr Staunton must have been either a publicity seeker or suffering from shell-shock, as the name of Staunton does not appear on any passenger lists for the *Waratah*. Needless to say nothing more was heard of this story.

STOKOE, John George, a ships' engineer, boarded the ship in Melbourne as a passenger. He was born in Durham and married Margaret *née* Donald and his son George was also a ship's engineer. After his wife died in 1898 he married a widow, Elizabeth Pearson.

Strangely, John George Stokoe appears on the passenger list for the *Waratah* leaving London on 26 April 1909 for Australia. He stayed a short time and rejoined the ship for its journey back in July.

TICKELL, George Herbert Allan was twenty-one when he boarded the ship in Adelaide. The passenger list states that he boarded in Melbourne but his father told the Board of Trade Inquiry that he watched the *Waratah* leave Melbourne and then took the train to Adelaide where he saw his son board the ship.

George was born in 1888 in Melbourne, Australia, the son of Commander Frederick Tickell, a naval officer who was born in China, and Mary Elizabeth *née* Figg. George's sisters were Charlotte Mary, Evelyn Lucy and Kathleen May. George's father Frederick had a long and distin-

Naval commandant Captain F. Tickell. (Courtesy of John Oxley Library, State Library of Queensland No. 161980)

guished career. In 1891 he was a lieutenant at the Royal Naval College in Portsmouth, England, and in 1897 he was a saloon passenger aboard the *Damacus* on his way back to Australia, where he was promoted to Commandant of the Commonwealth Naval Forces in Victoria later that year. He was mentioned in dispatches and appointed the CMG (Companion of St Michael and St George) for his part in the Boxer Rebellion in China. The Victorian Government had requisitioned the liner SS *Salamis* in 1900 and under Tickell's command 200 troops left for Hong Kong.

He was director of Naval Reserves, and in 1912 was appointed an aide-de-camp to the Governor-General. In 1919 he was promoted to rear admiral and died a few months later that year.

TURNER, David boarded the ship in Durban. He was from Fife, Scotland, and was accompanied by his wife and five children aged from three to fourteen years old. His wife was South African and the family had made several journeys back to Scotland. He was a successful businessman with a landing and forwarding business in Natal and London. The family had intended to travel to London earlier but some of the children were ill and sadly they postponed the trip.

WILSON, Mrs Annette *née* Baker was forty years old when she boarded the ship in Melbourne, her eight-year-old daughter travelling with her. Annette Emily Baker had married Hugh Thurburn Wilson in Melbourne in 1891 and they resided in Toorak. Hugh was the manager of the Royal Bank of Australia in Melbourne. He was born in Rathven, Banffshire, Scotland, in 1852, the son of John, a land steward, and Helen Wilson *née* Thurburn. Hugh was one of twelve children and his brother Charles was Writer to the Signet, the oldest legal society in the world as well as procurator-fiscal of Aberdeenshire.

Officers and Crew

FRANCIS, Alfred R., aged twenty-seven, was senior steward and waiter to the Commodore.

His widow Florence was living in Southend, Essex, and was awarded a total amount of £270 compensation for his loss in 1910. £140 was to be invested for her four-year-old son and £130 for her to start a business.

FRENCH, Charles, fireman and trimmer, was thirty-two years old. He was born in Hove, Sussex, the son of Charles, a farm worker, and Rhoda *née* Corke. He had three brothers and four sisters.

FULFORD, Dr Howard Cecil was twenty-seven and the son of Edward John Fulford and Emma (*née* Lortsmith) from St Kilda, Melbourne, Victoria. He was the ship's surgeon on board the *Waratah*.

GEORGESON, Abel, boswain, was fifty-five years old. He was born in North Shields, Northumberland, the son of Abel, a mariner from the Shetlands, and Isabella *née*

Thompson. He married Dorothy Harrison in 1883 and they had two daughters, Agnes and Mabel.

GIBBS, Harris Archibald, an apprentice, was eighteen years old. He was born in Bognor, Sussex, the son of Harris Hornsby Gibbs, a house builder, and Ella *née* Plucknett. He had three sisters. His parents attended the Board of Trade Inquiry.

HAMILTON, Robert A. aged forty-eight, an engineer born in Lanarkshire, Scotland, was married with seven children. The family lived in Australia for some time and five of their children were born in Queensland. They returned to Scotland in 1900 where another child was born.

HAYSOM, Charles Ernest, ship's butcher, was thirty-eight years old. He was born in London the son of George, a boot mender, and Harriett *née* Howlett. He had two brothers, one of whom, Sidney, was an omnibus driver, and a sister.

He married Kate Frances *née* Howlett (who may have been a distant cousin) in 1905 and they lived in Willesden, Middlesex. Two years after her husband died Kate was living with her husband's family in Willesden.

HEMY, Henri Frederic, Second Officer, was twenty-seven years old. Born in 1882 in Darlington, he was the son of Thomas Marie Madawaska Hemy and Anne *née* Dixon. His father Thomas was born at sea on board the *Madawaska* in 1852 whilst the family was travelling to Australia. They returned to England a few years later. His grandfather Henri Frederick, born 1818, was a professor of music and a composer; he composed 'Hemy's Royal Modern Tutor' for the pianoforte which had sold 300,000 copies by the late 1870s, amongst many other works. He had his own orchestra and was also a member of the Theatre Royal orchestra. A story that has been handed down in the

Self-sketch of Thomas Marie Madawaska Hemy, father of Henri. (Courtesy of Peter Searle and Norma M. Hemy)

Henri Frederic Hemy, grandfather of Henri.
(Courtesy of Doreen Oates *née* Evans)

Picture of the *Birkenhead* sinking by Thomas
Hemy.

Picture of the *Danmark* sinking by Thomas
Hemy.

Hemy family relates to Henri Hemy being the composer of *Jingle Bells*, and he sold it to an American who turned it into the song we know today. This may or may not be true; there is no concrete proof either way. Thomas was a marine artist of considerable note and his paintings are sought after today. His famous painting 'The Wreck of the *Birkenhead*' was exhibited in Bristol in 1893 and led to him tracking down one of the survivors of that ship who recounted what had happened.

The MV *Birkenhead* was a troopship carrying around 636 people, including women and children, which struck rocks off Cape Danger south-east of Cape Town and sank on 26 February 1852. About 200 people were extremely lucky to survive. It was a harrowing end for the people in the water, who were dragged down by sharks coming in for the kill. This tragedy resulted in the Great Whites becoming known as 'Tommy Sharks' in that area. This is believed to be the very first time that the call for 'women and children first' occurred. The men sacrificed themselves, well aware of the probable consequences. It later became maritime protocol, of course, but these were its origins and it was Thomas Hemy who first used the phrase 'Women and Children First' for his painting. Another well-known ship Thomas painted was the *Danmark*, an emigrant ship carrying around 735 people, including young babies and children, in March 1889. They sailed out of Copenhagen and after several days at sea were in danger of slowly sinking after the shaft broke and caused a large hole in the underside of the ship. The *Missouri* was passing on her way from London to America and everyone was rescued by Captain Murrel. Thomas Hemy's painting of this ship was exhibited as 'Every Soul Was Saved'. It is of interest that Thomas Hemy's mother had been lost at sea and perhaps this explains the deep empathy he had with the subject.

Henri Hemy's uncles Charles Napier and Bernard Benedict were also marine artists, Charles perhaps even more famous than his brother Thomas. When Thomas had learnt of his son Henri's ship disappearing off the coast of South Africa, his thoughts must surely have turned to the shipwrecks he had already painted years before.

HODDER, George William, chief engineer, was thirty-seven years old. He was born in Bermondsey, London, the son of George Hodder, master mariner from Topsham, Devon, a true seafaring town, and Hannah *née* Gribble. George William had two sisters and a brother Charles who followed in the family tradition and went to sea.

George William was married in 1902 to Florence Eliza Mountjoy and they lived in West Ham, Essex. They had two daughters, Roberta Hannah born in 1904 and Joyce Florence in 1907. When Florence was widowed she had two small children to take care of and was employed as an assistant teacher.

HUMPHREY, Thomas, third engineer, was twenty-five years old. He was born in Rochester, Kent, the son of Thomas Humphrey, a marine engineer, and Eliza *née* Johnson. He had three sisters and his brother Henry was also a marine engineer.

ILBERY, Captain Josiah Edward was born in 1840, the son of Walter Ilbery, a Customs man, and Elizabeth Vachell *née* Foley, and grandson of Josiah James Ilbery of Edge Hill, Liverpool, a railway superintendant who left Liverpool and moved to the Isle of Man by 1857 where he is noted in the directory. He lived to the ripe old age of ninety-nine years old.

Josiah Edward had three brothers and two sisters. His brother Edward was also a naval man rising to chief officer in the merchant service. Another brother, Walter Alfred, was blind and he studied music, becoming a professor.

By 1881 Josiah was a master mariner, having command of the *Delcomyn*, and one dark night while returning from Adelaide to London he went to the rescue of a lifeboat carrying some of the crew of the *Koning Der Nederlander* after they had abandoned ship. He was to be master of a great many ships in the future.

JAMIESON, James H., 4th engineer, was twenty-six years old. He was born in Aberdeen, Scotland, the son of James, a shoemaker, and Ann Grieg. He had brothers Jessie Grieg, Robert, Frederick, Stanley and Richard and sisters Annabelle, Barbara and Ann.

MEEK, George, a trimmer, was twenty-nine years old. He was born in Port Glasgow, Renfrewshire, Scotland, the son of Matthew, an iron ships driller. He had four brothers and three sisters. Two of his brothers were ships riveters. The family received £40 in compensation for his loss. His wages for the trip were £4.

MERRIN, Dr Patrick, of Dublin had a very lucky escape and considered himself a survivor of the *Waratah*. He had agreed to be the Medical Officer for her return trip to London, but a few days prior to the sailing circumstances arose which made him unable to go. Dr Merrin had moved to Australia in 1907 and held the post of Medical Officer of Health in Warrange, North Victoria. He returned home to Ireland later in 1909. It may be assumed that Dr Fulford was asked to take Dr Merrin's place at short notice as it is Dr Fulford who is listed as the ship's surgeon on the crew list

MORGAN, John Purton, third officer, was twenty-five years old. He was born in Aberystwyth, Cardiganshire, Wales, the son of Benjamin Ellis Morgan and Mary Beatrice *née* Purton. Benjamin Ellis was a Justice of the Peace for the County of Cardiganshire. John's grandfather Benjamin Morgan was a rector. He had two brothers, Charles Ellis and Hugh Phillips, and a sister, Enid Beatrice.

NEWMAN, Thomas, able seaman, was fifty years old. He was born in Tasmania, Australia, the son of Richard and Mary *née* Feneran. Richard Newman came from Devon and had arrived in Tasmania by 1841 as he took his first appointment with the government in that year. He was later a clerk to the Colonial Secretary's office. Thomas had siblings Arabella Blake, Mary Gertrude, Charlotte Susan, Margaret, Richard, George E. Feneran, Augusta Rennell, John Feneran and Robert William Sparke. It is possible that descendants of this large family are still living in Tasmania.

Thomas Newman's obituary was copied in *The Times*.

OWEN, Charles, chief officer, was thirty-nine years old and married with one child. In 1910 his widow Lilian was living in Swansea, Wales, and was paid compensation of £272 by the shipping company for his loss.

SHASAL, Frederick Wm, assistant pantryman, was seventeen years old. He was born in Clapham, London, the son of Frederick Wm Shasal, a clerk, and Mary Ann. The family lived in Battersea and he had three sisters.

SKAILES, Septimus George, chief steward/purser, was thirty-two years of age. He was born in Stratford, Essex, the son of Thomas Jackson Skailes, a manager to a firm of match manufacturers, and Caroline *née* Fitkin. He had brothers Percy, Frederick, Thomas, Alonzo and Sidney, and sisters Caroline and Alice.

Septimus married Harriett Minnie Strickland in 1905 and they had two sons, Frank Strickland in 1906 and George Arthur in 1907. Harriett was widowed with two very young sons to bring up and the Blue Anchor Line paid her the sum compensation of £300 for the loss of her husband.

STACE, Edward, boswain's mate, was thirty-eight years old and born in Ashford, Kent, the son of Norton, a fish hawker, and Elizabeth. He had siblings Anne, Norton and Thomas.

TEMPLETON, John, chief cook, was born on 8 January 1871 in Glasgow, Scotland, the son of John Fleming White Templeton and Elizabeth Adam Cochrane, the seventh of ten children. After Elizabeth died his father married Barbara Craig in 1874. At this time John was a jewellery maker but by 1881 the family were living in West Ham, Essex, and he had changed his occupation from jewellery maker to ship's cook.

John Templeton Snr gave his son his Christian names which must have caused some confusion, as two men with the names John Fleming White Templeton lived in the same household. John Jnr married Emma Gertrude Reeve in 1901 and their children were Ivy Gertie, born in 1902, and Violet Barbara, 1907. Two years after the ship had disappeared Emma Gertrude was living in West Ham with her two daughters, working as a dressmaker.

THURSTON, Guy, 4th officer, was twenty-one years old and born in West Bengal, India, the son of John Walter Thurston and Ethel Madelene *née* Trelawney.

TROTT, Frederick, pantry boy and general servant, was sixteen years old and the son of Samuel. Samuel had been on the *Waratah*'s maiden voyage as a passenger cook and Frederick had gone with him. Samuel Trott left the ship in London but Frederick rejoined the *Waratah* for her next voyage. Samuel gave evidence at the Board of Trade Inquiry.

WALKER, Robert, ship's carpenter, was twenty-eight years old. He was born in Glasgow the son of Archibald, a shipwright, and Agnes Docherly. He had brothers James, Archibald and John and a sister Jane.

He married Margaret Stevenson Stalker in 1907 in Govan, Glasgow, Scotland, the daughter of Adam, an engine fitter, and Elizabeth. They lived in Drive Road, Govan, and his widow was paid £282 in compensation for his loss.

A total of £14,000 compensation was said to have been paid to the relatives of the passengers and crew by the shipping company.

Waratah Crew List

Name	Age	Rank
J.E. Ilbery	69	Captain
C. Owen	39	Chief Officer
H.F. Hemy	26	2nd Officer
J.P. Morgan	25	3rd Officer
G. Thruston	21	4th Officer
R. Walker	28	Carpenter
A. Georgeson	55	Bos'wn
E.J. Schafer	26	Bos'wn Mate
E. Stace	38	Bos'wn Mate
W. Belshaw	48	Able Seaman
M. McIver	56	Able Seaman
H.G. Smith	37	Able Seaman
W. Rackliff	29	Able Seaman
T. Newman	50	Able Seaman
G.W. Ambrose	26	Able Seaman
C. Turkle	38	Able Seaman
W. Waite	33	Able Seaman
W. Harding	35	Able Seaman
C. Allen	37	Able Seaman
G. Shea	37	Able Seaman
R. Robinson	27	Ordinary Seaman
H.C. Fulford	27	Surgeon
A.P. Moore	29	Able Seaman
A. Martin	31	Able Seaman
A. Barr	29	Carpenters Mate
Jas Costella	44	Seaman
G.W. Hodder	37	Chief Engineer
A.M. Hunter	31	2nd Engr
T. Humphrey	25	3rd Engr
F.T. Hunt	26	4th Engr
J.H. Jamieson	26	4th Engr
J. Hamilton	23	4th Engr (jnr)
F. Monk	21	5th Engr
R.A. Hamilton	48	Refrigerating Engr
S. Pearson	30	Donkeyman
W. Smith	45	Greaser
Wm Walters	30	Refrig. Greaser
B. Steiner	33	Greaser& Fireman
J. Conn	34	Greaser& Fireman
A. Cumming	26	Greaser& Fireman
J. Jewers	26	Greaser& Fireman
W. Comper	29	Greaser& Fireman
J. Lydiard	27	Fireman & Trimmer

Name	Age	Rank
O. Schelier	44	Fireman & Trimmer
J. Immelman	26	Fireman & Trimmer
S. Nelson	44	Fireman & Trimmer
C. Butcher	28	Fireman & Trimmer
J. Clark	29	Fireman & Trimmer
A. Brown	26	Fireman & Trimmer
C. Samuelson	37	Fireman & Trimmer
J. Jacobson	38	Fireman & Trimmer
F. Dorander	28	Fireman & Trimmer
M. Seiffert	45	Fireman & Trimmer
R. Bocker	43	Fireman & Trimmer
W. Reinsch	38	Fireman & Trimmer
K. Lindross	36	Fireman & Trimmer
J. Steel	33	Trimmer
H. Dance	27	Trimmer
C. French	32	Fireman & Trimmer
A. Bellringer	25	Trimmer
A. Sandon	22	Trimmer
Geo Meek	29	Trimmer
H. McCrone	24	Trimmer
W. Thornton	22	Trimmer
T. Coulson	29	Trimmer
J. Kelly	31	Trimmer
G. Dixon	24	Trimmer
F.H. Benson	26	Trimmer
H. Taylor	39	Trimmer
W. McKiernan	37	Trimmer
S. Skailes	32	Chief Steward
P. Oxford	25	Barman & Storekeeper
K. Papineau	60	Pantryman
F. Shasal	17	Asst Pantryman
J.C. Clark	30	Steward
D. Dennison	23	General Servant
W.B. Rogers	28	General Servant
E. Rumbold	44	General Servant
F.M. Wellington	26	Gen Svt & Bathman
C. Baxter	19	General Servant
P.C. Bonham	28	General Servant
W.W. McPhey/McPhee	25	General Servant
W.R. Allan	29	General Servant
A.R. Francis	27	General Servant
W.T. Edwards	18	General Servant
P.J. Monaghan	18	Gen Svt & Waiter
W.G. White	37	General Servant
A. Woodcock	23	General Servant

Name	Age	Rank
C.H. Hammond	18	General Servant
E.J. Walters	19	General Servant
G. Wyborn	22	General Servant
M. Campbell	22	General Servant
Fred Trott	16	General Servant
A. Blake	18	General Servant
P.R. Alexander	21	General Servant
T. Ings	27	General Servant
W. Smith	?	General Servant
W. Thomas	45	General Servant
A. Nicholls	39	3rd Steward
S.E. Gorman	36	Pantryman
J. Templeton	39	Chief Cook
C.W. Southwell	26	2nd Cook
F. Sale	23	3rd Cook
A. Sach	19	4th Cook
A.E. Phillips	35	Baker
J. Jones	34	2nd Baker
C.E. Haysom	38	Butcher
F. Poland	24	2nd Butcher
P. Murray	26	Sculleryman
Sarah E. Whitehorn	35	Stewardess
Geo Sudbury	36	General Servant
Emma Swan	40	Stewardess
L. Burgess	23	General Servant
E. Sterne	17	General Servant
H.A. Gibbs	18	Apprentice
H.S. Clark	21	Apprentice
H.W. Harding	?	General Servant
H. Tanner	?	Fireman & Trimmer
P. Isaacs	?	General Servant

Passengers from Durban to Cape Town and London

Name	Age	Occupation	Embarked	Destination
Col. P.J. Browne	49	—	Adelaide	Cape Town
Miss K. Lees	23	—	Adelaide	Cape Town
Miss L. Cooke	—	Maid	Adelaide	Cape Town
Mrs Harvey	38	—	Sydney	Cape Town
Master Harvey	13	—	Sydney	Cape Town
Miss Miller	22	—	Sydney	Cape Town
Mr Charles Taylor	34	Miner	Sydney	Cape Town
Mrs Taylor	30	—	Sydney	Cape Town
Miss May Taylor	8	—	Sydney	Cape Town

Name	Age	Occupation	Embarked	Destination
Master C. Taylor	5	–	Sydney	Cape Town
Mr J.T. Blackburn	29	Dairyman	Sydney	Cape Town
Mrs J.Y. Wilson	58	–	Melbourne	London
Mrs Wilson	40	–	Melbourne	London
Miss L. Wilson	32	–	Melbourne	London
Miss Wilson	8	–	Melbourne	London
Mr N.W. Black	41	–	Melbourne	London
Miss M. Campbell	25	–	Melbourne	London
Mrs Govette	45	–	Sydney	London
Miss Lascelles	30	–	Sydney	London
Mrs A.G.H. Starke	60	–	Melbourne	London
Miss Starke	30	–	Melbourne	London
Mr John Ebsworth	45	–	Melbourne	London
Miss M. Hesketh Jones	25	–	Adelaide	London
Mrs A. Hay	45	–	Adelaide	London
Miss H.G. Hay	23	–	Adelaide	London
Mr William Cumming	32	–	Sydney	London
Mrs Bowden	55	–	Sydney	London
Miss G. Bowden	25	–	Sydney	London
Miss L. Schaumann	11	–	Sydney	London
Miss D. Schaumann	10	–	Sydney	London
Mrs J. Harwood	68	–	Sydney	London
Mr Wright	40	Master Mariner	Sydney	London
Mrs Wright	30	–	Sydney	London
Miss Henderson	25	–	Sydney	London
Mrs Allan/Allen & inft	40	–	Sydney	London
Miss Rose Allan/Allen	6	–	Sydney	London
Mr J. McS hunter	–	–	Sydney	London
Mr Bowden	40	Miner	Sydney	London
Mrs Bowden	34	–	Sydney	London
Miss Kathleen Bowden	6	–	Sydney	London
Master Harry Bowden	11	–	Sydney	London
Mr E.B. Page	34	Showman	Melbourne	London
Mrs Page	26	–	Melbourne	London
Mr P.J. Calder	29	Fireman	Melbourne	London
Mr A. Clarke	28	Bricklayer	Melbourne	London
Mr J.G. Stokoe	39	Engineer	Melbourne	London
Mrs A. Ibbett	49	–	Melbourne	London
Miss B. Murphy	25	–	Melbourne	London
Mr G.H. Tickell	31	Miner	Melbourne	London
Mr Lowenthal	47	Painter	Melbourne	London
Mrs Adamson	–	–	Durban	London
Mrs Ashe	–	–	Durban	London
Mrs E.A. Bradley	–	–	Durban	London
Dr J.T. Carrick	–	–	Durban	London

Name	Age	Occupation	Embarked	Destination
Mrs P. O'Connolly	–	–	Durban	London
Miss Connolly	–	–	Durban	London
Mr William Coote	–	–	Durban	London
Mrs Dawes & child	–	–	Durban	London
Mr Donaldson	–	–	Durban	London
Mrs Dunn	–	–	Durban	London
Miss D. Dunn	7	–	Durban	London
Miss B. Dunn	2	–	Durban	London
Revd Father Fadle	–	–	Durban	London
Mr M.J. Govendo	–	–	Durban	London
Mr R.E. Hugo	–	–	Durban	Cape Town
Mrs A. Lyon & child (1 yr)	–	–	Durban	London
Mr J. McCausland	–	–	Durban	Cape Town
Mr C.B. Nicholson	–	–	Durban	London
Mr P. O'Connor	–	–	Durban	Cape Town
Mrs Petrie	–	–	Durban	London
Master Petrie	–	–	Durban	London
Mrs E.A. Press	–	–	Durban	London
Mrs Sillery	–	–	Durban	London
Mr W. Stocken	–	–	Durban	London
Mrs Stocken	–	–	Durban	London
Stocken child	5	–	Durban	London
Stocken child	2	–	Durban	London
Miss Tayler	–	–	Durban	London
Mr J.F.J. Taylor	–	–	Durban	Cape Town
Miss Taylor	–	–	Durban	Cape Town
Mr David Turner	–	–	Durban	London
Mrs Turner	–	–	Durban	London
Turner child	14	–	Durban	London
Turner child	12	–	Durban	London
Turner child	7	–	Durban	London
Turner child	6	–	Durban	London
Turner child	3	–	Durban	London
Miss Young	–	–	Durban	London

Passengers Disembarking at Durban

Name	Age	Remarks	Class
Mr E.J. Mullen	36	–	Saloon
Mr F.C. Saunders	38	–	Saloon
Mr G.A. Richardson	36	–	Saloon
Mrs H. Cawood	37	–	Saloon
Mr M. Morgan	30	–	Saloon

Name	Age	Remarks	Class
Mr Claude Sawyer	54	Engineer	Saloon
Mr S. Pearce	76	Miner	3rd
Mr G.R. Boyce	38	Carpenter	3rd
Mr W. Hocking	48	Joiner	3rd
Mr W. Cousins	30	Storeman	3rd
Mrs Cousins & inft	26	–	3rd
Master Cousins	1	–	3rd
Mr Charles Swain	39	Carpenter	3rd
Mrs Mary Swain & inft	26	–	3rd
Mr H. Foord	34	Speculator	3rd
Mrs F. Morris/Norris	30	–	3rd
George Morris/Norris	19	Auctioneer	3rd
Mr Wynott	40	Detective	3rd
Mr De Beer	42	Detective	3rd
Mr McLaughlin	38	–	3rd
Mr Jas McNaught	30	Miner	3rd
Mr A. Brookes	24	Contractor	3rd
Mr E.T. Waters	47	Miner	3rd
Mrs Waters & inft	26	–	3rd
Mr Harold Grigg	25	Miner	3rd
Mr K. Grigg	48	Miner	3rd
Mr Wm Milburn	39	Miner	3rd

CHAPTER 4

THE DISAPPEARANCE

Following her departure from Durban on the return leg of her second – and final – voyage, the SS *Waratah* had the following officers on board:

Captain Josiah Ilbery, aged sixty-nine
Chief Officer Mr C. Owen, aged thirty-nine from Swansea
Second Officer Mr H.F. Hemy, aged twenty-seven from Darlington
Third Officer Mr J.P. Morgan, aged twenty-five from Abirys South
Fourth Officer Mr G. Thurston, aged twenty-one from India
Surgeon Dr H.C. Fulford, aged twenty-seven from Melbourne
Purser Mr P. Skailes, aged thirty-two from London
Chief Engineer Mr G.W. Hodder, aged thirty-seven from London
Second Engineer Mr A.M. Hunter, aged twenty-one from Perth
Third Engineer Mr T. Humphrey, aged twenty-five from Rochester

The return trip started at Sydney before going on to Melbourne, Adelaide, and crossing to Durban. She took on cargo at each of these ports, consisting of wool, wheat, tallow, skins, oats and flour. In Adelaide she took on lead concentrates. This comprised 300 tons of her cargo and there was to be conjecture about these substances later when questions were asked about her disappearance, as lead may become unstable in certain circumstances and is a regulated cargo today. It was stipulated that if the lead had liquified it could have created a shift in weight. The amount of lead she carried was clearly noted on the cargo hold loading plans. However, there seems to be a further mention of a leady substance and this also raised questions as to what may have befallen her. *Waratah* was a combined cargo and passenger ship and had on board a large quantity of refrigerated meat; this, along with the boxes of butter and grain, would have enabled the passengers to survive a considerable time on the supplies in the hold as well as the provisions for the trip, which was lengthy in a regular trip of this magnitude.

Some of the cargo was due to be unloaded at Durban and there she was to load up with coal for the journey back, via Cape Town. Some reports say she took on cargo at Durban although most report that she did not, just topping up her coal supply. This would have been necessary if she were to aim for a fast route home impressing all with her speed, and she had already made an unscheduled coaling on her maiden voyage due to unexpectedly low supplies.

There was discussion relating to her going aground off Kangaroo Island, Adelaide, on her maiden voyage which could have made enough of an impact on the rudder system to have caused a problem later on. Again, as with the entire story of the *Waratah*, there

'*Waratah* At Her Best Steaming Ahead' by de Rosset. (Courtesy of Emlyn Brown)

are many conflicting reports on this, but how important this incident may have been remains to be seen. She had since been dry-docked and passed with flying colours.

Her trip to Durban was reported as uneventful, with the passengers enjoying some fine weather and presumably taking good advantage of the ship's promenade decks and sheltered deck spaces. However, there was one unhappy traveller and he was most vociferous in his misgivings. Mr Claude Sawyer, engineer, first class passenger and seasoned traveller, was decidedly anxious about the way the ship was behaving and declared to all that he felt she was unsafe. To add to this, he alarmed folk on board with the news that he was having premonitions of an apparition coming out of the sea with a sword covered in blood calling '*Waratah, Waratah*'. Whether concerned for the ship's safety or by his premonitions, Mr Sawyer did mention his fears to the officer in his lifeboat group during a drill and it seems he was not alone in his unease. He thought that the ship was top heavy and made a point of studying how she returned after heavy seas, remarking that she did not behave normally within his scope of experience. Indeed this was how he explained his disembarkation at Durban to his wife when he wired her. One of his fellow seers was Mr Ebsworth, a solicitor from Melbourne involved in shipping who had been to sea himself as an officer, and Sawyer declared that he too was unhappy with the performance of the ship. He said that the ship had come in hard against the dock at Adelaide, but it was the strange way she dealt with the waves which made him the most concerned and he pointed out his bathwater was not draining properly and that passengers had sustained injuries from being thrown about in what would be considered fairly good conditions. Sawyer tried in vain to persuade others to leave the ship but they perhaps were a little unsure of this man and his pre-monitions. True to his word, Mr Sawyer disembarked at Durban and, although it was said he forfeited his ticket money on to Cape Town, it was also reported that he was

'Tug *Richard King* Which Took *Waratah* out of Durban On Her Final Voyage Shown Crossing Durban Bar' (twin funnels unusual on a tug).

due to disembark at Durban but tickets were made through to Cape Town at no extra cost, allowing the freedom of choice. Ultimately, for whatever reason, he disembarked, he was saved and the others were not. He was to continue to Cape Town aboard the *Kildonan Castle* some week later. One can only imagine how he reacted on hearing of the non-arrival of the *Waratah*.

At Durban, she coaled up for the voyage back to London and apparently took on no cargo at this port but around thirty-four passengers bound for Cape Town and London (Colonel P.J. Browne, Miss K. Lees and her maid Miss L. Cooke for Cape Town and the rest for London). These new passengers joined a ship which was already filled with families brimming with excitement at this voyage on board a modern cruise ship, all with their own agenda and plans for their arrival at their chosen port. With crew outnumbering passengers, they were bound to have plenty of attention on board. It also has to be said that some may well have been more than a little relieved at continuing without their self-appointed soothsayer, Mr Claude Sawyer, and to relax and enjoy the rest of the voyage.

Indeed one newspaper printed a letter from a member of the public who was most scathing about Mr Sawyer's opinion, stating that it was quite normal for ships to list as far as fifty degrees in extreme circumstances and also normal for the so-called jerk to be the result of a beam sea, or often with a following sea – it was the ship righting itself. He dismissed the stability issue, citing the knowledge of the commander in question and his attention to detail. He quoted the case of a steamer which had disappeared for months between Kobe and Yokohama and finally popped up in the Philippine Islands little the worse for the experience.

At 8.00 p.m. on Monday 26 July the SS *Waratah* left C Shed and the shelter and comfort of Durban Harbour with the pilot Lindsey on board to guide her out, ably escorted by the tug *Richard King*, to travel out to one of the most treacherous coasts on earth.

She was to be seen by several ships; the first was the *Clan McIntyre* at around 6.00 a.m. on 27 July and, as the *Waratah* overhauled the smaller, slower vessel, they exchanged the customary signals and information on who they were, where they were bound (both London) and wished each other a good voyage. *Clan McIntyre* was heading on without visiting Cape Town whilst *Waratah* for bound for that city. They continued to be in view

'*Waratah* Plunging
Into Heavy Seas.'
(Courtesy of
Emlyn Brown)

of each other for a few hours until finally, somewhere roughly 15 miles off the entrance to the Bashee River mouth, the *Waratah* with her superior speed steamed ahead and over the horizon and the *Clan McIntyre* never saw her again. They were to play a major role in the Inquiry which followed, although of course they knew nothing of her disappearance until reaching England. They did, however, report weather so bad they declared it the worst storm they had been in, and yet they had managed to survive it, as had other ships in the area, so that it seems strange that anyone would have assumed that the *Waratah* had gone to the bottom of the ocean when far smaller vessels had survived without injury or damage. Moreover, this report of its possible loss in the storm was not received until the *Clan McIntyre* arrived back in London in August – as she had no radio either – and she was not to know what had happened to the ship which had passed her so majestically that night.

There were other reports at the time of the storm, however, and one ship, the *Illovo*, which had also left Durban bound for Cape Town, arrived a day late into Cape Town reporting huge seas and monstrous gales through which she had struggled for days. They said the seas presented such a perilous threat that Captain Kinloch took the difficult decision to ditch many tons of coal in an attempt to save his ship, but that clearly helped, as she hobbled into Cape Town very late, having had a dreadful ordeal, but intact and with all on board fine. This helped fuel the hope that *Waratah* had in some way suffered at the hands of the gale but would appear with full explanation very soon. Another ship reporting being in the vicinity was the *Guelph* whose captain, Culverwell, stated that he had exchanged signals with a ship but could not clearly make out her name, only catching the last three letters as being t-a-h. This happened in the late evening of 27 July and is at odds with where the *Waratah* would have been, given the confirmed sighting of the *Clan McIntyre*. TAH at the end of a name was hardly unusual given the international traffic which frequents that area. There were to be some futher sightings which did not tie in.

Harlow was another ship which claimed to have seen her that night, although the captain and first officer were not in full agreement in their recall of the incident. Lights were seen which at first were believed to be either steamer lights or fires on shore, a regular occurrence in that area. It was also deemed possible that there could have been a

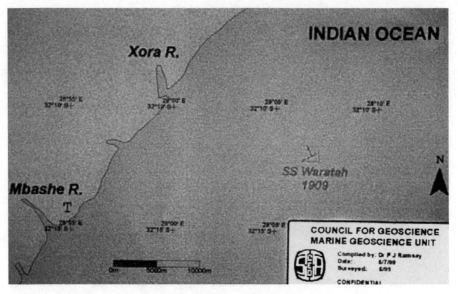

Area of the last sighting of the *Waratah*. (Courtesy of Emlyn Brown and Council for Geoscience)

ship on fire. However, the facts did not tie in with the position and sightings of the *Clan McIntyre* and so this sighting was discounted, although considered a truthful account of what they believed they had seen.

One man on patrol on the coast claimed to have seen her roll over and not come back up again. This is covered in more detail in Emlyn Brown's account in Chapter 9 as he searched for the possible wreck in the vicinity described by this man, as well as a pilot who flew over the area years later and claimed to see what appeared to be a wreck off the coast there.

Evidence was given from a man claiming to be a Captain Brendon of the *Talis* who said he had seen the *Waratah*, yet on investigation neither he nor his ship were to be found on record anywhere – it was in all probability a hoax.

Messages in bottles appeared purporting to hold the keys to the tragedy; all were fake. There is little one can say.

The lack of any wreckage was the catalyst for the searches as was the fact that boats had gone missing before and some had turned out well; these things spurred on people's hopes and at first the newspapers carried reports full of optimism. The area where she was last seen is notorious indeed, yet other far lesser vessels were able to limp into port safe and sound.

Other reports of bodies in the water, in particular that of a little blonde girl in a red coat or dressing gown, were dismissed later at the Inquiry and certainly the tug sent out to follow up these claims, and the other ships who were out looking for any signs, had seen nothing at all to back up those reports.

It is worth mentioning that ship owners were understandably dismayed if their crew spotted anything untoward, such as a body in the water, as the resulting inquiries were very disruptive to their schedules. There is more about this in Chapter 8.

CHAPTER 5

THE AFTERMATH

It was to be a while before there was grave concern about the missing liner, so convinced were people of her unsinkable design and power to beat anything the elements could throw at her; sinking was simply unimaginable, so there had to be a reasonable explanation. It was not unheard of for ships to arrive in port even weeks late, as happened to one Pacific liner which reached Queensland three weeks overdue. The *Waikato*, too, had been long overdue and still turned up months later, so panic did not set in at first. The mood changed as it became evident that the *Waratah* was not about to limp into port and the realisation grew that something would have to be done to discover her whereabouts.

There was no news, no wreckage, no sighting which could be relied upon; the owners were inundated with inquiries about the families on board and it was decided by the agent in Cape Town that a search should be launched. On 1 August the tug *T.E. Fuller* was sent out to look for any sign but was forced back after some dreadful weather. She was to return out later and continue her extensive search along the coast. Three continents were to be galvanised into action as South Africa, Australia and Britain pulled together and joined forces with a massive common goal – to find the ship, her passengers and crew. The communication and unity enabled the searches to be both effective and thorough. Back in London the Admiralty was in communication with the London Salvage Association and were issuing more orders to South Africa to continue the search. The British Royal Navy ships HMS *Forte* and HMS *Pandora* were in the area and they were also called upon to join the search. Based on the combined experience of the maritime experts, captains and ship owners, it was the belief that had the *Waratah* been disabled she would have caught the current off Cape Agulhas which would have carried her eastwards, and therefore they had an idea of where to plan the search tracks using the template of the *Waikato* recovery to plot their planned route. The New Zealand steamer *Waikato* was built in 1892, 400ft long and a spar deck design ship which broke down on 2 June 1899 on the Algulhas Bank after being disabled by a fractured tailshaft. She drifted for 100 days, covering around 3,000 miles before being towed an unbelievable 2,500 miles through the most inhospitable seas by steamer *Asloun*, arriving safely in Freemantle, Australia. She was discovered on 15 September and arrived in Australia on 8 October – a most remarkable rescue.

Meanwhile, there was heated debate in Britain amid rumours of *Waratah* having loaded coal on her bridge deck and thereby having potentially risked the stability of the ship, and other even more disturbing accusations. This was all discounted at the subsequent Inquiry, but would have done nothing to reassure those who had family aboard the ship. On three continents, prayers and church services were focusing upon the stricken ship and the souls

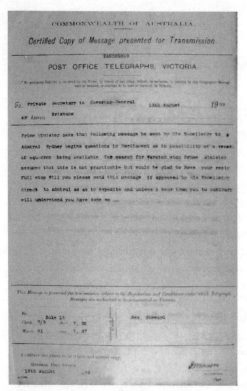

Left and below Telegram communications
from the Australian government.
(Courtesy of National Archives of
Australia: A6662, 1479)

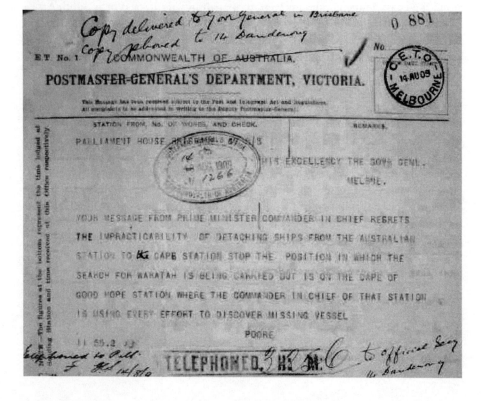

on board. As long as there was no wreckage, there was hope, and considering the success with the search for the New Zealand ship *Waitako* and her lengthy drift, there was still an air of justifiable optimism. Of course, with lack of radio equipment being the norm, shipping around the South African coast was signalled or asked whilst in port to keep a lookout for her. At least they would be able to report in, offer bearings and comment on the condition of those on board and the safety of the ship, if not actually be in a position to effect a full rescue. By now anything would be little short of a miracle for the relatives.

Forte began her search on 1 August from Durban with *Pandora* leaving just two days later from East London, but they had to take on coal and prepare for the trip so it was a few days later that they actually left for the detailed search. *Forte* searched for around sixteen days, returning back to Simonstown, *Pandora* longer at around twenty days, returning back to East London.

It was reported that the Royal Navy flagship HMS *Hermes* would be arriving from Beira and would take part in the searches. In addition it was also reported that a ship had been seen slowly making tracks towards Durban and it was believed that she was a Blue Anchor vessel – hopes soared for the end of the tale and all to be well with her arrival back in the port she left. It was not to be. *Hermes* joined the search and was involved between 12 and 17 August.

At this time reports began emerging about bodies in the water. Steamer *Insizwa* reported having passed four possible bodies around the Bashee River (where *Waratah* was last sighted) and this precipitated a search starting with the steamship *Miltiades* on

The tug *T.E. Fuller* of Cape Town during the search.

14th instant to the following effect, and was conveyed to

Mr. Deakin, by telephone, as a matter of expediency im-

-mediately upon receipt:-

    "Commander-in-Chief regrets the impracticability

"of detaching ships from the Australian Station to

"the Cape Station. The position in which the search

"for 'Waratah' is being carried out is on the Cape of

"Good Hope Station where the Commander-in-Chief of that

"Station is using every effort to discover missing ves-

"-sel".

                    Yours faithfully,

                                        Melbourne,
                                    16th August, 1909.

Dear Mr. Shepherd,

        On Friday last, at the instance of the Prime
Minister, the Governor-General informed the Admiral that
the question of the practicability of detaching a ship
or ships from the Australian Squadron to take part in the
search for the S.S. "Waratah" had been raised in Parlia-
-ment; and the Admiral was asked whether there was any
probability of a vessel or vessels being available for
this purpose.

        A reply was received from the Admiral on the
                                                    14th

This page and opposite Telegram communications from the Australian government. (Courtesy of National Archives of Australia: A6662, 1479)

her way to Cape Town. The *Tottenham* had also reported seeing bodies in the water and at the Inquiry they confirmed seeing bodies and birds around. There was confusion about why they had not mentioned it to the authorities at the time, with the chief officer stating he had been cautioned to keep quiet as the owners would be unhappy about them stopping to pick up bodies.

Tugs and police on the coast went out searching for the supposed bodies. Whilst these were discounted as being whale offal discarded at the Durban whaling station, they reported that they had not dumped any whale off-cuts into the sea at that time. The tug *Harry Escombe* from East London was sent to search for the bodies but again found none. *Waratah*'s sister-ship the *Geelong* was also involved in the search around 13 August. At the same time, the commander of HMS *Hermes* (Commander Wills) was involved in an inquiry into the safety of lighting on the coast and life-saving measures in the aftermath of another shipping disaster, the loss of the *Maori*. The inquiry was set up by the Cape government.

Another ship which had suffered and yet survived a severe storm, the steamer *Solveig* out of Norfolk, Virginia, arrived at Port Natal. The storm had been so ferocious that her deck gear was carried away.

The Elder-Dempster-owned steamer *Canada Cape* had left Durban heading for Montreal and, on her arrival at St Helena, declared that they had searched for the liner along 36 parallel to 17 East from Delogoa Bay but had failed to see anything at all.

By now, letters were flying back and forth, with conjecture spinning out of control as to the fate of the liner. Passengers who had previously travelled aboard the *Waratah*, some confident in the ship, others not so, engaged in contradictory debate about coal on deck, top-heavy design and her inability to recover from waves. Mr Claude Sawyer was sought-after during this time due to his colourful descriptions of the behaviour of the ship. It was a matter of interest that he did not continue his journey on the first available ship down to Cape Town, but waited for a week before moving on, suggesting he might have really intended to go to Durban anyway, perhaps visiting friends. The agents were in each port doing as good a job of public relations and fire-fighting as possible, trying their best to keep the known facts to the fore.

At this time those who believed *Waratah* had been disabled by engine failure seized the chance to remind newspaper readers of the importance of keeping machinery in perfect working order at all times. They preached that there should never be the opportunity for disaster to strike as a result of poor maintenance, and pointed out that, for the majority of the time, it was a matter of pride that so many steam ships crossed the seas with no mishap.

Whilst all of this was happening in South Africa, and amidst the heated discussions the world over, the Australian public and the distressed victims' families were desperately looking for ways to help with the searches, as the majority of the people on board the stricken ship hailed from her shores. The telegrams show how they were encouraged to raise the matter in Parliament and to see if it was viable to send shipping from the Australian squadron to join in the searches in South Africa. It was deemed impractical from a logistical stand and the Melbourne Search Committee would eventually be set up to take matters into their own hands.

When they returned to South Africa empty-handed, the British warships were deployed to their original orders, the search all but over in spite of the many miles covered and great dedication on the part of all involved. However, while some still clung to the chance she might be drifting there was a small but determined voice of hope. So it was that a combined group, including Blue Anchor and the victims' families from Australia (who had set up a fund), alongside South Africa, chartered the cargo steam ship SS *Sabine*, owned by the Union Castle, on what was to be the first of the gruelling sea searches. *Sabine* was previously owned by the Elder-Dempster Line, which was bought out by the United Steamship Company UK in 1898 when she had formerly been named the *Matino*. '*It is this day mutually agreed between the Union Castle Mail Steamship Co. Ltd., owners of the SS* Sabine *and Messrs William Lund & Sons, Managers of the Blue Anchor Line Ltd.*,' and so it was agreed.

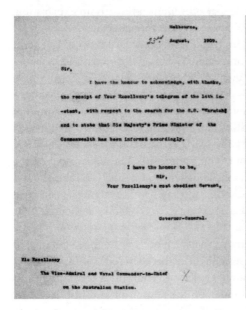

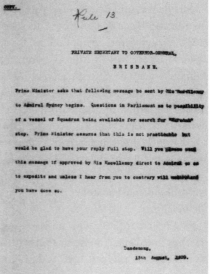

'Home for Months – Crow's-nest Constructed Primitively from a Barrel.' (Courtesy of B. Putt)

This *Sabine* had been mostly cargo-hauling coal over the seas when suddenly the captain, S.H. Owen, received orders to take her off somewhere with no explanation. Finally he was told that his ship had been chartered to carry out an extended search for the missing *Waratah*. Owen was to carry his own crew and a naval crew of five from HMS *Hermes* (Smith, Bird, Phillips, Light and Paull) to extend the search and lookouts, and also Lieutenant Beattie to command the naval group of searchers on behalf of the Admiralty. Captain Owen's account of this is beautifully written. He was clearly a man with vision and tolerance and, when many were voicing doubts about the wisdom of taking naval men on their ships, he was staunchly philosophical and declared he had never been treated less than courteously by the Navy. Perhaps this was in no small way a result of his good manners and demeanour. So it was that his ship was set up with the appropriate coal for the trip (Welsh, apparently, being less combustible) and the ship was fitted out to take on the extra hands needed. She already had her engineers and crew but took on another stoker and cook and adapted areas for the bunks and quarters for the naval men.

SS *Sabine* was filthy with coal and she must have been quite a shock for the men of the flagship *Hermes*! She was fitted with a searchlight so that they could assume lookout all through the night as well as day. Nothing was left to chance. It is most impressive that the team consisted of just five naval men and the lieutenant and I can see how the stories of there actually being seventy-five men began – it would make far more believable reading. However, space was limited as it was and they had to allow for the possibility of finding the ship and her passengers, so the emphasis was on the equipment – plenty of rope, supplies and stores – and the knowledge required to do the job. The men were described as 'special ratings', presumably due to their skills and personalities, which would have had to cope with non-stop work and dreadful conditions without complaint. And there were no serious complaints.

As it turned out, Captain Owen and the lieutenant were in full agreement on the approach to take and both took the task to their hearts, devoting every waking moment to their goal. The same went for all of them. It was to be a trip which demanded every last ounce of energy from the men, as well as outstanding seamanship, requiring the right decisions in some of the most demanding seas in the world. They saw few other ships but they must have had to keep a hopeful vision in mind or it would have been bleak beyond measure.

Two first-hand accounts of the *Sabine* trip are given in this book, from completely different views, but both full of details and providing an insight into another world. Endless fog and rain, cloud and gales were the norm and at times in the fog the whistle was sounded almost constantly, as was laid down by marine law, and that in itself must have been incredibly irritating – the captain noticed he was being worn down by it but insisted they stick to regulations, perhaps his way of coping with it all. That and the faint hope that a drifting ship would hear the whistle and be rescued – a slim chance but one well worth the annoyance.

These men were used to having a schedule, and following orders whatever the weather, but this trip was another demand altogether. No days off, just turn on, turn off of the searchlight, and standing in a crow's-nest which was no more than a simple barrel strapped to the mast. There was no respite from the elements and just a few men to work almost non-stop. Even changing into dry clothes was a challenge in permanently wet conditions. Walter's account of forever being in water on these trips is amusing for someone reading it at home but will bring back many memories for those who have been at sea!

The SS *Sabine* left Cape Town on 11 September and conducted a 14,000-mile search, zig-zagging across the path of the New Zealand ship *Waikato*, successfully found after months of drifting, and whose path was been the template for these searches. The success of this search was bound to have buoyed up the rescue teams.

It has been suggested that the teams were actually searching in the wrong place as they were carried out later in the year than the *Waikato* disappearance and the currents and weather would have affected the drift. However, this was why the teams took a zig-zag across the path of the former rather than simply following it, adding this extra insurance in case she may have drifted slightly differently. Analysing the pattern of drift when the searches were going on was rather irrelevant; the important fact was that the drift at the time of her loss was established.

Sabine visited Possession Island, where they landed and left a board, card and bottle with a message in it. This landing is at odds with many reports and it makes interesting reading. At St Paul's Island they landed again and here they found a crater and graves with crosses. They made a note of the names upon the graves and it was clear that the island had been a French observation station at one time. A letter written in French, which nobody could understand, was taken with them for translation on their return. They picked up some penguins as a record of wildlife on the island. All of this detail can be read in the journals and certainly confirms that they carried out a detailed search.

They returned to Cape Town on 7 December after an exhausting and disappointing trip. Resuming their duties, the naval men went back aboard their own ship and the *Sabine* continued her coal carrying.

Many Australians declared the search fell short of expectations and demanded another, this time going further south as well as visiting more of the Crozet group of islands. So it was that the Melbourne Search Committee raised the funds to charter the SS *Wakefield*. They had to wait for her to arrive in South Africa from England and for her to be fitted out in the same method as *Sabine* with the searchlight, crow's-nest, ropes, supplies and, of course, coal. The captain on this jolly was a man named Putt and we are most fortunate to have his journal and log as another perspective on this ongoing saga.

Walter's ship, HMS *Hermes*, was due to depart for St Helena for a month but he was asked if he would volunteer for a further secondment to search for the *Waratah* again. He recorded in his journal that he did not want to see a job half done and so took on the formidable task yet again.

There was a change of lieutenant in Hobart Seymour, and he was also given the added task of taking bearings and checking charts as they were travelling well outside normal shipping routes. This he did and we also have sections of his journal which explain certain finds and discoveries. Walter does note, however, that this ship was very different, as she was a larger ship with a greatly diminished crew, perhaps because she was a dedicated charter ship.

This search was intended to put the minds of those who had family on board at rest: all that could be done would indeed be done.

The SS *Wakefield* left Durban on Sunday 27 February 1910 and followed a path to the Crozet group of islands, and onwards. They visited Prince Edward Island, Marion Island, the Twelve Apostles, Hogg Island, Penguin Island and Possession Island once again. They covered the sea to the Heard Islands, Kerguelen, St Paul's and Amsterdam Island and on to Melbourne where both ship and men arrived equally battered and dishevelled. They had put pen to paper throughout and the story is a real ocean adventure. Walter, Captain Owen, Captain Putt and Lieutenant Seymour all wote accounts of the trip. Again, much of what has hitherto been written about these searches is inaccurate at best. These are first-hand accounts of exactly what happened, when, where and by whom. There was nothing but hard work and dedication from the men, despite running out of food, rum and the endless testing weather, as well as the loneliness of seeing just a handful of ships in months and months.

These fascinating journals construct a journey for us all into the ice and the bleak southern seas.

CHAPTER 6

KEY FIGURES IN THE SEARCHES

Walter Smith

Walter Smith was born the ninth child of Catherine (*née* Montgomery) and William Smith on 3 January 1878 in Hastings, Sussex, England. The eight children before him were equally divided between boys and girls and two others born later were also a boy and a girl. One daughter, Ellen, died in infancy but about seven years later another girl was born (in Scarborough) and Walter's parents decided to call her Ellen in memory of the child they lost. Throughout Walter's journal, possibly because she was the youngest and the namesake of her deceased sister, it is clear that he doted on her and made humorous remarks for her amusement.

Walter joined the Navy in Portsmouth aged eighteen and had an exemplary record. He was immensely happy at sea and his father and older brothers all followed careers

Walter's parents Catherine Smith (*nèe* Montgomery) and William Smith. (Author's collection)

Walter on duty.

connected with it. In fact, Walter's brother George was a captain. William (his father) had run away to sea at just twelve years old. He had gone off to Portsmouth and joined up – one can only imagine how his mother Mary felt at her son signing up so young. William was to continue to communicate with George Giffard, brother of the *Tiger's* commander, for many years and they visited each other regularly. William had been based on board the *Tiger* when she was hit and sank and he became close to the well-known maritime family, with many letters still being in the author's collection. George wrote of Walter on Monday 28 December 1903: 'I hope your son Walter does not remain long in the *Torch*. As you say, it is a pity he did not go with me. He would have been a Yeoman before this.' Giffard says of Walter's brother George Smith: 'I hope all your family are well and that the Captain of the *Royal Prince* is making successful voyages. If he is ever in the same port as myself I hope he will come aboard and see me.'

Walter's nephew was to become Captain 'Dick' Smith of the British India Shipping Company, and one of his cadets for a brief time was round-the-world yachtsman and all-round adventurer Sir Robin Knox-Johnston. Dick was also known as 'Lifeboat Smith' as he was passionate about ships' crews being able to sail and to survive should the worst happen. He taught his crews to sail and Sir Robin Knox-Johnston recalls being a cadet on board one of Dick's ships and being made to row around the harbour in a big heavy boat! Sir Robin said:

> I sailed on the *Nardana* or *Nyanza*, with Captain Smith when I was a cadet. It was on the way out to join a ship in the coast, in Bombay I think. ... I did meet him once in Hamble when I lived there as well. The locals told me he claimed to have been an MN Captain, I was able to assure them he had been.
>
> He was known as Lifeboat Smith. He would sail lifeboats, indeed he would sometimes have an additional bit of keel welded on beneath the boat to improve its performance. I do remember him taking us cadets to row him around in a Lifeboat when anchored off Karachi in 1960. Hard work, those boats were not light!

Above and right Walter's service record. (Author's collection)

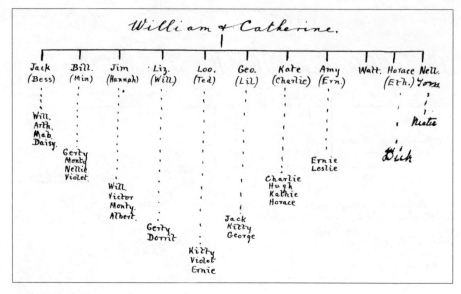

Walter's large family tree in 1910. (Author's collection)

Captain Putt

Seafaring tends to run through families and it was the same for the Putts. Captain Putt, from Glasgow, was to command the SS *Wakefield*. His home was in the beautiful, thriving, sea-faring port of Salcombe on the south-west coast of England where he lived with his family. He was born F.W. Putt on 28 October 1865, married the daughter of a sail-maker and had one son, Nicholas. Captain Putt died on 18 January 1943.

It would appear from his diary that he had given notice in to the company he worked for, Harrison Dixon & Co., and had been taking cargo to South Africa when he was diverted from his original plan and ordered to take on the second search for the *Waratah*.

His son, Nicholas, himself in the Merchant Navy, held a Master's Ticket (Certificate of Competancy) and was serving as chief officer on board the Athel Line tanker MV *Athelqueen* in 1933. The Athel Line was previously known as The United Molasses Company. These cargo ships, which became known as 'molasses ships', remarkably doubled up on cargo: they would go from carrying crude oil, petrol etc. to foodstuffs in the form of molasses, the tanks being thoroughly washed out prior to putting the molasses into the empty hold. Whilst all tanks were routinely cleaned between cargoes, it goes without saying that for a tank previously employed in carrying fuel to follow it up with food would require a far more thorough clean.

This was a dangerous task as pockets of gas could build up and, combined with static electricity, create the perfect conditions for an explosion; sadly that was exactly what

Captain Putt with family at Salcombe. (Courtesy of B. Putt)

Captain Putt and family. (Courtesy of B. Putt)

MV *Athellaird*.

happened to Nicholas off Yokohama. When the cargo of fuel had been discharged, he went down into an empty tank to see how it was progressing. An explosion killed him and also the chief engineer, the carpenter, an apprentice and an able seaman. This was a tragic and not uncommon occurrance, yet this doubling up of cargo from fuel tanks was frequent and the cleaning out essential. Fortunately today the system is more sophisticated and far safer, although for while in the 1960s and '70s it appears there were more problems in spite of the improved systems as it transpired that the hot water spray in the huge expanse could cause electrical activity and create the same issue. It was accepted as a dreadful job and the men would often be paid extra wages to complete the task. Crews in the tankers were incredibly hard working; they would travel great distances and, when in port – which was seldom – take on cargo and be away again in a sharp turnaround.

Captain Putt's grandson Bryan also went to sea in spite of his father's accident, which occured when he was just six months old. His mother sent him off with the same company as his father and he too carried out the cleaning of the tanks, noting that the only way to clean oneself off afterwards was with paraffin.

His description of filling the tank is excellent:

> … many a time I have stood on a tank top with an ullage stick (an 8ft piece of 2' x 1' with a 6" wide short crosspiece at the top) measuring the level of incoming oil as it neared deck level. Each time one withdrew the stick to check the level one would be showered with a spray of hot oil dripping from the end of the stick and blown up through the six inch ullage plug on the tank top by the pressure of the escaping gas.

What a prospect – yet I am sure many reading this will be remembering their own experiences or similar stories they have heard.

Bryan joined contrary to his own wishes in 1949 as an apprentice deck officer and attended the School of Navigation at Plymouth, signing Indentures before joining his first ship the SS *Athelstane*. He was to remain on board for about a year and, after leaving it, joined the MV *Athelviscount*. After seven months on board he joined his third ship, the MV *Athellaird*, and his final ship was the MV *Athelknight*. He left in 1952 having had quite enough of life at sea. His mother bought him out of his apprenticeship but had wanted him to stay and follow the traditions of the sea. Bryan lives near the sea in the West County and has no regrets, the sea being close enough to enjoy but not his master!

The families of Walter Smith, Captain Owen and Captain Putt have generally known little of their relatives' plights, including how extreme it really was out there on the searches. These men were quite literally in the same boat, but had wholly different experiences. The captains' primary concerns were for their ships and ensuring the safety of those on board, followed by delivering the naval party to the required search area. The naval party were there to man the searchlight, observe from the crow's-nest and search the islands. Thus the views in the accounts are both spellbindingly captivating and completely different, with many details completely missing from each account, almost as though the men were on different ships – which in many ways they were.

There are no first names given in the diaries, and little familiarity; these men were out in the middle of nowhere, in uniform and following the guidelines to the letter. These journals have never appeared in the same publication, and indeed Walter's has never appeared anywhere else in its entirety.

Lieutenant Hobart Seymour

Lieutenant Hobart Seymour was born in 1887 in Florence, the son of the Revd Edward Seymour MA Canon of Christ Church Cathedral, Dublin. He was related to Rear Admiral Sir Michael Seymour. He joined the Navy as a boy and was on board the flagship *Britannia* in January 1902. He was a midshipman in 1903 and a sub-lieutenant by 1906. In 1909 he was promoted to lieutenant and served on a number of ships including the flagship *Hermes*. His naval record makes mention of his command aboard SS *Wakefield* when she joined the search for the missing *Waratah*.

Walter mentions Seymour's seasickness, which was surprisingly common. Walter's brother George also suffered terribly. Even Captain Putt noted on his way out from Glasgow to South Africa that he felt he might be off his Christmas dinner due to seasickness, so it was not at all unusual.

The Revd Seymour. (Photograph by Dr Stuart Kinsella reproduced by kind permission of Christ Church Cathedral, Dublin)

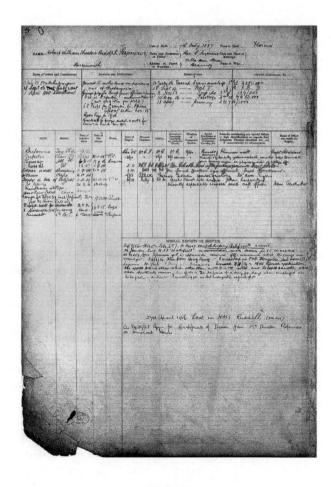

Seymour's service record.

Whilst reading his journal it becomes apparent that he was highly intelligent and also something of an anthropologist who appreciated the wildlife and surroundings in spite of their bleakness. His dedication to his orders to take note of currents and survey the islands – seldom visited as they were so far off the shipping routes – was indicative of his immense passion for his life at sea. His service record was excellent and he was fluent in French and German, winning prizes for his language skills.

On 11 January he was a passenger aboard the P&O Steam Navigation Company ship *Nubia* on his way to Hong Kong, where he was in command of a torpedo boat, P40 *Mongolia*, on patrol up the West River. He was on his was back to England in 1914 when war was declared and his next ship was the *Miranda*. His last ship was the HMS *Russell* which he joined in March 1915. He was killed on 27 April 1916 when the ship was mined off the coast of Malta and died along with 100 of his men. He had previously served on board the HMS *Russell* as sub-lieutenant from May 1907 to September 1908.

Lieutenant Seymour was clearly a popular and efficient leader for the search parties and his summing up letter to the Melbourne Search Committee is interesting. His journal ends during the endless and tiresome zig-zag course which drove them all to distraction, but the most important and interesting details of the islands and their landings are all intact. We are most fortunate to have this remarkable young man's journal.

⋙·◆·⋘

Captain Stanley Howard Owen

Captain Stanley Owen was to be called upon to take his merchant ship SS *Sabine* to search for the *Waratah*, using the template of the *Waitako* drift which concluded satisfactorily with the safe return of her passengers. The challenging search saw them given orders to go to remote areas checking for clues to the fate of the stricken liner. Juggling the safety of the ship and the need to land the naval parties on the islands they encountered to make more detailed inventories was a demanding role and one which the men could never have been prepared for.

A highly experienced captain with Union Castle, Stanley Owen was born in Islington, London, in 1865, the son of John and Pheobe Hutchinson *née* Cambell. His father John was a chemist and was originally from Ceidio, Caernarvonshire, Wales. Stanley was one of four boys; his brothers were Walter Cambell, John Edward and Granville Jackson.

Stanley ran away to sea at the age of fifteen and joined a ship from the Black Ball line. For a brief time he was on board a barque-rigged steamer, *Foyle*, later returning to sail and take command of the *Mary Jane* after the captain fell sick.

The Castle Line was to merge with the Union Line to create the tremendous Union Castle Line and Owen was destined to command many of their prestigious ships over his time at sea; across his career he commanded an impressive fifty-six ships, the last of which was *Arundel Castle*.

Captain Owen was to search for the *Waratah* in 1909. He had clear misgivings, aware that his was a role which could become burdensome should things prove less than positive in outcome, and to some extent his fears were founded. It is beneficial that Walter

Above Captain Stanley Owen as a young man. (Courtesy of Vincent Owen)

Left Letter of thanks to Owen and the crew from the passengers on board *Dunvegan Castle*. (Courtesy of Vincent Owen)

Smith's journal can shed some light on what happened and reveal some of the comments and judgements were inaccurate.

Owen was to transport the first British troops to France in 1914, just three days into the war, and he carried these duties out commanding the *Carisbrooke Castle*. His first mail steamer was the *Kenilworth Castle* in 1926.

It was in 1914, whilst commanding the *Dunvegan Castle* off the coast of Africa, that an incident occurred which elicited great praise and gratitude from the passengers toward their captain and crew. Above is a picture of the beautiful cover of a letter of thanks, a poignant piece of personal history. The particulars of the incident have been lost in the mists of time but it is known that it involved a ship holed up in a delta.

Owen was to make several trips to South Africa with his wife Gertrude Robinson and their last trip was taken on board *Dunluce Castle* in 1933. Described as a 'typical British skipper' during his life at sea, he was to retire and become involved in local council in Kingston, Surrey, where he had settled on marrying his wife in 1914. He died there in 1935, leaving Gertrude and two sons, Alexander and Edward.

CHAPTER 7

THE SEARCHES

The primary material here speaks for itself; it has never been published in this way and the journals have ever been read in their entirety before. Having rediscovered Walter's diaries in a case of family documents, they became the inspiration behind this book and before long the primary material began to swell with the diaries and journals and many contributions from friends who share a passion for the lost ship.

By the time these two searches were organised, there had already been extensive forays out to sea attempting to locate the *Waratah*. Nonetheless, the friends and family of the missing were still convinced that there was a chance that the liner could still be adrift. Thus the SS *Sabine* was chartered from the Union Castle Line and fitted out with the equipment required for searching and with anything they might need should they find the *Waratah*. The Melbourne Search Committee proved tireless in their campaign to ensure every possible avenue was explored for the safe return of their loved ones; failing her return, they at least wanted answers. This was the start of a long wait for news and the beginning of a perilous journey for those undertaking the challenge.

The SS *Sabine* was to be followed by the SS *Wakefield*. The ships already had crew as they were merchant ships, but as it was the British Royal Navy who supplied the search parties they put their own lieutenants on board to oversee the search operations. There were to be four men to operate the searchlight by night and a lookout in the crow's-nest by day, one man in charge of the dynamo and an appointed lieutenant to oversee it all. Fortunately this was to prove a satisfactory whilst physically demanding arrangement and all were united in their ultimate goal: to find the *Waratah* and return her to a place of safety.

The journals are written by the follwing men:

Yeoman of Signals Walter Smith on board the SS *Sabine*
Captain Owen of the SS *Sabine*

Lieutenant H. Seymour on the SS *Wakefield*
Yeoman of Signals Walter Smith on board the SS *Wakefield*
Captain Putt of the SS *Wakefield*

Walter Smith was the only man involved in both searches – hence his journals feature twice. All of the journals are very different in style and content and I have deliberately started with Yeoman of Signals Walter Smith's, as his writing is very relaxed and readable, which I trust will introduce the section in a slightly less formal manner. Following Walter is Captain Owen of the *Sabine*, who was given confusing instructions at first and

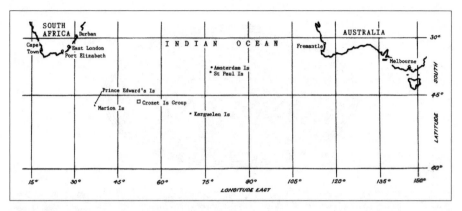

Map of search area for SS *Sabine*. (Courtesy Emlyn Brown)

who was in a bewildered state for a while before taking to the task with his customary professional zeal. He and Lieutenant Beattie RN were to be in total accord throughout and they certainly had their work cut out for them.

Walter volunteered again (having read the first account you may, like me, find yourself wondering what made him agree so readily when asked) to assist in carrying out a rather different second search. So we move with Walter onto the second ship and hear of problems with food, rum rations and rodents. Captain Putt kept his account of hurricanes, fog and endless snow and Lieutenant Seymour was there both to command and to check charts and note anomalies, which he did with great determination. Their travels took them outside the main shipping routes, presenting an opportunity to discover new information, and they found plenty to write about. So I shall leave the story to these Victorian/Edwardian men who truly pushed the boundaries of endurance. It is believed that the *Waratah* is the most searched-for ship in history, these searches spanning around a year, carrying out twenty-four-hour lookout in treacherous conditions. It does make one think – if these search ships succesfully endured this level of punishment, what could possibly have happened to the *Waratah* following a storm of equal, but certainly not greater, ferocity?

So we start with Walter's tale; he arrives at the *Sabine* coming from the comparative comfort and cleanliness of *Hermes* and begins his journal as a letter home to his enormous seafaring family.

PART ONE

SS SABINE

WALTER C. SMITH

Sunday 10th (Oct)

A month ago yesterday we left Cape Town and we have not seen anything in the shape of a piece of earth since that day and there's no telling when we shall and even when we do, I don't know if we shall be able to send a mail, but as this is the first fine day we've had since we started I thought I'd kick off and then I can do a bit more another time if we get another fine day.

Well now I'll tell you a little of the picnic. I suppose you got my letter I left in Hermes *and I suppose you got some newspaper cuttings as they came aboard and took our photos just before we left, for the* Cape Times, *so that if it turned out at all I expect you have got one by now, but it was raining hard and the ship was coaling (not us) at the time, in fact we were making our miserable lives happy.*

Well, here goes. We left Hermes *on Friday 10th September and joined* Sabine *in Cape Town docks about 11 a.m. Everything smothered in coaldust but that didn't trouble us much, as we'd quite made up our minds for it and guessed we were not going on a gigantic yachting cruise. Well, we introduced ourselves to the skipper and the bloke in the charge of us, Lieut. Beattie R.N., and the best they could do for us was to send us ashore to the Sailors' Home till the ship was ready to sail tomorrow, so without any further arguement we proceeded in execution of previous orders and walked round the town looking at all the ostrich feathers etc. that we were going to buy with the salvage money we were going to get when we found the* Waratah, *and after having a few feeds in case we shouldn't get any more for 3 months we made tracks for the Home and turned in. (Had a long yarn with the Boss about Ern – his brother.)*

Turned out and Broke the Fast and took a cab or the cab took us, down to the ship. It had started raining the previous evening and it knocked off last night just to cheer us up for the 2nd month at sea. Well when we got aboard we found they had nearly finished building a Rabbit Hutch for us to hang the spare moments out in, so after going inside one at a time and surveying it we came to the conclusions that it would do <u>Fine</u>, and still smiling as we stood hanging round in the coal dust, or coal mud for it was all wet, and who should appear but Our Admiral and Flag Lieut. with the Skipper. He had a look (or chanced one eye) at our Abode of Rest and then came out to have a few words with the representatives of the Royal Navy. Well he says 'Are you alright?' 'Yes Sir.' 'Got everything you want?' 'Yes Sir.' 'How do you hook up for warm clothes?' 'We've got a full kit Sir.' (If we'd said anything else he might have inspected it) so he asks the Skipper if he could let us have a blanket each to make an overcoat with, he says 'Yes Sir, certainly' (but we have not got it yet). Then the Admiral wished us a pleasant passage and shoved off back to his House in Simonstown where he will be able to read in the papers, some day, how we are having that pleasant passage, praps.

A page from
Walter's original
journal.

So then the Lieutenant asked us if there was anything else we wanted ashore as we were not
going till after dinner, and after a few moments' consideration we suddenly remembered there was
a bottle of beer and some bread and cheese ashore that we hadn't had so we left the coal mud once
more and saw the Beer, Bread and cheese off the premises, then once more wended our way down
to the colliery that was to be our home for the next 3 months, if not more, well then the newspaper
bloke wanted us to pose and in between the drops of rain he took our dials and then it was out all
visitors. By the way, these visitors were the blacks who had been working in the four thousand tons
of coal for us to wander round the Briny Ocean with. Next there was a noise like shoving off and
to the tune of A Life on the Ocean Wave and I Wouldn't Leave my Little Wooden Hut,
played by 2 of the Bluejackets, we started on this ramble. Then several people in different ships
made signals wishing us success and our Skipper told us to reply 'Thank you, I intend to bring
her back'. I don't know whether he meant this packet or the Waratah but up to the present we are
alone with 2 more months to go, so that later on we might be able to tell you the Tale of 'How we
found the Waratah'.

Well, I forgot to tell you before, but from the moment we left Hermes we had made up our minds to crack chums with the Cook, whoever he was, and so when we got aboard and found that Gentleman was a West Indian and his suite of rooms were on the same landing, in fact next door to ours, the job was done and we found him a perfect white man (bar his colour). Well, he said, between the sips he was having from a bottle, 'Gentlemens I'll look after you' and so he has to the best of his abilities and whenever there's anything on the board for the officers, he always puts enough for us five on a separate dish so that as regards food we are doing great and that's half the battle ain't it.

14th Oct Just found out the date (18th now)

Well it's Thursday. Don't know the date but it's the first Thursday in this week and we are still at C with the same things in sight as we had last Sunday, with a fresh supply of water from above and a thick fog for the last 4 days by way of a variety but otherwise everything is about the same old nip. We are still going ahead but the only place we seem to get any nearer to is the sky. I don't know if we are really going up that way beings as we've searched all there is down here, but it certainly seems like it for the clouds are nearly down on deck and I might add it's cold up in the sky. Well that's not telling the tale is it. I knocked off just after saying Ta Ta to Cape Town and now I'll endeavour to continue the punishment. Well the next thing of any importance was tea. They had to give us that in the Engineers Messroom as someone had just noticed that we had no table in the rabbit hutch, but it didn't matter whose Mess we were in a long as Cookie knew who he was serving and we looked out he knew that. Then we got to work lifting and shifting and I think we convinced Cookie that we should not make a fool of him by having stuff on the table so we did as other New Brooms do (sweep clean). Then the Skipper wanted to see Naval Brigade and up we wandered to his cabin and after looking at us (we were smothered in coal mud) he told us that he didn't want us to mix up with the ship's company too much as we were, or at least he thought, Intelligent Men. Capital I and M.

I started coughing, it was better than laughing and then he nearly knocked all the pleasure out of a yachting cruise in the Indian Ocean and elsewhere by telling us that this was how he intended to work us during our stay and he hoped we should get on alright and make ourselves as comfortable as possible. Well the Stoker would look after the Dynamo all night and wrestle with his bunk by day and us four would work 2 in a watch day and night, one signalman and one torpedoman in each watch doing 2 hours out of 4 at the Masthead in the daytime and the other 2 hours on the bridge, a sort of Pageboy to the officer of Watch, you know, go and get my oilskin, make me a drop of Cocoa, see what the log shows and what's the time and so on till your 4 hour watch was up and then we could go below and at night time instead of going aloft we would burn the searchlight in the same manner 2 hours about.

Well, needless to say we didn't sort of fall in love with that routine, but being as we have been brought up in the Navy to think a lot and say nothing we all said that and went on our way Quite Satisfied, saying, we're not to reason why, we're but to do or die.

Well after we got down to the Verandah, I mean the top of the main hatch, and talked it over a bit we said we'd try it for a point and we did for about 3 or 4 days when just as they were getting used to their Messenger etc. we were getting tired of it, so we held a conflab in the Cottage By The Sea and concluded that we would say nothing about it but simply work out our own plan of campaign and when we come down from the masthead at 10 a.m. remain down on deck and see if he'd send for us and so on for the remainder of the watches. But their conscience would not allow them to do that and so we scored the point and now we do the 4 hours between 2 of us at the masthead by day and the searchlight by night and of course that gives us 6 hours off instead of four which in 3 months would have been quite a nice period (I don't think).

And the officers seem to get on quite as well without that luxury (A Naval Footman). Well, after that we settled down all kiff and the Skipper comes along to our Grot every day and wishes us good morning and those who are awake return the compliment whilst the others pull the blanket up and turn over. Whilst we are burning the searchlight the other officers spin a yarn and on the whole we're doing grand and everyone is satisfied and none of us are in a hurry to rejoin the Navy. We get plenty to eat and can't go ashore so we're getting fat and wealthy.

We get quite a change of climate as we are steering a ZigZag course and so when we are going South on the Zig it's a lot colder than when we are going North on the Zag but the worst part is when we're neither zigging nor zagging but simply doing a Waratah for it and simply drifting. It's always raining or foggy then and up in the Crows nest it's rotten and we have renamed it Seagulls nest for no crow would live up there I'm sure.

We have only passed 3 sailing ships since we started and only signalled one of them. In fact I think it must have been the same one twice, but we nearly frightened him with signals and when we ask him if he'd seen anything of a disabled liner he said he was very sorry he had none, so we left him to it and by the way he was going he'd get a long way in a long time, but there's one thing he won't get run down for there seems to be nobody but us out here. A nice place to spend a Honeymoon, nobody to see you.

And now I think I'll pack up again and see if there is any change of scenery by Sunday next and if there should be a chance of sending a mail you have got some to get on with and I will keep up the supply till we get back to Cape Town when I hope to get your back numbers and to hear you are all going strong.

Monday 18th October Forenoon

As it was snowing hard yesterday and a couple of my jerseys were hanging up in the galley I had to turn in and wait for them to get cooked, but managed to climb into them last night and swore that I won't wash them again till I take them off for good.

Well, we had quite a flutter in the camp last night. Soon after it got dark the 1st Mate fancied he saw a rocket fired on the horizon and as we had just been burning the searchlight, thought that they had seen the Rays and let go the rocket so we altered course about 4 points to starboard and burnt the light again but nothing more came of it so I suppose it must have been a star shooting.

But it was rather amusing for about an hour to hear the different yarns going round down below. Capt's steward and others whose duty it is to dish up cups and saucers for officers had heard the Capt say that today was the day he reckoned on seeing the Waratah as in accordance with such and such a current she would have drifted so and so and allowing so much for the wind she would naturally be in Lat 000 Long ditto ditto ditto and then of course us steaming so and so for so long would bring us just about here and that's how we got here, but what we are trying to find out now is, where did the Waratah drift to whilst this lecture on 'what to do and how to do it' was going on. Oh, that wasn't all. Others had dreamed a dream in which they heard the very same man who was on the lookout report the missing liner off the starboard bow and the same officer had altered course the same no of points in the same direction, in fact one Salvation Army Captain (an AB belonging to the ship) was telling the others how he had heard a voice say starboard bow, and we were beginning to believe that we had her when one by one they turned in and I can say that I was on watch from 10 to 12 p.m. and if the Waratah was on the starb bow I shall have to get a new pair of spectacles for I couldn't see her. Well don't know what state of mind the people in the Waratah *are in but if we keep on keeping on like this with the same scenery for a few more weeks we shall all want seeing to.*

By the way, I forgot to tell you before but we all swore off shaving when we left Hermes *and you ought to see some of our dials. I've knocked off biting my fingernails so as to get hold of the ends of the musstash and by the time we get back to earth and face the camera we should make a pretty good collection. I will send them home Nell when I have finished with them. They will do to go with the ostrich feathers. They are a mixture of seals whiskers and porcupine quills and should look all kiff in a hat, especially one like Mary Wheatland wears. And now I think I'll back up again till something else happens so ta-ta.*

Page 16 26th October 09 at C

Here we are still zigging and zagging but we have made a call, for on Saturday 23rd inst after groping about for 5 days in horrible dirty weather and a thick fog we sighted Mud and winded our way Mudwards, then another surprise came our way for as we neared the land the Mate came down and asked us to jump in the chains and heave the lead as if we could, they wanted to anchor, now that was really <u>one</u> *we had* <u>not</u> *bargained for.*

As I can assure you it's quite cold enough at the masthead with hands in the coat pockets, leave alone breaking water up with a lead and juggling with a coil of 20 fathoms of half frozen leadline, but as I said before 'We're not to reason why etc.' and so we go on with the mangling and picked up bottom and let go anchor. Yet another, they told us to jump in our whale boat, which is an extra boat she carries on this trip as emergency boat and, after looking at our Cottage By The Sea and wondering if we should see it again, we found our way into the boat and put on lifebelts so as the fish could eat us feet first, then they passed a big board and a post down, also a shovel and told us we had to stick this up on the island which was one of the 'Crozets'. On the board was the name of the ship and the date etc. There was also a bottle with a letter in and a tin with some other message in, in case anybody else is fortunate enough to drift that way they will have the satisfaction of knowing that someone else has had the luxury before them.

They gave us rockets, fireworks and handflags to signal with in case they had to put to sea while we were away (as it was blowing hard). In fact everything that Robinson Crusoe would want, but nobody thought we might want food or water and, thinking that if we took any it would only prolong the agony, we let her shove off without it and after a hard slog with 5 long heavy oars we came across the

A contemporary view of sea elephants – a first for most! (Courtesy of B. Putt)

funniest sight I have ever seen, heard or dreamed or read about. For where we landed, lying asleep on the sand was quite 300 seals and sea elephants, in fact sea-anythings. One could never believe such a sight possible, some of them were 20 or 25 feet long and as big as an ordinary elephant with of course no legs, but they had about 2 foot of trunk. In fact a nose like a parrot with the upper part of the beak as thick as an elephant's trunk and hanging down over the lower part all same, whilst others were smaller, about the size of me if my legs were like a mermaids (you know). Well we had our Lieutenant and the 2nd Mate in the boat and they didn't know what to do best but a Russian Fin AB in the bows says it's all kiff Sir; they won't hurt us and so we landed. We no sooner touched the shore than out jumped the Russian Fin and walked a few paces up to the first one with the shovel we had bought to bury the pole with and hit the seal a Bang on the snout and he was out to the world. He then stuck his knife in and ripped him up and started bemoaning his fate because his knife wasn't sharp enough to skin him with and it was too rough to load the boat with 1 each to take aboard with safety but we all had to have a go at outing one when we found out how easy it was and then we went up the hill to stick up our visiting card (for there was not another human being on the island).

Up the hill we found thousands of penguins and nests full of eggs so we took the eggs, but the Russian told us that by the penguins skins they were moulting and it was breeding season but he said some of the eggs might be good so I took off a towel I had for a neck tie or comforter and filled it up and the others put some in all sorts of things and took them down to the boat and after throwing stones at the seals etc. that were laying asleep and awake and starting them all fighting with each other we shoved off. The Russian AB told us they won't tackle a man unless he is cornered so needless to say we didn't corner them (Brave Boys). Well after another struggle we got aboard and when the boat was hoisted we went up to rescue the eggs and as luck would have it most of them were whole, but when we got them below they were nearly all full of birds and parts of birds so we gave them a sailor's grave and proceeded to sea before dark as it's not at all a nice place to scull around in the dark with fog and a gale of wind blowing. The Skipper gave us an extra tot of Rum for our bravery and we carried on zigging and zagging to St Paul's Island.

Now all that lot happened on Saturday 23 and on Sunday we had the strongest and coldest wind I ever wish to be in, but she is a good old Bus and behaves remarkably good although of course she is getting light and therefore does a lot of rolling and pitching and us being quartered right aft, so far aft in fact that if we were to fall out of the back window we would be mixed up with the screw and logline.

A contemporary view of penguins on Possession Island. (Courtesy of B. Putt)

It's Tuesday today and getting finer and warmer every hour as we are going East and crawling up to the Northard a bit, but still not the faintest sign of the Waratah *and it was 6 weeks of the 3 months search gone last Saturday, but still we have hopes, although naturally they are getting fainter as the time flies past.*

Now I don't know if you can follow my tale of the visit to the island for its more like a ghost story but it's a fact and I will tell you more about it next year down at the 'Ship' at Christmas.

Here we go again and this time it is Wed 3rd Nov 09 so you see we are journeying along but still no signs of the lost property. We had another exciting 5 minutes on Monday 1st November, sighted a steamer ahead and steamed for all we were worth, of course wondering if it was the Waratah, *but soon saw that it wasn't and after making several signals asking him if he had seen anything of her they told us that they left Durban for Freemantle, West Australia on October 25th and that there was no news of* Waratah *there then, so we told them we were alright and ask them to report us at Freemantle and told them where we had been, where we were going, and that we had seen nothing and then we parted company and have not seen anyone since. Oh, I found out the name of that Island we called at was Possession, Crozet Group and the steamer's name was* Grifida, *and she was the first and only steamer we have seen since we left Cape Town and that's 7 weeks last Saturday so that you see we are not in a very busy thoroughfare with our Zig-zag business. I expect you will see this report in the papers soon after she reaches Australia, but I don't expect you will get this till the New Year for it takes 17 days from the time it leaves the Cape and we're not due there till the 11th December.*

I daresay we should have asked that steamer to send our mail from Freemantle but it was too rough to lower a boat, in fact to tell the truth we have not had 4 fine days all the time we've been at sea and every word of this scribble has been done with the ship rolling, 'heavy' it would be called in the Navy but in this tramp it's an everyday occurrence and if I wait for a fine day you don't look like ever getting an account of 'How we Did Not Find the Waratah'.

I don't know what date it was when I knocked off but today is the 16th Nov and by ways of a change it is raining. Well I left off writing soon after we sighted that steamer and we were wending our way to St Paul's Island, we met an Italian barque on the way, but she had no news of the Waratah, *and we arrived at the Island on Saturday forenoon to find nobody.*

But the Bluejackets manned the whaler and took our Lieutenant and the 3rd Mate ashore to have a look round and plant another visiting card. Now this lump of mud used to be a volcano on its own, but as nobody seemed to care about living on it and do a Messina for it, I suppose the owners let fires die out, with the result that the Crater (I think that's what they call the centre of it) burnt right down and now there is 27 fathoms of water inside with just enough room for a boat to go in through a gap which couldn't have been formed better by a crowd of workmen, and into this we humped the whaler and lo and behold what should we find but 5 huts, and 6 or 7 small boats which had been built by a shipwrecked crew who appeared to have lived on there up till 1904, but I don't know when they started as there were dates on the rocks as far back as 1824 - 54 - 57 and a few graves with wooden crosses and names of foreigners cut in. But we found a letter written in French and as nobody on board here can savvy it we are taking it back to Cape Town, but I should think it was left by the rescue party as there was also a box containing candles, matches, writing paper, etc. and 3 bottles of Rum and 1 of Whisky which of course we left there in case someone else gets left there under much worse circumstances than we were. Then we caught 5 rather curious type of Penguins and came back to the ship and left again after dinner in a NW direction, which means shaping up for Cape Town, but I think we shall do a bit more zigging and zagging on the way and by the look of things we shall go back without the slightest bit of information of the missing Waratah. *All we do know is that she has not drifted where the experts think she did and if she has gone further South then I'm sorry for their chances, for the weather we have had has been quite as much as any ship with her machinery in proper working order wants, to keep touch and go, so I don't know how she has managed with hers broken down and knocking all about at the mercy of the wind and sea for over 3 months now. We passed a large steamer outward bound to Australia in the Middle Watch on Saturday but too far away to signal and he was in too big a hurry to stop, but let's hope either we find her on the way back or else we hear some news of her when we get there otherwise it will be 3 months at sea for nothing, when we might have been swinging round the buoy in Simons Bay. You can bet we are getting pretty light now and well out of water and to walk about the ship is like walking on a spring bed, the deck comes up to meet you and of course we are getting our usual amount of rolling and pitching chucked in.*

Oh the penguins are doing all kiff up to now and suppose they will pick up some museum in Cape Town or somewhere but its no good us thinking of keeping them. There is not much more to tell you of the last week or two's happenings so I think I'll pack up again and let you have some more the next fine day.

All the time we are going NW we are getting into warmer weather and by the time we get another week gone we should be in good weather again and I can assure you we can do with it.

Tuesday 8th Dec 09

Even a 3 months search for the Waratah *comes to an end and sad to say not the faintest sign of her has been found. We are just past where she was last seen, in fact I think we are nearer to her now than we have been all the time but we can't get down far enough. Well we get into Cape Town tonight and the mail leaves for England tomorrow so I am going to post this lot right away before I go down to Simons Bay and get the 3 months news which I will answer next week by the way. I hope its all good news and now I have just reckoned up you should get this on Xmas Day and so I must wish you all a Merry Xmas and a Happy New Year and many happy returns of the 3rd for me.*

And now I must make this the Final Gallop. We have been having more dirty weather until a couple of days ago and now its grand again but being light we are still rolling and jumping round but tonight we let go the mud hook in Table Bay and tomorrow rejoin the Navy, not much worse for the Life on the Ocean Wave of the last 3 months.

I don't know if I shall be able to stick it with this doormat round my dial till I get a picture taken but I'll try just for Nell's sake. She won't laugh much I'll bet. Well now with another kind love, wishing you all you wish yourselves.
I remain your affectionate son Walter.

This was the story from the perspective of a naval rating whose job it was to keep lookout all day in an impossibly open crow's-nest, to operate a searchlight at night and to visit the islands when they found a place safe enough to land. It was a terrible time for the officers who had to put the ship's safety first while trying to find signs of life or wreckage on dreadfully inhospitable shores; certainly reefs were aplenty and many were uncharted. It is interesting to note that whilst away Walter was looking for the *Waratah* with great fervour, but at the end of the journal, on coming back to South Africa along the coast, he mentioned that he felt they were closer to her then than ever, they just couldn't get far enough down.

CAPTAIN OWEN

I have never written anything until now for the public and am not quite sure if I shall make what I am now going to write, public.

The first thing to think of is will it be sufficiently interesting for people, the public, to read. Next is will anybody other than seafaring people be able to appreciate the difficulties and the gigantic task that has been mapped out for me.

I will now open my story and introduce myself. I am Master of the SS Sabine a (vessel lately engaged in carrying coal) steam vessel of 2992 tons. 270 horse power belonging to the Union Castle Line engaged in carrying coal from Natal to various ports on the S.E. African coast either varied by an occasional trip to Mauritius and Port Nolloth. I sailed from Port Natal September 2 1909 for Mossel Bay and Cape Town. Just before leaving Port Natal, the Marine Supt. informed me that there was every likelihood of my hearing some important information when I arrived at Mossel Bay. Naturally this excited my curiosity, and I implored him to tell me the nature of the information, but he declined as he said it was of a private nature and he had given his word of honour that he would not tell anyone. After this I fenced a bit with him, and asked him if it would be to my advantage, and he replied that if he were in my shoes, he would feel highly honoured, of course this set me thinking and wondering what was in store for me.

On my way down from Natal to Mossel Bay I experienced fairly fine weather so I hadn't much to worry me in regard to navigation and I had plenty of time for thinking of what was in store for me, for the life of me I could not think of anything. I arrived at Mossel Bay at midnight on Sunday Sept 5 1909. At daylight I saw the tugs working the lights off to the ship and I wondered what was the matter as it was very unusual for us to work cargo on Sunday. Shortly after this the Port Official and our Agents representative came on board and the latter gentleman handed me a long cable message from the managers telling me that I was to work out as much as possible of the Mossel Bay cargo, and then proceed with the utmost dispatch to Cape Town, as I was to go and search for the missing steamer Waratah. I sent for the Chief Officer and told him the news and instructed him to work as quickly as possible. After my breakfast I went on shore, with a view to seeing if I could find out any further details, but the agents had received no more cables. I took my departure from Mossel Bay at 10pm and had a more or less foggy passage down to Agulhas from there to Cape Town. I had mod. winds and fine clear weather. I arrived at Cape Town at midnight on Monday and went into dock at daylight on Tues.

As soon as I had seen everything alright on board, I went up to the Coy's Office and had an interview with the managers and explained to them what I wanted doing on board, of course I was very much worried as there was so little time to do anything but I had made a good few notes and Mr Duff and myself sorted these notes out and organised them so that the orders might be sent to the different depts. to be carried out and we also decided it would be necessary to provision the ship for six months, these arrangements had to be made for tow ropes etc. and accommodation for extra hands as it was decided that we were to have four extra men in the engine room, four extra deck hands, one extra hand in the Galley, one extra steward. The next thing that cropped up was that orders came from the Admiralty that we were to carry four naval signalmen, one stoker to work the dynamo for the searchlight and one Naval officer to look, which had been ordered by the Admiralty. Then I asked if I could be supplied with two whale boats and one extra chronometer.

No doubt anyone who has much knowledge of S Africa will easily understand that there are many difficulties in the way of procuring things like tow ropes, boats, chronometer and such like

Drawing of SS *Sabine*, signature H. Wyllie 09. (Courtesy of Vincent Owen)

Captain Owen's map of the search area for SS *Sabine*. (Courtesy of Vincent Owen)

things. Mr Duff asked my advice on these matters and I suggested that Harbour Board for ropes, the Guano Islands Department for boats and the Admiralty or Observatory for chronometer. On enquiry it was found that the harbour board could supply us with an 18' coir hauser, but no 5' wire so other sources had to be tried.

Eventually we managed to get a 5' wire from a store in town and a 6' from Sir John Jackson's Worter at Simons Town. The next thing that had to be attended to was the chronometer, on enquiry at the observatory I found that with the sanction of the Admiral they could supply me so the admiral was asked and he immediately granted permission.

After doing this we had to make arrangements about the coal for consumption on the voyage and we calculated that 2400 tons would be sufficient to last for the voyage of 90 days and I asked for another 1600 tons for ballast purposes as the ship would not be able to tow unless she had a fairly good hold in the water. The next thing to decide was about getting rid of the bulk of the Natal Coal as most of it was useless for our purpose and some of it we considered dangerous on board for any length of time. We finally decided to retain on board 1000 tons of Natal coal and make up the balance with Welsh coal. As soon as all these arrangements were completed I went down to the docks to consult our Supt engineer about the extra accommodation that was required and after looking at various parts of the ship we decided to build it under the poop abaft the present seamen's accommodation. And then after these details had been arranged I paid the crew off and signed on most of the old hands again.

I hadn't much time for thinking while I had been making these arrangements but in the spells I had while going from place to place I had sufficient time to realise what a tremendous task I had before me and could not see how I was to carry it out successfully. All my friends envied me my luck (of course I am speaking of men who are not conversant with the sea) and could not understand how I could fail to pick up the Waratah. They seemed to think it was as easy to pick her up as it would be to find a collar stud that had been lost under the bed in their bedroom, they had no idea of the magnitude of the vast S Indian ocean and I could quite see what an immense amount of benefit it would be to me if I could only find her but she had already been adrift for 44 days and anyone who knows anything about the Agulhas Current and the currents in the Indian ocean know how difficult it is to even estimate the position she had reached, leaving alone any idea of a correct calculation. The more I thought of these things the more I realised the enormous responsibility that had been placed on my shoulders and I was almost tempted to refuse to accept the undertaking of the expedition. Of course I knew if I met with success it would mean a handsome reward but I can truthfully say that the pecuniary advantage was the last thing I thought of.

The one thing that buoyed me up was the thought of how proud I should be if I could only manage to pick her up and tow her to a place of safety and also the thought of bringing relations together again who had been parted for such a long time. I tried to picture to myself the look of happiness on the faces of the people when they saw the Sabine coming to the rescue. I thought of separated husbands and wives and mothers separated from their little children. These things alone would be sufficient reward for me but then again came the dreadful thought, supposing my efforts prove a failure and that is where the trouble comes in, how shall I be received when I come back. I hardly dare think of it. Everyone will have suggestions as to what I ought to have done, one will say why didn't you go in this direction and the other will say why didn't I go in the other direction and so on.

During this time the ship was in a very dirty condition. I have been engaged in the coal trade in this vessel for nearly two years but I have never seen her in such a dirty condition. There was coal coming in and coal going out and this was going on night and day. Under ordinary conditions we could keep the alley way doors closed but as there were so many workmen making various altera- tions and additions to the ship this was rendered impossible as the traffic would have been impeded, and I was anxious to prevent any delay. My cabin was in a filthy condition. Everything I touched was covered with coal dust. It was useless to grumble at the stewards, they were as busy as busy could be and were endeavouring to hurry the work on so I had to put up with these discomforts and try to be as cheerful as possible.

The Engineers worked very hard and the poor Chief Officer was worried to death in trying to keep things going. He had to get all his stores in and he was a bit handicapped by some of his men getting a little drop too much and occasionally overstaying their leave and coming back to the ship in an unfit state. Sailors are a given that way, they can never realise how necessary it is for them to stick to their ship and have everything ready and efficient before proceeding to sea. It makes me very sad to see sailors the worse for drink. When they are at sea and away from temptations, they are the finest creatures in the world, but once they get into the hands of land sharks who ply them with liquor and rob them, they become as stupid as mules and are useless to themselves and to the people who employ them.

On Friday September 10th Cunningham and Gearing had the searchlight on the Bridge well under weigh. This addition to the ship's equipment gave me a great deal of anxiety, owing to it being placed so near the compass, but there was no help for it, we could not place it in any other part of the ship, as the Bridge is the only place where we could use it with any useful effect. During this time I was anxious to meet Lieut. Beattie R.N. who was to accompany me on the Expedition and believe he was just as anxious to meet me, but we were both so much engaged that it was difficult to meet. When I was at the ship he would be at the office, so it was a game of hide and seek. This business was put an end to by Mr Duff inviting Beattie and myself to lunch with him at the City Club.

When we met I was immediately impressed with Mr Beattie and felt sure we should get on well together and I was very pleased as it would have been a most disastrous affair if he had been a difficult man to deal with. I could see at a glance that Mr Beattie realised the responsibility that we were undertaking and like myself was to a certain extent glad that he had someone to share it with.

Many of my friends tried to make me believe that I should have trouble with a naval officer on board. I listened to all they had to say and said it will be time enough to think of the trouble when it comes, but all the same the idea of trouble never entered my head, as I judged the man by myself, arguing that if I were in his place it would take a great deal of inducement to make me interfere in another man's work unless he was making an errant fool of himself or endangering the ship. I expressed these views to Messrs MacLean and Duff and I think they were pleased that I had adopted this idea.

There are many men in the merchant service who are rather aggressive towards naval men but the reason being they know nothing of naval men and they don't understand the duties that naval men have to perform. Whenever I have come in contact with officers in the navy I have always been received kindly and treated with the utmost courtesy.

After lunch Mr Beattie and I went to our office and on arrival there we received our sailing direc- tions from Mr Duff – which had been cabled from London. We very soon set to work with these and plotted them out roughly on a chart in the Pargiter's Office.

The area of our search was enclosed between lines joining Lat 40' 0'S Long 20' 00E and the Crozet Islands. The Crozet Islands to St Paul's Island and then a line joining St Paul's Island and Gordon's Bay better known as St Johns Ri and we had to make a special search of a circle and centre of it being situated in Lat 39' 0'S Long 40' 0'E, the diameter of this circle being 400 miles. We were rather dumbfounded at the enormous area mapped out for us to search.

While we were studying the chart Captain Whitehead came in and joined us in the study. He agreed with us that we had construed the cabled instructions correctly but still that did not lessen the magnitude of our task.

In the evening Lieu. Beattie, myself and Mr Duff dined on board the SS Gailea with Captain Whitehead. After dinner Beattie and I laid down the area of search on a chart for the use of the Cape Town office and after this Mr Duff gave me final instructions, then I went on board Sabine to see the searchlight at work, and I soon saw that this innovation would give me a good deal of worry and anxiety but it was fixed into place and there was no time to make any alterations. I won't go into any details about this as they would be too technical and would be very uninteresting to general readers.

On Saturday morning Sept 11th everything was nearing completion. To the uninitiated the ship looked far from being ready as the coaling was still going on and stores were coming in, the deck was littered everywhere with empty cases, straw, coal dust and hatches, but I knew once the coaling was finished, she would very quickly be made to look shipshape. At 10am I went up town to finish up a few details at the office and also to see Messrs MacLean and Duff the managers and there I met Admiral Egerton and we had a chat together and then he came down to the ship with me and Lieut. Beattie accompanied us. By this time a few rain showers had fallen and this did not add to the tidiness of the ship and I was rather afraid the Admiral would be rather disgusted with her appearance but I took comfort in the fact of his being a sailor man and realised that he must have often seen plenty of vessels in a dirty and untidy state.

As far as I could judge by his manner he seemed to be fairly satisfied with everything. When he had finished I asked him if he would kindly speak a few encouraging words to the officers, engineers which he kindly consented to. I asked all the officers and engineers up into my cabin and introduced them to him and he addressed them. The gist of his speech was to this effect. That we were going on an errand of mercy and a very responsible mission and the whole world would be anxiously watching our movements and praying that our efforts would meet with success and he also said that we must all endeavour to mutually assist each other in our various duties and that when any hardships came along that it would be well for us to bear them cheerfully. Then he reminded us that we were going to a very cheerless and inhospitable part of the world where we were likely to encounter very violent and lasting gales with high and dangerous seas, finally he said we must go out with hopeful hearts and a firm determination to find the missing steamer and not only find her but we must tow her to some place of safety. Then he bade us all good by and wished us good luck.

At 1.30 pm we were ready for sea and made preparations for hauling out of dock. Just before leaving a photographer begged me to allow him to take my photo. I consented as I did not want to prevent him from making an honest penny if he could. At 1.40 we proceeded out of Dock and I decided to take Dr Thomas out with me so he could examine any of the crew who had not been examined. As soon as he finished, I sent him on shore. Whilst he was examining the crew we were exchanging signals from the SS Gailea and SS Ascot; they both wished us good luck. I thanked them and signalled back that I intended to bring her back. After this I steered round the breakwater. Just as we were passing the breakwater we passed a motor launch crowded with ladies and gentlemen belonging to Y.M.C.A. One of them stood up in the launch and semaphored to us, wishing us good luck and a safe return. One of the naval signalmen answered them, giving them united thanks of all the crew. I steamed round Green Point and took a wide course down for Slang Kop. As we proceeded along the coast we encountered a strong SW wind and a high SW sea, accompanied with intermittent drizzling rain and as the day grew older the wind and sea increased and by midnight it was blowing a mod. Gale and she rolled and laboured considerably.

Soon after passing Slang Kop Lieut Beattie and myself decided that we would part company till tea time as we both wanted to straighten our gear and get everything secure and comfortable. Both our cabins were in a very untidy state. My cabin was littered up with many parcels which all had to be opened and sorted out and their contents stowed away.

After I had finished tidying up I had my tea and when I came back to my cabin to have my smoke a feeling of relief came over me as I had leisure to think over the events of the few days I spent in Cape Town. It was a relief to be away from friends and acquaintances who were forever firing volleys of questions at me about the missing Waratah and there was a certain amount of satisfaction in being freer from the office and being entirely my own master. I felt that there was very little fear of any disaster overtaking me as I had carefully thought everything out and everything that could be procured in Cape Town that I had asked for had been provided for me so as I had a good sound vessel under my feet and good reliable officers & engineers. I had very little to fear and everything to hope for.

On Sunday at noon the weather had moderated. We obtained good observations and found she had made a fairly good run. In the afternoon Lieu Beattie and I drew in the track of the SS Waikato on our respective charts and there we made tracings of these and on the tracings we filled in the tracks of all the steamers that had left the South African coast for Australia and New Zealand after the Waratah had gone a missing. We did this so as to be able to form an opinion as to the best track we ought to take to find this Waratah. The tracks of the various steamers looked very close together and it seemed impossible that they could have escaped seeing the Waratah, but when we analysed them and took the scale of the chart into consideration it was palpable to us that although the tracks looked close in reality there was a large space in between them.

In the evening after tea we had another consultation over the chart and laid down various tracks in pencil to give us ideas as to the best way of finding her, and we also calculated the average drift of the Waikato when she was broken down. In doing this we soon found out that the most likely place to find her would be in the circle that we were ordered to make a special search, as she remained in this circle for a long period, and her drift was irregular in speed and direction, so we decided to make for the circle as quickly as possible, and when we arrived in the circle we would zig-zag it as much as possible and while in it to keep in view the track the Waikato made and also the length and direction of her drift in any given number of days. We worked away at these ideas till we were tired out and then we cut out all the paragraphs from the newspapers relating to the Waratah and Waikato then we decided to give up working, have a smoke and a sociable chat but we very soon came back to the Waratah and our chance of picking her up. We were both hopeful but at the same time we wondered what was the cause of her going a missing. We suggested all manner of accidents that could have befallen her. I expect we shall be daily wondering about her and our conversation will be mostly of her.

Monday morning Sept 13th 09

After taking over morning observations, the officers, myself and Mr Beattie had another consultation about the best method of proceeding and the officers agreed with Mr Beattie and myself so we decided to adopt the plans that we had agreed to on Sunday night and now we are carrying them out. On Sept 17th we arrived at the edge of the circle and we commenced making our zigzag track and we settled down to go up, down and across the circle and explore it to the best of our ability. Today is the 10th day we have been in the circle and we have met with no success, day after day

Beattie and I go to the chart and look, & look at it hoping and hoping that each tack we make will bring us to the Waratah. *This may seem strange to people who don't understand it, but if anyone will just think the maths out they will soon see what a difficult task we have — some days we have the current setting one way and then it moves in some other direction and we seldom have it running at the same rate. Up to the present we have been very fortunate in regard to obtaining observations. On one day only have we missed getting sights. On the whole we have had very fine weather, but very heavy WSW swell and as our course is more or less at right angles to the swell she rolls and labours considerably. Day after day we pursue our monotonous search and we don't see anything but water and hundreds of birds. Each day passes away much in the same manner. We cannot go in for any recreation beyond a little reading. Most of my time is occupied in keeping my various calculations up to date and my Abstract of Log and Mr Beattie has his work to keep going for the Admiralty. I think some of my friends who desired to accompany me on this expedition would by now be praying to get back to their houses and civilisation.*

On Saturday Sept 25th 09

I stopped the engines to allow the engineers to overhaul some of the machinery. I stopped at 9 am. and set sail and was agreeably surprised to find the vessel kept a certain amount of way on her which enabled her to steer. At 10 am Mr Beattie sighted a vessel hull down to the N'd of us and on looking at her with our glasses we found her to be a barque steering to the ESE. I took a bearing of her so that when the engineers had finished the necessary repairs in the engine room I could steer for her. At noon the repairs were completed in the engine room and I steered to where I thought I could find the barque. It was rainy weather and I had lost sight of her. At 1 pm Mr Wright sighted her from the crow's-nest and I set my course toward her. At 4pm she observed the signal I made to her (heave to I have important news to communicate) and I steamed up to her, and signalled asking if she had seen anything of the Waratah *or any wreckage and she replied in the negative. Then I asked her to report me to my owners on arrival at her next port or to any passing steamer then I asked her where she was bound to and found she was bound to Padang in Java. Her name was the Anitroo [?] belonging to Poroground [?]. As soon as I had finished signalling I steered away to the northard and she continued her course to the ESE so we soon parted company. I expect the people on board were rather excited and wondered what was the matter when they discovered we were chasing them. They were a bit slow in making up their minds about heaving to but once they made a start they were very quick in shortening sail and bringing her to the wind.*

Every day we transfer coal from no 1 hold to no 2 and this does not add to our comfort more especially so when the wind is fresh from ahead as the dust flies everywhere.

I am afraid this journal or narrative would be very uninteresting if I write it every day because each day is practically the same as the previous day. My conversations with Mr Beattie generally end up with — my goodness, I wish we could find the Wararah.

Sept 30

One of the sailors caught an albatross and we fixed a brass tally with wire on to his neck, on the tally we put the ship's name, position and date on it and then released it. After releasing it I wondered how long he would fly about before he was caught and in what part of the world he would go, perhaps this message will be found long after I am dead and probably the person who gets it will wonder what it means.

Oct 2

It is three weeks today since we left Cape Town and still we have only seen one vessel and yet we have been going backwards and forwards across the tracks of vessels. It only goes to prove the vastness of the ocean we are plowing and we are only about 1000 miles as the crow flies from the African coast and the distance we have steamed is 3985 miles and only one ship sighted! It makes you think our chance of finding the Waratah is very remote. Last night we experienced a fairly heavy gale. The wind whistled round us and the sea was heavy. At 10pm a heavy cross swell got up and where it came along it made the ship roll heavily. I forgot to mention a curious thing that happened a few nights ago. While working the searchlight (as we do every night) a cape Hen flew at it and dropped dead on the bridge. It seemed to have died from fright as we did not see it strike anything. It might have struck one of the awning stretchers above the searchlight.

Tuesday Oct 2nd 09

1.42 pm. We observed a piece of wood about 8' long and 6' square floating in the water so I immediately turned the ship round and went after it and steamed close up to it. When the ship was about 50' from it we carefully surveyed it with our glasses and found it was thickly covered with barnacles and must have been in the water for about 6 months at least. It appeared to be a piece of wood belonging to a boat carrying cattle.

I would like to have picked it up but there was rather a heavy sea running and there were frequent rain squalls so I thought I wasn't safe to lower a boat and had to leave it.

Day after day goes by and they are all pretty much alike and a good deal of my time is taken up in making sure of getting good observations, to obtain a correct position at noon. The last few days have been very unfavourable for obtaining observations owing to the overcast sky and frequent misty rain. This weather has retarded my progress more than I appreciate as I have to go at a very moderate speed owing to my limited view.

I daresay there are many people who would condemn me for moving at all but if they take thought for a minute they must see that is my only chance of finding the Waratah as she must be continually drifting to the eastward with the current. The only guide we have to go by is to calculate the drift of the SS Waikato and keep somewhere in the limits that she drifted in and not to pass to the eastward of her supposed drift.

Wed Oct 6th 09

We experienced a nasty bit of weather in the morning. We had thunder and lightning and the barometer was rapidly going down and the sky before noon was covered with thick misty cloud and frequent showers of misty rain kept passing over and the wind was unsteady veering between NE and N. At 1.30 pm this misty covering cleared away and revealed a very angry and threatening sky which was covered with clouds, rolled and bucked [?] up like marble. It was a dull leaden colour, it was a sky once seen could not be forgotten. About 2.30 pm the sky was again covered over with mist and frequent rain and wind squalls passed over. I was dubious as to what course to pursue in regard to handling the ship. At 6 pm the weather was anything but reassuring so I said to myself that I would have my tea and then see how it looked after I had finished. I went on the bridge at 6.30 and had another look at the weather then decided the safest thing to do was to heave to and accordingly did so. At 7 pm the gale broke on her from the NNE. The squalls were very violent, in fact I might almost say terrific. The wind fairly shook the ship from stem to stern and it was accompanied with incessant vivid fork lightning, thunder and deluges of rain, making it impossible to see anything. The rain was driven so hard that it almost cut one's face and the sea became very high and dangerous. We blew our whistle in accordance with the Board of Trade instructions but it stood a very poor chance of being heard more than about 50 yard distance. This state of weather lasted about 2 and half hours and then the wind began to shift to the NW and the weather improved. By 10.30 pm the weather cleared up and the stars came out.

During the full strength of this breeze I kept congratulating myself on having decided to heave her to when I did. I should have been in a very anxious state of mind if I had been running before it and might run into something. It would have been rather dangerous to bring her round in such an angry sea and it would have been madness to run before it.

Friday Oct 15th 09

Since Oct 6 there is nothing very particular to remark except on the weather. On the 8th I experienced a heavy gale from the WNW and a very high sea was running which necessitated my bringing the ship to the sea [?]. This gale lasted for about 15 hours and the only redeeming feature connected with it was that the weather was fine and clear throughout. I gave myself a nasty knock on the head just before dinner. It happened this way. I went on the bridge to have a look around and had not been up more than a minute or so and she shipped a sea just before the beam and part of it expended itself on the bridge and as I tried to dodge it my foot slipped and I struck the crown of my head against the table in the sheltered corner. It made me see quite a lot of stars. Every day we are transporting Welsh coal from no 1 hatch to the reserve bunker and the dust from it flies everywhere and the bridge in particular. We manage to shift about 35 tons a day, sometimes we do more. Of course the weather makes a great deal of difference. When she is rolling it makes it very difficult for the men to wheel the barrows along. The men are working very well and so far I have had no complaints from them. They all work with a will and they seem to have settled down to the work and appear anxious to get finished with it. On the 12 and 13th we had dense fog nearly all the time and I calculate that we had 36 hours fog out of 48 which was very trying. I was getting very tired of it and the incessant whistling was beginning to get on my nerves. The weather was absolutely vile. Now and again it would clear away and I thought I had got through it then it would come down round us again and our range of vision was limited to about 100 yards. Of course I stopped during the very dense fog and proceeded slow ahead when there were clear intervals. It was very annoying to me because valuable time was passing away and it is palpable to anyone that this wasted time would have to be made up by making my courses wider apart to enable me to keep up to my contract time and it must be borne in mind the Waratah is all the time being carried to the Eastward with the ever flowing Easterly set, which runs at the rate of from 20 to 40 miles a day, at times it attains a greater velocity.

On the 14th the weather cleared up, and we were all delighted to see a bit of blue sky now and again, and I was more delighted than anyone as I was able to find out the ship's position and was agreeably surprised to find that the position was not very much different to what I calculated it would be, only a few miles. I expected to be out of my reckoning at least 20 miles.

During the middle watch of the 14th an ice bird became dazzled by the searchlight and fell on the Bridge. Mr Wright (2nd officer) picked it up and kept it for me to see; it is a very pretty little bird about the size of an ordinary pigeon. Its colour is lavender with occasional dark pencillings. He kept it in a cask and we noticed that it had a very good idea of defending itself with its beak. He killed it after breakfast and skinned it. He had the carcase cooked and tried to eat it, but after a couple of mouthfuls decided that a person would have to be starving before he could eat it with any degree of relish.

Oct 29 09

I see I have not written anything up since the 14th Oct. the reason being that we experienced more unusual amount of bad weather and I was behindhand in some very necessary work and this had to be made up. Day after day we go plodding on our way but we see nothing but birds and whales. The birds are ever with us and the whales come as a kind of treat. I am getting tired of writing in my private report. Nothing sighted during the 24 hours. On the 18 Oct the Chief Officer reported to me at 7.50pm that he saw what he took to be a rocket bearing East and I went on the bridge and steered in that direction for about an hour and worked the searchlight vigorously but we could not see anything more so I came to the conclusion it must have been a shooting star and resumed my course.

On the 19th Oct we had a strong NE gale and very rough sea accompanied with hail, sleet and snow which was anything but pleasant and then there was no snow or hail we passed through banks of fog. On the 20th the wind shifted to the NW in a hail and snow squall and then increased to a violent gale accompanied with blinding hail squalls and a tremendous high sea and I was compelled to haul the ship up and bring her nearly head to sea and reduce the speed of the engines. This weather continued till Friday 22 Oct with occasional lulls. The weather was exceptionally trying and it was seldom clear.

On Friday Oct 22 at noon I was as near as I could calculate about 10 miles to the Nth of Apostles (Crozet group) but the weather was too thick for me to see anything so I decided to waste no time looking for Apostle Island or Hog Island and shaped my course for Possession Island (the biggest island in the group). At 3pm it set in very thick so I decided to slow down and I gave up all hope of sighting Possession Island that evening. At 7.30 pm the weather again cleared up but it was too late to try and find the island so I kept the ship going as slowly as it was possible for her to go. At 3am on Saturday it was very clear. The stars were all shining brightly and I decided to go full speed, calculating that I should sight the island at daybreak (4.30 am). At 3.30 am to my great dismay the fog set in exceptionally thick and I had to stop and I was beginning to be quite downhearted and thought I should never be able to find the island. At 6.22 am the fog cleared away and there were fine patches of blue sky but fog was still hanging round the horizon but I decided it was clear enough for me to run full speed and did. At 7.12 am I sighted a small black peak poking above the cloud and then saw two or three with patches of snow here and there and decided the peaks were the peaks of Possession Island. They very soon covered up again but I had bearings on them and shaped a course to clear Dark Head, the NW corner of the Island. At 8-9 am the fog came on again as thick as ever. I stood on for a bit and as there was no sign of the fog clearing I decided to let the ship steam round in circles. At 11.15 am the weather began to clear up and at noon it was clear enough for me to see the two extremes of Possession Island and this enabled me to obtain a more or less correct position and I steamed in toward American Bay arriving off the bay at 1pm. I had to be very careful as the chart of the island is of a very small scale and gave very little detail. As we approached the bay I made out a house in the NW corner of the bay which I took to be a storehouse used by the whalers. There were also some posts erected which looked like goal posts and I concluded that these were used for drying and stretching skins. I stood in to about half a mile and blew the whistle continuously but there were no signs of any human beings. After satisfying myself that no one was there, I steamed round to Ship's Cove and arrived there at 2.15 p.m. and anchored in 21 fathoms of water, about 400 yards from the cliffs, and after taking a careful survey of the place, decided to send the 2nd officer ashore in the boat to see if he could find anything or anybody. Before sending him ashore I wrote a short statement that the ship had called there, had seen nothing on the way and was proceeding towards St Paul's Island. This was directed to whom it may concern with a request that if anyone found it, that they would forward it to Messrs Donald Currie & Co. The statement was enclosed in an air tight tin, and the tin was securely lashed to an upright with a whisky case firmly nailed on the upright, and this was erected on a small mount on the shore of the Cove about 200 yards above High Water mark. After the boat had been ashore about an hour I recalled her as the weather was wearing a very ugly and threatening appearance. When she returned Messrs Wright and Beattie reported to me that they found the foundations of what had been a wooden house, the remains of a boat and two iron blubber pots [but] that there were no signs of any human beings or recent habitation. The shores were simply swarming with penguins and seals, in fact they had to kick them out of their way as they walked along. They told me they had no difficulty in landing and once inside the cove the water was very smooth, excepting a slight swell setting in.

I was very disappointed with Ship Cove. From the sailing directions and the chart I had formed an idea that it was a fairly good anchorage but the instant I saw the place my ideas were quite changed. I could see at a glance that it was very unsafe for a large vessel to stay at anchor there with any degree of safety.

I was very sorry I arrived there so late as I had made up my mind that if I had arrived at day break I would have stayed there till the evening to give the Chief Engineer a chance to give his engines a slight overhauling and I also wanted to send one of the officers on shore with some reliable men to have a good look over the island to see if they could find anything. If I had arrived at day break it would have given me time to have sent a boat ashore at American Bay and then another Beacon could have been placed there.

At 6.15 pm with the wind began to freshen from the NNE and as the vessel began to sheer about in an alarmingly wild manner I decided to heave up anchor and get to sea and was very soon under weigh again stood to the N'd and as the night wore on so the wind increased in strength. At 5am it was blowing a terrific gale and there was a tremendous high sea running so I had to heave her to with the wind on the port bow. At 6.30 am a heavy sea struck the accommodation ladder and wrenched the bolts away and it went overboard. After this I put five oil bags over the weather side, and this seemed to smooth the sea a little, anyway she did herself no serious damage, but she took some gigantic rolls. This rolling was caused by her falling off when the heavy squalls of wind came on as I could not keep sufficient way on her to make her head the wind and seas. At 4 p.m. the wind and sea began to moderate and I was able to keep her on her proper course.

Monday 1st November

We have more or less had bad weather all this week and yesterday we fell in with another heavy Wly gale and I had to bring her up head to wind and sea. At 10.45 a.m. she rolled very violently and some of the coal in the holds shifted over to Starboard which gave her a list of about 7 degrees. At midnight the wind and sea moderated a little and I kept her away on her course again. Today at 5.48 p.m. the Chief Officer sighted a steamer bearing NW/W and I immediately steered toward her and on close approach we found her to be the Gryfevale of Glasgow. We asked her if she had any news of the Waratah and she replied that she left Durban October 25th and up to then nothing had been heard of her. I signalled to the Gryfevale that I had called at Possession Island (Crozet group) and found no one there and that I was making my way towards St Paul's Island and asked the Capt of the Gryfevale to report me to Lund's Agents on his arrival at Fremantle where he was bound to. He replied that he quite understood my signal. I wished him a pleasant passage and good bye.

Seeing this vessel has relieved me of a lot of anxiety as I know that with a little luck she will be in Freemantle in twelve days and then the whole world will soon know that we have seen nothing of the Waratah. *This is the first steamer we have seen for thirty seven days. It made us all quite cheerful. I am afraid our news will make many people very sad when it is published.*

Nov 11 09

I have very little to report since I made my last remarks. Day by day goes by in much [the] same way. We get coal up to keep the engines going and we take our sights at regular intervals. On the 9th instant the Chief Officer called me to let me know that a sailing vessel was in sight. I immediately went on deck and directed my course towards her but made a very poor shape at overhauling her. She was under very small sail but she was evidently a fast sailer. By 10 am I gave up all hope of catching her as I could see she was gaining on me. At 11.45 am she tacked to the S'd so she was then meeting me. At noon she was close to us and I manoeuvred the ship and kept close to her and signalled to her asking her to report me on arrival at her destination or to any passing steamer. I gave her the usual dismal news that I had nothing reassuring to report. She was the Italian full rigged ship Australia *bound to St Leonards (Queensland) in Ballast. I did not ask where she had come from. On the 10th instant we had a great variety in weather. During the morning we had a moderate Ely gale and high seas accompanied by misty and foggy weather. In the afternoon the wind veered to the north east at 5 pm the wind was north west and at 5.30 pm it blew a very violent gale from that quarter. The force of this wind was terrific and the sea was simply lashed into a foaming mass of driven spray which drove over the ship from end to end. It was much too strong to last long but I took the precausion [sic] of hauling her up head to wind and kept her heading that way until the wind abated. There was a decided improvement in the weather at 8 pm and at 9 pm I was able to resume my course. At midnight the weather was quite fine and there was a very heavy swell which made the ship roll heavily.*

The 11th inst.

We had a really fine day and a smooth sea which everyone appreciated. It is the first really fine day we have had for over a month and the Chief Officer did a very good day's work at the coal. The ship is beginning to get very foul, the grass is quite thick on her sides and in rough weather the wind and sea beats portions of it from her side and they are blown up on to the deck, this makes me anxious about her speed on the return journey. Even now I notice an appreciable depreciation in her speed, and now the grass and barnacles have got a hold of her, her foulness will increase by leaps and bounds and I shall congratulate myself if I mange to make some more than 7 knots in fine weather.

Friday Nov 19 09

Friday Nov 12th at 4.15 am I sighted the island of St Paul. I was rather anxious in regard to making this island owing to its being small and not very high. I managed to obtain very reliable stellar observations on the previous evening so was not very anxious about my position but was afraid the weather might be foggy the next day. I was up at 2.0 a.m. and kept a lookout in case the current might make her over-run her distance. It was a perfect morning hardly a cloud in the sky and the day began to break at 3.45 and at 4.15 I sighted the island on the port just on the bearing I had steered for and found by observation that it was 32 miles distant. At 8 am I was close to its southern extreme and at 9am was safely at anchor in the anchorage on the East side of the island. I anchored with my Star anchor in 19 half [?] 7 cables from the Ninepin Rock.

The island of St Paul is 2 and half long north and south and 1 and half east and west. Its highest points attain an elevation of 862 feet and is situated in Lat 38' 43'S and Long 77' 35E and is a volcanic island and some time or other it must have been an active volcano.

On approaching it from the W'd there is nothing very remarkable about it, it wears the same appearance as all other volcanic islands but as one draws round to the Eastern side and just about the middle one is immediately struck with its remarkable formation. At some very remote period this island must have subsided into the sea and a portion of the East side has fallen into the sea and what was the mouth of the crater is now almost a circular lake about 1300 yards in diameter carrying a mean depth of 25 fathoms of water and the sides are almost perpendicular and the water is quite deep close round the shore. The gap in the side of the island which forms the entrance is about 400 yards and the channel into the lake carries a depth of 7 ft and is about 50 yards wide so the lake would be quite easy of access to a vessel of light draught, in fact mention is made in the Sailing Directions that small schooners have entered the lake and one schooner was wrecked in the lake by breaking from her moorings during a whirlwind. The island has from time to time been inhabited by fishermen and it has been the scene of two known wrecks. HMS Megocea [?] was beached June 1871 and English four masted barque Holt Hill was wrecked on the Western side of the island Nov 13th 1889. Close to the entrance of Crater Lake and a little to the Noth'd is a remarkable rock named Ninepin rock which must have been named on account of its resemblance to a ninepin. It is 255 feet high and is separated about 20 yards from the island.

I sent the boat ashore in charge of Mr Tilllng the 3rd Officer, Lieut. Beattie accompanied him and the naval men formed the crew. They returned to the ship after being ashore for an hour and a half and they furnished me with the following information. They had no difficulty in landing and obtained a depth of 6ft over the Bar at the entrance to Crater Lake. Close to the landing place were five huts all of which were roofless save a few rafters.

In the first hut visited were three white painted boats, being marked respectively No I Rêve Réunion No 2 Rêve Réunion , no 3 Rêve Réunion (they all appeared to be in good condition) and also some empty bottles which had a strong odour of fish oil.

In the second hut were found six boats one having on her stern Stella Maris the others were unmarked. Inside the door was roughly painted 'Holt Hill lost Nov 13, 1889. 32 hands' followed by some other words which were undecipherable and the Direction Board for directing shipwrecked people to the huts where the provisions and clothing which are stored there by the French Govt was inside of these boats. There was also a wooden box with a canvas cover marked Bôite aux Lettres which contained a tin of tea, matches, fishing line and hook, a knife and a bottle. Also a piece of plain writing paper in an envelope and in the corner was a large quantity of salt in sacks.

In the 3rd hut was found a boat bottom up, several broken casks and a small wooden box with a gable shaped lid containing tea, candles, matches, sugar, fishing lines and hooks, a knife and three letters and some writing materials. Two of the letters were addressed to Madame Ver Felise Fleurie St Denis Reunion and the other a Monsieur Commandant de Passage, all three were unsealed so they were brought on board and given to me.

Secured to one of the beams in the hut was a board bearing the following inscription: 'Salerie Fleurie a perms Moisces sapin constuite en Nov Rêve 1904' and close to this was a tin containing a piece of canvas on which was printed SS Kent visited this island in search of the missing dredger Walrus from Durban.

A G McGibbon Master

J MacLean 1st mate
HA Causton e2nd
EJ Cloke 3rd
C J Grantly 4th
Jany 18 1904 [?]

[This piece of canvas is now in my possession.]

In the fourth hut were found 10 casks, 5 of which were broken open and contained empty tins. There was also a large pile of salt covered straw in the corner.

The fifth hut was empty.

Near by were three graves close together, surrounded with ship's cable, having wooden crosses erected, on which were carved as follows: Octave Potin 25. Xbre 1903, the next one Repose Henri Medom Dec. the rest was obliterated. The third grave besides having a wooden cross had a granite cross on which was inscribed Aremateur du Rêve Raoul Fleurie DCD 10 Xbre 1904, there was a wreath of everlasting flowers secured to the cross with wire. Some distance away was another cross having on it Iracha Joseph Emilien, Dede le Janvier 9 1901, nearby was what appeared to be two more graves surrounded by a wall partially covered with cement, but there were not crosses.

In all directions were scattered iron bolts, blocks, wire, tanks, pots, small spars and near to the landing place was an old marine boiler (small). On the Northern Spit which forms the entrance to Crater Lake was found a square block of light brown stone on which was roughly painted 'Coup de Venus du 5 Janvier' followed by some words which were undecipherable '1885'. Attached to this stone by iron dog bolts was a granite block having the following inscription cut into it: 'Passage de Venus, sur le Soleil Observatoire Francaise 8th Dec. M.D C C C L X X I V L38' 42' 51' Lg 75' ll 09'.

The flagstaff marked on the chart had disappeared. A piece of board on which was painted the ship's name, date of visit, was nailed to a wooden upright and an air tight tin containing a statement of our mission and where we had come from was secured to this upright. This beacon was placed in hut no 3.

Today is Sunday Nov 21 and at noon we were in Lat 41 24 S and Long 54 2E. After leaving St Paul I sailed along the Northern boundary of the area of search midway between the boundary and the northern points of the zigzags we had made on our way out to Lat 36 35S Long 59 20E and arrived at this point at 4am Nov 18th 09 and then steered for a position Lat 42 20S Long 54 0E and arrived at this position at 4am today. On the way down I encountered an exceptionally strong current which set me to the Eastward and also experienced moderate Wly gales, very high seas and more or less dirty weather. This is a portion I did not explore on the way out as I had not time to do it and I decided to make one run down to this Latitude hoping there might be a chance of seeing something. I am now going up to Lat 36 0South and long 54 0E and from there shall make short zigzag courses towards the African coast as we all think there is very little likelihood of picking the Waratah up at the S'd of Lat 40 0S.

[This bit was crossed out.]
On the 26th Nov I spoke [to] the SS Maithara bound from Durban to Port Adelaide. I signalled him but he was rather too conversational to get reliable news so I bade him goodbye and proceeded on my course.

Dec 3 09

Since Nov 21ˢᵗ 09 we have had no really bad weather only light gales and moderate heavy seas and occasional rains and mists and we have made much better running than I expected and…

Sadly this account comes to an abrupt ending but the majority of the trip is outlined here. Captain Owen's ship's log was also incomplete. Fortunately, what is here is in order and makes great reading.

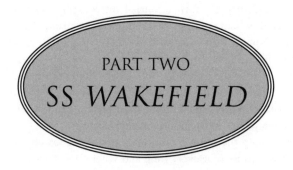

PART TWO

SS WAKEFIELD

This part of the book follows the far more treacherous search carried out by the *Wakefield*, in which the intrepid adventurers encounter some hair-raising moments, including many hurricanes, all endured from an open crow's-nest. Each crew member was responsible for a different task and their varied accounts and priorities speak for themselves, but they all shared the same overall experience.

Of the three journals which follow, the first is Lieutenant Hobart Seymour's; his task was to liaise with Captain Putt over how best to perform the requests of the Melbourne Search Committee and Admiralty. The lieutenant was charged with noting and surveying the territory as it was so remote and charts proved inaccurate in a few cases. He also observed currents and drifts, so he comments quite frequently on these developments, and of course he was an active presence on the islands, organising the naval party searches. His entries focus heavily on the things the crew saw when landing, as well as the geography and conditions.

Walter's account comes next and his focus is more on what the islands could provide in the way of food, and on survival and human nature in all its glory. Written in a con-

SS *Wakefield*.
(Courtesy of B.
Putt)

versational style rather than as a formal journal, his contribution relays the day-to-day experiences involved in being put ashore on uninhabited islands.

Finally comes Captain Putt's account. He had to negotiate treacherous harbour entrances, leaving his crew on islands and hunting out reefs. His journal is less about the islands – it appears that he did go ashore once but he does not mention it himself, leaving that to Walter – but due to his remit dwells on the *Wakefield* and the safety measures in place. His journal considers the weather, their position and other such matters. His description of arriving back in Melbourne is captivating.

I have aimed to keep the more interesting parts of the searches intact but there is simply not the room to present everything and where the journals report little activity and focus only on noting position I have edited them down. Captain Owen of the *Sabine* had a typed log which is also available to read at Greenwich.

There are great gaps, which are accounts of the zig-zagging – the complete scouring of sea on a 300-mile x 40-mile course. It was to take weeks in horrific weather and there was hardly any other sea traffic. Clearly during this time the logs were up to date but for the purposes of this book have been condensed down.

The team left port on Friday 25 February, casting off at 10.40 a.m.

———————◆———————

LIEUTENANT HOBART SEYMOUR'S JOURNAL

MARCH
Thurs 3 March

6 am wind shifted to South. Lookout in crow's-nest.

8.30am sighted land ahead viz Prince Edward and Marion Islands and the hills of which were covered in snow.

Position at noon Lat 46.26S Long 37.50E and by x bearings Lat 46.22S Long 37.45E. course and distance made good S13E 176.

Current for the 24 hours S58E.

11.20 reduced speed and proceeded to steam down lee side of island to find suitable landing place but too much surf was observed to enable boat to attempt landing with any degree of safety. Turned and steamed slowly back at 4pm stopped engines and allowed ship to drift to observe currents. When steaming along the lee side of the island current was against ship but when steaming in the Northerly direction at about 2 miles off the land current was observed to be with ship 2 per hour N30W (true) ship was moving over the ground about 5 knots. This current was experienced as far as NE Cape. North of that point the general set was SE half knot per hour. The currents which are separated by the island rejoin about 5 to the eastward of it, the general set then, as before the island is reached, is Ely about half per hour. Compass was affected by island to the extent of having 5 more Easterly error than before. Shifting drifting to the leeside of the land all night.

Fri 4 March

At daylight steamed up close to the land and at 10.16 am landed search party of 4 in surf boat. Although it was blowing fresh from WNW there appeared to be less surf on the beach than on the previous day, it was, however, only with the greatest difficulty that the party were able to land at all. The beach is of large rounded boulders and in the surf the boat damaged her keel and garboard shake [?] both when landing and bringing off the party. The ship's carpenter, however, was able to perform the necessary repairs. The party consisted of the Dr, myself and two naval ratings. On landing we separated and the Dr and I going North and the two men South. We searched thoroughly from the North point to the South point of the island, finding nothing at all. We were unable to proceed any further owing to a range of mountains barring the way. The two men met with similar obstruction. The searching had all to be done on grassy cliffs some 50 feet or more above the sea. The going was extremely bad and, ground being like a sponge, every other step taking one up over the ankles and occasionally we sank down up to the knees. Also the country was intersected by innumerable gullies conveying the water down from the snow on the hills so that we were constantly climbing and descending and we were all absolutely tired out when we arrived on board at 4.30pm.

The island presents no objects of interest except the penguins and seals which are very beautiful. It is of volcanic origin and covered with long grass and higher slopes with a course [sic] moss and the whole island is boggy and swampy. The drawing of the island on the chart is incorrect. From NE Cape the land runs in a big bight to a long low lying point just to the Northward of which is the only landing place. This point which should be named E Cape is roughly in Lat 46.37S Long 38.1E. From there the general trend of the land is SWly (true) till a similar point is reached to E Cape only it faces South and should be named South Cape and is roughly in Lat 46.38S Long 37.58E and from there the land runs up to High Bluff. It will thus be shown that there is no SE Cape.

The skipper of the sealing schooner Beatrice L Corkam whom I interviewed in Cape Town (on the subject of the islands about to be visited) also informed me of this. I have made alterations in pencil on the charts and the Capt of the Wakefield is of the same opinion. The area searched by the landing party is shown in red ink.

Kelp extends off the land from Ross's Rocks to S Cape on the eastern side, but the whole of the Western side is steep too, the mountains run down to the sea and the water thus is clear of kelp. The only evidence of human habitation on the island was the name Agnes Dounshire a sealing schooner, painted in a cave just by the landing place.

Sat 5 March

Ship drifting under lee of Prince Edward Island. At daylight attempted to steam round. Went coast of island to examine portion which search party were unable to explore on the previous day, but abreast of the Ross Rocks such a strong head sea was encountered that ship had to turn round and make for shelter again. About 8am the wind shifted to the southward so ship proceeded to Marion Island arriving there about 10.30am. There was no difficulty finding the landing place which is in a little cove and well sheltered and as some huts were seen from the ship it was proposed to leave a search party ashore for a couple of days. So I went ashore to find out if huts were inhabitable etc. Considerable difficulty was experienced in hoisting out and manning the boat owing to the strong wind and sea, which caused the vessel to roll heavily, but once inside the Cove we got a smooth water, the thick kelp outside acting as a breakwater. Inside the Cove we found the wreck of the SS Solglimt of Christiania. Her port bow with the name on it was the only intact portion but there was other wreckage besides which uncovered at low water so that caution should be exercised when entering the Cove.

We landed in a slight surf on a hard sandy beach enclosed in a curious sort of semicircle of cliff which must have been the crater of a volcano at some time. On the beach were three large iron tanks used in boiling down blubber, presumably out of the wreck, and a large quantity of timber. There was also a shed with boiler arrangements so that the place must have been used as a whaling station some time. On the beach on some boulders high up were two boats belonging to the wrecks and higher up just at the foot of the cliff was a lifeboat with air tight compartments and covered in with canvas. There were several lifebuoys from the wreck ashore and all the hatch covers, wooden fittings have been used to make a path along the beach and lower slopes to some huts which I shall presently describe.

The ship herself is so curiously placed, there being only just room for her in the Cove, and so much of her gear is on the shore that it certainly looks as if she had been placed there on purpose, possibly to act as a breakwater against the heavy sea which would roll in with a Northerly wind. High up on the lower slope of the cliffs is a wood and canvas hut with 'Engineering House' painted on the outside, it was found to be full of brine.

On following the wooden path over the rocks we came to a hut full of rubbish and above that was another hut built up against the cliff having on the outside a board with the words 'FOR MEN' painted in block letters. Above the hut on the rock of the cliff was painted in big letters the word DOLBAKKEN and this was visible from the ships outside.

Descending once more to the wooden path we climbed a ship's ladder which brought us to another hut having an old stove and 4 bunks in it. We also found a small store of medicine. Proceeding further we came to a small hut containing stove and six bunks, which the doctor and I used as our sleeping quarters afterwards. Alongside of this was a big hut with bunk accommodation for about 8 men, two tables and a couple of forms and a couple of wooden stools. This we afterwards used as a general living room and the three men who landed with us slept there. Just across the wooden path facing this shed is a store room containing a large stove and the shelves were covered with every possible necessity in the way of food. This is evidently used as the headquarters of the sealers when they are on the island and there were signs of recent habitation. The wooden path stops short here and a grassy slope commences which is the only out of the small semicircular cove.

Returned on board and ship returned under the lee of Prince Edward Island for the night. There is a reef covered with the kelp extending N1/2 (half) E (true) about 2 miles from a point just to the Eastward of the landing. There is also a small reef covered with kelp just to the Westward of the landing and several similar ones off the North coast. The set of the current being Easterly it was unsafe to remain for the night with that big reef under the lee. The Captain returned under the lee of Prince Edward Island and remained there afterwards also when the search was ashore.

Sun 6 March

Lying to leeward of Prince Edward Island.

5am proceeded at full speed for Marion Island.

9.15am launched surf boat. Doctor myself and three of the naval ratings proceeded ashore with provisions etc. expecting to be taken off again on Wednesday morning at daybreak. We also intended to beach the boat but had considerable difficulty in doing so and spent most of the day in dragging her clear out of the water so that no searching was done on the island that day. After dropping us the vessel steamed round Marion Island to search for wreckage. There was a man in the crow's-nest all day. The ship was within two miles of the land but nothing was seen. Ship then proceeded to Prince Edward Island and steamed from the High Bluff round the West and North sides, stopping under the lee of the island for the night. Nothing was seen on this island either.

Original page from
Lieutenant Seymour's
journal, 6 March 1910.
(Courtesy of B. Putt)

Mon 7 March

Ship lying all day under the lee of Prince Edward Island. On Marion Island started searching the coast at 8am and got as far as Cape Davies returning to the hut at 5.15pm having seen nothing.

The distance covered there and back is only about 12 miles but the walking is so bad that it is equal to 30. All the walking has to be done on the grassy slopes on top of the cliffs and the ground is so boggy and wet that sea boots are necessary. Also there are high hills which come right down to the sea, which are covered with long grass and full of deep holes into which one frequently sinks up to the knee. These have to be climbed in order to get to the edge of the cliffs beyond. So that the walking altogether is just about as bad as it is possible to find. For this reason it is not possible to get any further in one day, consequently we were unable to explore any further in that direction. Had the ground been dry and had it not been raining almost all the time we were on the island we might have carried the tent round with us, thus walked all round the island, but camping under canvas in that country and under those weather conditions – the mountains are covered in snow and it is very cold – was absolutely out of the question.

Tues 8 March

Ship under lee of Prince Edward Island. At Marion Island – 8am started searching to the Eward and got within a mile of C Hooker and then had to return and got back about an hour before dark. I personally did not take part in this expedition nor did the doctor as we both had badly blistered feet from walking in sea boots the previous day. The men reported the going to be bad, but rather better than we had on the previous day as far as the East Cape and from there on it was very bad. Nothing was seen on this expedition.

Albatross, seals and penguins are seen in great numbers on this island. The beautiful King Penguin is especially common and during the course of our various expeditions we came across several rookeries of them containing many thousands, the noise from which was deafening. Owing to the north and NW winds on this day the tides were exceptionally high so that the stern of the surf boat was afloat at high tide. We were however only able to shift her about 4 or 5 feet higher up with her bows right up against the boulders of which the top part of the beach is composed. We made her painter fast round a big rock, filled her stern with water and put in a cask full of stones to prevent her lifting, aft wedged her with baulks of timber on one side and a cask full of stones on the other, but even then I was very much afraid she would not last out the night.

Wed 9 March

Ship lying under lee of Prince Edward Island.

9 am she proceeded for Marion Island but such a mountainous sea was running that she had to turn back again and make for her previous shelter where she remained for the rest of the day. At noon there was a whole gale blowing from the NW with terrific rain squalls and everything was battened down on board. Owing to these winds the tides were so high and such a heavy surf was beating in that in spite of our efforts of the previous day, our boat was afloat aft at high water. With great difficulty we managed to get her 3 or 4 feet higher and secured her as before. Throughout our stay on the island she was visited at every high tide, but it was impossible to get her any higher up and on examination at low water next morning it was found that her garboard [?] had opened up nearly the whole length of the boat.

Thur 10 March

Still weather-bound on Marion Island with the ship unable to get over and take us off. Fortunately the sealers had left a good store of provisions as ours was pretty well finished. In the afternoon the weather moderated and the ship steamed over to the island but owing to the heavy sea still running she was not able to come in close enough for an exchange of signals. She then returned to her previous shelter under Prince Edward Is.

Fri 11 March

At 7 am ship arrived off the island and we signalled her to send a boat as ours was damaged. Lifeboat with Chief Officer in charge was accordingly sent in. The ship's carpenter was also sent in the boat with tools and he effected temporary repairs to the surf boat and we launched her with the assistance of three of the other boat's crew, our intention being to tow her off to the ship, leaving a man in her to bale out. There was a moderate surf running at the time and on launching she bumped on the sand in the surf and this caused her to open out and she filled. We took all the gear out of her including oars and rowlocks and attempted to tow her off as she was, but she was such a drag on us that instead of making any headway, she was dragging the lifeboat astern into the surf again so we had to cut her adrift lest the crowded lifeboat should get swamped and broken up too.

Noon, lifeboat returned to ship. 12.30pm left for the Crozets. Full ahead course SExE 3/4E.

1 pm streamed log, placed lookout in crow's-nest. Observed a very large iceberg about 5 due East of E Cape travelling East.

3pm Afe to ExS 3/4S.

8pm reduced speed to 6 knots for the night and burnt searchlight as before.

Mon 14 March

Lookout in crow's-nest from daylight to dark.

10.45am sighted whaling barque with Schronerin [?] company. Afe course for speaking barque who proved to be the Alice Knowles of N. Bedford USA. She had heard of Waratah being missing but had seen no signs of ship or of human habitation or wreckage on the Crozets which she had just visited.

Noon Afe to SE 1/4E. position at noon Lat 45.4S long 49.40E. course and distance made good N77E 170. average speed for day 7.1 hour.

1.30 pm sighted Twelve Apostles group right ahead and shortly afterwards Hog Island on the starboard bow. Between 2 and 4 hours experienced currents setting ENE 3 per hour. Steamed around Twelve Apostles Group passing within a mile of North Rock. Nothing was observed at all and although a strict lookout was kept both from bridge and crow's-nest, no signs whatsoever of the Cairn alluded to in the Sailing Directions were seen.

5pm shaped course for Hog Island and remained under the lee of it all night. Burned searchlight as before.

Tues 15 March

Dense fog with NNW gale. Ship steaming on a North and South course at slow speed all day and supposed to taker her 2 miles off the Five Giants.

4pm sounded in 90fths black sand and turned ship's head south.

4.10 pm fog suddenly lifted to the northward for a few minutes when it then set in thick again. Found ship to be about 1and half off the southernmost Island of the Twelve Apostles Group and 1 and a half distant from the rock that was awash and breaking heavily. To have been in this position the ship must have had a strong NEly set as the ship was placed on the chart at 4pm about 4 miles to the westward of her actual position.

5.45 pm fog lifted and weather moderated. The centre of Hog Island bore WNW, dist about 12. The ship was then allowed to drift for the round. Manned searchlight as before.

Wed 16 March

4.15 am steamed full speed towards the island and at 8.30am I landed with the four naval ratings. Proceeded as far as NE Cape and about 2 along the North coast of the island when we found the way barred by a range of mountains running down to the sea. So returned getting on board about 4.30 pm. The walking, though very bad and of the same nature as the two islands previously mentioned, was slightly better as the ground was a little harder. The only thing seem worth noting was an ordinary domestic cat which however had become wild and [could] not be approached. It would indicate however that the island has been inhabited fairly recently.

The provision depot hut is broken down and all the provisions and clothing are absolutely rotten and will want replenishing. The hut too should be built of something more substantial than wood. The provisions appear to have been untouched. We could not however find any signs of the hatchets, spears and cooking utensils alluded to in the Sailing Directions. I left a small bottle in a conspicuous place by the ruined hut with a note inside written in English and French to say the island had been visited requesting anyone finding it to report to that effect.

Thur 17 March

8.30am landed again on the Hog Island with one man and proceeded South along the coast getting as far as the South Eastern point. On arriving I noticed that the fog which had been on the hills all day was creeping down so I turned back and made for the landing and got on board again about 2pm. It is not safe to stay on that island with a fog as the hut is broken down and the provisions rotten and it might last for several days and not safe for the vessel to approach very close owing to the outlying reefs.

We saw nothing whatever on our search. While we were ashore the ship steamed around the western coast of the island and got as far as South East point when the fog came on and, as he did not know what dangers might exist between that point and the landing place, the Captain deemed it best to go back the way he had come. The ship also saw nothing. About one o'clock the fog lifted so as soon as we were on board, proceeded for Penguin Island, passed within half mile of the Herione Breaker reef and observed it to be two rocks about 4 feet above water close to one another.

Experienced a slight Easterly set between Hog and Penguin Isles. Steamed around Penguin Is and saw nothing.

5.35 pm shaped course for Possession Island.

Burned searchlight as before.

11.30pm stopped engines and allowed ship to drift. The breaking rock to the SE of Penguin Isld is correctly placed with regards to the Island.

Fri 18 March

5.10 am proceeded course SExE.

8.15 aft ExS. Could not make out Possession Island owing to thick fog. About 11am the fog lifted and we sighted the island on the strbd beam, a bearing at 1.35pm placed the ship 5 North of Perforated Rock. Closed in on the land and examined the coast between Perforated Rock and American Bay but saw nothing. The whole of the Northern side of the island is steep too, high mountains drop down to the sea. It is consequently impossible to search that part of the coast on foot. Stopped off American Bay for the night. The current in these waters are probably surface current and affected by whatever wind happens to be blowing.

Monday 21

A very fine day and smooth sea.

8.30am landed with one man and proceeded to search the coast between American Bay where we landed and also Ship Cove. We found nothing relating to the Waratah *[but] on the beach was a lot of wreckage belonging to the Norwegian sealing schooner* Catherine.

The castaways from that vessel built a large hut from the wreckage in which there is berth accommodation for about 15 to 20 men. They also erected a gallows to which were attached a pair of gymnastic rings and a swing. This is visible from a long way to seaward.

The hut showed signs of habitation in the way of plates etc. left about and there is a board bearing her name secured on the outside of the hut. This latter is in very bad repair and needs restoring. Inside it simply swarmed with rats whom we found nesting in some canvas on top of the provisions. The bunks are eaten away by them and rotted by the damp and the place is at present uninhabitable. The provisions however seemed intact only I saw no signs of any clothing. This however may be have been stowed away under everything else. Most of the gear was in big tins and painted with red lead. We also saw a box of tinned milk. We found a box having a complete metal box inside and probably containing ammunition to judge from its size and weight and on the outside it was addressed to the SS Solglimt from SS Alpha from Christiania. Curiously enough, on returning on board, one of the men forward had been reading a back number of Chambers Journal *April 24th 1909 and came across the following passage which I quote word for word:*

In Decr 1906 the Norwegian Sealing schooner Catherine was driven ashore by a gale on one of the Crozet group. Her crew waited patiently for a month in the hope that some ship might pass close to the island and effect a rescue and then Capt Rae left with two sailors in an open boat determined to reach Melbourne or perish in the attempt. Meanwhile the castaways had discovered the depot of provisions left at this remote o'post by the Government in 1880 and there was an abundance of fresh water, seals and penguins. After having sailed 1000 miles on their errand of mercy, the dauntless trio were picked up by the German ship De Ruyter on her way from Japan to the USA and were transferred to a tug boat not far from Melbourne and were soon in touch with the shore authorities. The Federal Premier immediately cabled to the Cape Government and in response thereto the SS Turakins was ordered to call at the island. She found the castaways in good health and brought them on to Hobart and the Norwegian Consul provided the necessary clothing and other comforts for his countrymen. Mr H J Bull of Christiania, the owner of the Catherine wrote a letter of thanks to the British nation on behalf of himself and his fellow castaways and HM King Haakon VII conferred the order of St Olav on Capt Forbes of the rescuing steamer and the Norwegian Government has taken the opportunity of the departure of the SS Solglimt on a similar expedition to replace the provisions which were used from the depot at the Crozet Islands by the crew of the Catherine. The Solglimt evidently landed the provisions and then went on to Marion Island and was wrecked.

[It is not clear where quote ended.]

Near the hut were three graves on a little hill. Two of them bore epitaphs but the third had nothing. Those two were as follows: In Memory of Charles Engelbrecht a native of Stralsund Prussia, died 12th September 1867 aged 22 years, and In Memory of Henry Stapleton Born Queenstown 1825, died January 5th 1866 aged 41 years. On a hillock close by was a small signalling gun as used in some liners. The walking to Ship Cove was very bad, boggy in part and consisting of volcanic ejections in others, but always very hilly and intersected by numerous gullies down which rush the mountain torrents. On arrival at Ship Cove we found the notice put up by the SS Sabine still standing and we found the tin at the bottom of the notice board but the fastening with which it had been secured to the post had been severed and the sealing wax with which the lid of the tin had been fastened broken and the message inside extracted, but there was no message to say who had found it. I accordingly placed a fresh message in the tin noting the name of ship and date and requesting anyone finding it to report accordingly. We returned back on board about 5.30pm. Ship lying off American Bay for the night.

Tues 22 March
Ship lying off American Bay.

5.40 am Proceeded for East Island and proceeded to steam around it. In NE Bay could be seen two or three uprights in the Western portion of it. These are probably the remains of the huts alluded to by Captain Simpson in Dec 1901 but no signs were seen of the post or Cairn mentioned. The island is well worth seeing, cliffs rise from the sea to a height of 6000 feet almost sheer and numerous cascades some of them of great height are to be observed. There are two or three beaches leading to low boggy valleys, otherwise the island is absolutely steep too. The island must also be larger than shown on the chart as it took the ship steaming at 7 knots 4 hours to get from NW point round the eastern side to SW point, a distance of about 17 miles. An easterly current was experienced during this rip round the island from one and a half to two knots per hour. On reaching SW point shaped course for Ship Cove but on arrival there it was found that landing was impossible owing to the heavy sea breaking on the rocks. So proceeded to steam round south end to search for wreckage and half way up the west coast of Possession Island but such a strong head wind and sea was encountered and fog banks were seen approaching that the vessel was turned around and made for the lee side of the island where she remained dodging for the night. Dense fog and light breeze. A breaking patch was observed about 3 off shore and whose line of bearing ran through the position of the breakers reported by Capt Simpson of the Australian [?] in 1886.

Wed 23 March

7.30 am landed search party and planted a notice board alongside of that left by SS Sabine. It had painted on it 'SS Wakefield in search of SS Waratah landed March 21st 1910.'

The Chief Officer of the ship also left a bottle with a message in it at the foot of the notice.

Proceeded to search between Ship Cove and a spot about 1 mile beyond SW point but saw nothing.

2.45pm returned on board. Proceeded full speed and shaped course SE ½ E for Kerguelen Island. When off East Island took sights. Capt sight placed the island 3 to the westward and the mean of two sights of mine with the ½ hours run in between placed it 4 ¼ to the westward which gives a mean of 3 ½. Moreover, from 2.45pm when the ship started 1 degree east of Ship Cove till 4pm when ship was about 1 degree south of the SW point of East Island the log showed 9, thus making the distance between that point and Ship Cove 10 miles. Burned light for 5 mins every 15 mins.

Sun 27 EASTER SUNDAY

8.30am sighted land ahead which proved to be Roland Island and shortly after made out Bligh's Cap and the remainder of the islands. In view of the strong SWly wind blowing at the time the heavy sea running and a falling glass with every appearance of dirty weather, decided to proceed direct to Christmas Harbour and search that immediately and then be free to proceed should the weather clear, otherwise take shelter under the lee of the island.

11.5 am Roland Island abeam. Afe to SExS ½ S.

Noon ship 2 east of Cape E'Eastaing, reduced to slow speed.

12.30pm wind shfted to NW and on arrival off Christmas Harbour such violent squalls were blowing that we were unable to launch a boat and land. Remained under the lee of the land working engines as required to maintain position.

Burned searchlight whenever main engines were working.

Fresh gale with very violent hail squalls and round NW sea.

Wed 30 March

Weather moderated considerably during the night but there was still too much sea to land. Early in the forenoon about 11am the sea appeared fairly smooth in Foul Hawse Bay and though still too rough and squally for landing in Christmas Harbour, decided to attempt a landing in the former. A landing was finally effected near Arch Rock in Foul Hawse Bay though not without difficulty and proceeded to try and get to Christmas Harbour overland. The boat ran alongside a ledge of rocks and the force of the sea was broken by the kelp which lies on them otherwise we should never have managed it. After walking for over two hours, I noticed the wind was freshening and fog coming down from the mountains so turned and made for the landing getting on board about 4pm and only just in time as the ship had to steam away from the land owing to fog as soon as we were aboard. Burned searchlight at intervals.

Naval search party on Possession Island. (Courtesy of B. Putt)

Thurs 31 March

Ship lying well clear of the land owing to thick weather.

4.10am weather cleared with a freshening wind shaped course for Christmas Harbour.

6am very heavy storm rising and glass falling rapidly. Turned and steamed full speed away from the land. Course NE whole gale of hurricane force blowing and mountainous cross seas and thick rain.

10.20 am reduced to half speed.

Noon afe to NNE same weather conditions with violent squalls.

4pm afe to North about 6pm the weather cleared. Afe to NW increased speed to ¾. Position at 7pm by stars Lat 48.17S long 69.55E.

8.45 increased to full speed.

Burned searchlight during the night.

APRIL
Fri 1st

3.30am reduced to half speed, weather improving slightly.

4.10am shaped course West and increased to full speed

2.40pm arrived off Christmas Harbour but found wind and sea too high to attempt a landing so lay off the Bay working engines as required to maintain position.

Burned searchlight whenever steaming. During the night the ship drifted towards the Sentry Bose Rock giving a SSE set of the current about ½ and the same was found on the night of the 30 March — these were the only two occasions owing to the high winds and sea that we experienced during our stay at Christmas Harbour.

Sat 2 April

6am slight sea and wind moderate though frequent strong squalls were blowing, decided to land and search Christmas Harbour. After great difficulty effected a landing on the rocks about ½

Entrance to Christmas Harbour in calm weather. (Courtesy of Hans Helfenbein)

mile from Cape François. The squalls were too violent to enable the boat to pull right into the beach. Walked to Christmas Harbour and found the flagstaff still standing and at the foot of it a notice board reading 'Eure 1893'. I turned the board round and left it in the same place, scraping the name Wakefield on the back with a bit of broken glass as I had no knife. We have brought a board with the name of the ship and the date in the boat but it was too far to carry it so placed it near where we landed, up clear of the rocks so that anyone passing close in a boat would see it.

While I was ashore the wind and sea got up and we had considerable difficulty in getting off to the ship. Twice the boat was nearly swamped and it is a marvel she was not. She was slightly damaged when hoisting her on board owing to the rolling of the ship. As soon as we were on board at 9.20am proceeded full speed course as requisite for clearing Terror Reef.

Noon afe to ExN whole gale blowing from the Northard and high sea with thick rainy weather.

2pm when clear of the Reef afe to SExS ½ S and reduced to slow.

6.30pm position by stars Lat 48.41S long 70.19E. strong gale and high following.

Burned searchlight for 5 min every 15 min.

Mon 4 April

6 am strong gale and heavy sea. Weather clear with violent snow squalls at short intervals. As it was too rough to land, decided to steam in to Royal Sound and try and establish communication with the Norwegian settlement there. Consequently at 9.15am shaped course WSW shortly after passed SS Jeanne d'Arc who was steaming towards Hillsborough Bay. Exchanged signals relative to the SS Waratah and they informed us they had seen nothing. He then asked her to report us all well on her return to Durban. Proceeded into Royal Sound as far as the lighthouse on Murray Island then as the wind was increasing and the snow squalls thicker and more frequent and also as it was getting late, it was deemed advisable to get clear of the land before dark so turned and proceeded to our previous berth of Cape Digby. We saw nothing in the southern part of Royal Sound and no signs of life in the way of a lighthouse keeper on Murray Island.

Burned searchlight.

Thurs 7 April

Steamed into Hillsborough Bay. Lookout in crow's-nest.

10 am spoke [to] Norwegian whaler Ornew *and I boarded her to ask for information. On board I found a French whaling captain who very kindly consented to Pilot us in to Gazelle Basin so we proceeded full ahead. 1pm stopped and came to port anchor in 8 fthms of water. Although it was blowing fresh outside there was no wind or sea in the Basin and the Frenchman said that the plan of Gazelle Basin was absolutely accurate. There is however a clear passage between Schulz Reef and the island off Cape Wackenhusen through which the ship passed both on her way in and out of Foundry Branch. Our Pilot informed us that this was perfectly safe and infinitely preferable to going straight into Foundry Branch as the Reef charted in the Southern portion of that bay extends further to the Northward than shown and does not break except in heavy weather. He also told us he had been in Irish and Whale Bay and seen nothing and that these two harbours though affording a certain amount of shelter are very unsafe as anchorages as owing to violent squalls experienced there and a rocky bottom a ship is very liable to lose her anchors. He said the same of Christmas Harbour and gave an instance of a small 100 ton whaler moored there with there [sic] anchors and cables who parted the whole three in a squall. Fairweather Harbour he said was a good anchorage, as regards shelter, but the holding ground is indifferent and the only two really good anchorages in Kerguelen are Gazelle Basin and inside Long Island off the settlement in Royal Sound. The holding ground of the latter is not entirely reliable he informed us and steam should be always kept handy whilst there. Island harbour is stated to be a good anchorage for small ships and as having too much kelp for a large steamer to manoeuver [sic] in. This Frenchman has lived 18 months in Kerguelen and says the finest weather is always experienced at the new moon and the worst at the full moon. The tides are very unreliable but the highest and lowest tides generally occur in fine weather. The currents depend solely on the wind, the prevailing wind being westerly. The general set of currents is Easterly. He stated he had discovered an uncharted island in Weinick Bay nearly a mile long and 100 feet high and also that the northernmost of the three bays situated in Royal Sound between Observatory Bay and Long Island extends to the westward as far as Long 69.30E. He has walked from the settlement in Royal Sound to Gazelle Basin and it took 4 days and 4 nights. With the wind south of west and with snow, fine weather may be expected, especially if the glass is steady, no matter what height the mercury may be, but with the wind north of west and unsteady barometer rain and heavy weather may be expected, the worst blows always being from the NW. He also stated that it seldom blows hard for more than 24 hours and that if a gale commences at daylight it generally moderates at sundown and vice versa. The average duration of a strong gale being 12 to 15 hours. Inside Gazelle Basin we found the SS* Mangora *at anchor and in the little bay just to the northward of the entrance to Gazelle Basin was the* Jeanne d'Arc *secured alongside the rocks in deep water and discharging coal on the shore. Her Capt was on board the* Mangora *when I called and both the Norwegian Capts confirmed all the Frenchman had said, and they all three confirmed the Northerly and NEly set of the current (about 10) experienced by us between the Crozet Grout and Bligh's Cap. They said 2 or 3 degrees further North we should find the easterly set. The Captain of the* Mangora *also informed me that 20 to 25 miles NNW (true) of Bligh's Cap he sounded in thick weather getting 20, 15 and 12 fthms. He could see nothing owing to the fog but on getting the last sounding turned and steamed away from the place.*

Landed search party at the southern point of the little rocky promontory, on the eastern side of which is Boat Cove is a small white staff and the words 'Brev Hen' painted in big white letters on the rock. This means in Norwegian 'letters here' and the spot used to be employed by the whalers as a letter box. The Cairn alluded to in the Sailing Directions is still standing and is surrounded by a sign which from the Anchorage looks like a cross and is two strips of the top of a cask nailed crossways to a post.

The provision depot and the wording above are as described in the Sailing Directions. The entrance to the Cove being closed with stones, I went into the cave and found it damp with water dropping on to the stores which however were coated with tar and covered with a big strip of canvas. The provisions have been tampered with, probably by some of the whalers, and these were only two big casks and about 80.9lbs tins of meat remaining out of the original number. The flagstaff with the French Flag (made of tin) is still standing but there is nothing buried at the foot of the shrouds, the reports having been extracted long ago by some of the ships frequenting the place.

8pm let go starboard anchor as the ship was veering about. Got soundings over the stern 11 fthms. Ship Hd WSW 10 pm sounded in 10 fthms into mud. Ships had SWxW.

Fri 8 April

6am weighed starboard anchor.

8am landed search party who walked across Jackmann Peninsular to Irish Bay and about two miles in a Westerly direction along the South shore of the Bay returning on board shortly after 5pm when it was too late to go [to] sea owing to the darkness coming on and the difficulty in negotiating the entrance to Gazelle Basin. Nothing was seen on this expedition.

Sat 9 April

At 6am the Frenchman came on board weighed anchor and proceeded to sea. When clear of the Schulz Reef, put him on board the whaler Orman. He was very kind to us during our stay and gave us every assistance in his power for which he would accept nothing, as he was only doing it to oblige us. The Norwegians in the whaler however though they had only stopped for a few minutes on two occasions when there were no whales in sight, asked for £20 to compensate them for loss of time. We gave them £5 which I thought was quite enough.

9am shaped course ENE and proceeded full speed out of Hillsborough Bay. Fresh northerly gale with rain and high sea. On leaving harbour placed lookout in crow's-nest.

Noon afe to SE Kent Reef bore S ½ E true 4 ½.

3.30 pm ship 8 degrees off Cape Digby afe to SxW. time commenced for Charterers Afe. Strong gale blowing and very high following sea, weather rainy and at times thick.

Burned searchlight 5 in every 15 mins.

Mon 11 April

7.30 am made Heard Island on Port bow. Lookout in crow's-nest. Moderate northerly gale and very heavy Wly swell. Proceeded to steam along the western side of the island, our intention being to steam down that side, round the south point and under the lee of the land up the East coast and to land if possible.

Discovered an uncharted reef about ½ miles long and breaking heavily about 5 degrees N50W true of Cape Arcona. This position is only approximate as although 4 different sets of bearings were taken, they did not cut in owing to the land being inaccurately charted. I think the island should be turned from 15 degrees to 20 degrees from left to right or with the hands of a watch to get the correct position. This is borne out by the fact that when about 2 off the land at noon the estimate SE bore ESE by compass or N78E true, also there is no big bight immediately to the southward of Cape Arcona. The part marked low land is very low indeed being only a few feet above water. When we started steaming down the coast the wind was North, this shifted to NW, SW, South and East and finally when we got to the position at noon above mentioned it was blowing a whole gale from the NE and the weather was thick and hazy. That we were in shallow water was obvious as in spite of the strong wind blowing it was quite smooth water and there was no land to shelter us. Taking this into consideration and also the fact that it was thick weather (we only got the bearing of the point in a momentary clearing) that the locality is but poorly surveyed and that once round Spit Point we were on a lee shore in a light ship who would not steam against a heavy sea. We decided to turn and steam away. The Capt of the Mangora moreover had informed us that he had visited the island 17 days previously to hoist the British flag and that he had steamed right down the East coast in a small whaler as far as Spit Bay and seen nothing so we considered it would be a waste of time, besides being dangerous, to hang about this locality, so shaped course for Cape Bourbon so as to pass close to McDonald Island. Whilst sheltered by the high land we got little or no wind but as soon as we were clear of that we got the full force of a strong NEly gale.

3.20 set course NNW.

6pm afe to NW ½ N.

7pm afe to NW. These last two alterations of course were so as to make sure of passing the leeward of McDonald the weather being at the time thick with misty rain. Experienced a NEly set of the current which moderated the leeway the ship would otherwise have made with such a strong gale and high sea. Burned searchlight.

Wed 13 April

Strong gale and high sea. Weather cloudy with hail squalls.

8am afe N ¼ E noon afe to North.

Position at noon Lat 50.18S. long 68.56E. estimated current NEly 12.

2pm sighted Bernadet Islands, Solitary and Round Islands and also the mainland.

2.30 pm saw an uncharted breaking patch about ¼ long S50E true from the SEastern of the Bernadet Group. It is probable this reef, though only a few feet below water, only breaks in bad weather. This would account for it having been previously unreported. The same applies to the reef previously mentioned off Heard Island and which we named Wakefield Reef.

At 3.26 pm obtained a sight which fixed the ship in Long 68.52.45E and the South Eastern islet of the Bernadet Group then bore N17W, a bearing of it at 3.10pm cutting this line of bearing placed it in Lat 49.54S Long 68.49.15E (finished time for charters afe).

No bearing was obtained of Round Island as it was not easy to see but its position at a guess would be 5° NNW of Solitary Island Cape Bourbon at 3.10pm bore N7W but this bearing was not good as the Cape was very hard to make out owing to haze.

3pm shaped course SExE.

5.30pm reduced to half speed.

6pm afe to SSE.

6.15pm position by stars Lat 49.59S Long 69.23E. afe to SxE. This position argues a strong northerly set of the current as the course was laid down to pass about 10 to the southward of Salamanca Rocks. 10 afe to ExS and reduced to slow.

Awaiting daylight. Burned searchlight.

Thurs 14 April

4.10am Afe to North.

5.30am increased to full speed.

6.20 afe NE ½ E.

Steamed into Royal Sound intending to proceed up to the settlement. From 10.45 to 11.30 sounding continuously with no bottom at 12 fthms. 11.30 obtained bottom with hand lead in 7 fthms mud. This was in the centre of the triangle formed by Sulin and Hayes Reefs and the SEstn position of Grave Island. Proceeded as far as a position due south of Green Island when in view of a rising wind and falling glass and very ugly appearance of the weather and also bearing in mind the uncertainty of the holding ground near the settlement (of which we were informed by the Frenchman in Hillsborough Bay) it was considered more prudent to make for the open, turned therefore at noon. At 1pm stopped off Cat Island and went ashore to investigate the appearance of Island Harbour from the summit. As I could see very little kelp and that all close in shore, I returned on board and the Capt decided to go into the harbour and anchor.

2.40pm let go starbd anchor in the centre of the harbour in 10 fthms black mud.

At about 3.30pm landed on Grave Island to inspect the graves we could see from the anchorage. Found these to be 15 in number. The graves of men who had died in the American whalers in about 1860. The epitaphs were all written in English but some of them were hard to decipher owing to age. Observed two broken down huts on Hog Island in the position marked on the plan. Both Cat Island and Grave Island are full of rabbits and there are also a few duck, one of each were shot with a rifle.

The breeze died away towards evening, some difficulty was experienced in landing owing to kelp, but it is all close in shore and the centre of the harbour clear.

Fri 15 April

Ship at anchor in Island Harbour with strong Sly gale blowing and party unable to land or do anything.

9am let go the Port anchor to steady ship. Wind increasing with violent westerly squalls. 1.15pm weighed both anchors owing to ship having dragged and drifted berth 5 cables further west, close under Hog Island. 60 fthms on starbd and 30 fthms on Port cables. Weather still continued the same with very violent squalls and hail and snow.

Ship at anchor in Island Harbour with strong gale blowing. Very violent snow squalls. At 6am owing to an exceptionally violent squall the ship dragged both anchors and dragged right out of the harbour, narrowly escaping the NE point of Hog Island. Weighed both anchors at once which came up simply covered in kelp (no doubt this was the cause of the vessel dragging). Proceeded out of Island Harbour into Royal Sound where the ship spent the day steaming slowly off and on between Sulin and Long Island (East) in the hope that the wind would drop and enable us to get to the Settlement. On the previous day I forgot to mention a small vessel, probably the Norwegian steamer (Eclipse), was sighted apparently making for the anchorage in Island Harbour but when she saw we were there she anchored outside between Cat and Grave Islands. She got underway about 5am on the 15th and steamed off presumably to sea. Glass rising but strong gale blowing every very violent snow and hail squalls so about 4pm proceeded outside Royal Sound for the night and burned searchlight. Vessel dodging.

Sun 17

Ship outside Royal Sound and gale still blowing. Course and engines as requisite to maintain position. Noon observed an uncharted breaking patch NE ¾ N from Balfour Rock or just covered by

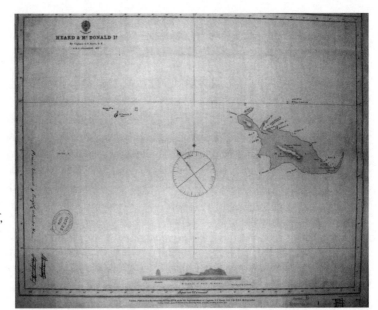

Chart prior to
Wakefield Reef,
1874. (Courtesy
of the Archives
of the United
Kingdom
Hydrographic
Office)

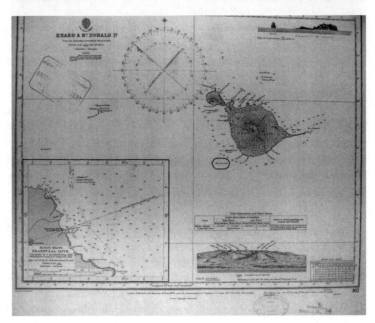

Chart marking
Wakefield Reef,
1950. (Courtesy
of the Archives
of the United
Kingdom
Hydrographic
Office)

*the red or just covered by the red section of the light on Murray Island [...]. It was only breaking
occasionally and must be a good depth below water as we only saw it on this particular day when
there was a heavy SWly sea. During the afternoon when the wind was moderating experienced a
strong NNW (true) set of the current of from 1½ to 2 knots an hour. The ship was steaming slow
about 4 knots making good 6 over the ground. As regards the light on Murray Island we saw it
burning on the nights of the 16th and 17th but when close enough to see it we were always in the
white section. I was however informed by the Frenchman that it was found the green sector was not*

sufficiently easy to distinguish from the white so the Northern Green section has been changed to red. It is probable that the southern green sector one has also been changed but my information did not allude to it.

Burned searchlight as before.

Mon 18 April

Steamed into Royal Sound intending to go straight up to the settlement but we were delayed by fog. This, however, lifted about 10.30 am so steamed up as had been our original intention. The settlement is on the Northern side of the Southward of the five bays at the Western end of the large inlet sheltered by Long Island (West). The third one is Suffrly [?] Bay. We steamed up to within 1 mile of the settlement but did not land as it was nearly 3 oclock and it was desirable to allow sufficient time to get out into the Sound clear of Hayes Rock before dark which sets in about 5pm and it had taken us 2½ hours to get in from there.

The Capt did not consider it prudent to anchor there for the night in view of a falling glass with every indication of wind, especially after our experience of Island Harbour. The holding ground for the latter is supposed to be good whilst the Frenchman had told us that off the settlement was unreliable. Moreover we knew that nothing had been seen by the people of the settlement as we questioned the Capt of the Jeanne d'Arc and Éclair in Hillsborough Bay and they told us that nothing had been seen in Royal Sound.

Turned and steamed away from the settlement. 4pm wind and sea rising and weather thick with rain. As there was no more searching we could do in Royal Sound I did not consider that we should be justified in waiting two or three days for another fine day to steam up to the settlement and land, knowing as we did that nothing had been seen, so decided to shape course for St Paul's.

The settlement is a large one with a wooden jetty running out and there are two large mooring buoys close to it. There is a large factory from which smoke and steam were issuing and that is probably where the boiling down of the blubber is done. The houses appeared to be wooden on the point of land separating the settlement inlet from that running in a SEly direction towards Greenland Harbour is a post with several arms which looked like a sign post though I can't imagine why one should be placed there unless it is to direct to the settlement anyone who being in doubt as to the directions, should land there to find out.

6pm shaped course NExE.

6.10pm Balfour Rocks NNW 2½. Streamed log. Burned searchlight as before. Fresh NWly gale and very rough beam sea. Ship rolling heavily.

The whales are all caught in Hillsborough and Whale Bays and have to be towed round to the settlement in Royal Sound by the small steam whalers, who consequently make this trip about twice a week each way thereby burning an enormous quantity of coal. The scenery throughout Kerguelen is grand and mountainous, closely resembling the Norwegian Fjords.

Sat 23 April

4pm proceeded full ahead for the Island.

8.30 am landed search party. The wind was NNE true and the glass at 30.51. There was a heavy swell on the beam which broke right across at intervals and it was only by watching our opportunity that we were able to cross it.

We landed about 9.30am and during our stay ashore the ship remained two to three miles offshore and stopped. She at first drifted NW true but about 11am or just about one hour after high water the current changed and she drifted SE true at about ½ per hour. After landing in a tiny cove which was just big enough to hold our four-oared dinghy, we proceeded to investigate the contents of various huts. There are four in number. There were also several ruined huts but as these contained nothing there is no need for further allusion to them. All the huts are built of rough stones piled up and have been thatched with coarse grass (which grows on the island), long poles and bamboos being used as rafters. The roofs however have been blown off them all and the interior is open to the sky. In number 1 hut we found one boat in fairly good condition, 3 empty barrels (which are missing from the provision depot).

In one of these barrels was a post and notice board left by the SS Sabine when she visited the island. Attached to this by wire was a tobacco tin containing a statement signed by the Capt and Mate of the ship and also Lieutenant Beattie RN stating that nothing had been seen of the Waratah by that ship and giving a list of the ships spoken. There was also a request that it might be forwarded to Messrs McDonald Currie and Co which I shall do on reaching Melbourne. I left a message in the tin giving the name of the ship and date of landing and requesting anyone finding it to report to that effect. I also left a notice board in the hut with the name of ship and date on it and fastened a bottle containing the same information by the wire which the Sabine's tin had been secured to the post.

In no. 2 hut I found some letters written in French which I took, also directions in English and French for the use of shipwrecked mariners and a complete list of the Officers and Chiefs, company of the French War vessel Bourdonnais when she hoisted the French flag on these islands in 1892. This latter I look but left instructions for the use of shipwrecked mariners.

In this hut were 6 boats in fair condition, one named Stella Maria and alluded to in one of the letters in my possession, appearing to be the most seaworthy. On the inside of the door of this hut was painted 'Holt Hill lost Nov 13th 1889. 32 hands. 1 lost now 31' saved.'

I also found a good supply of fishing lines. Continued ★

A letter written in English by the skipper of the fishing schooner Angele Eliza found at St Paul's:

Instructions for Captains who have lost their vessel to St Paul 13 April 1893

Stores — *the ware vessel Eure has deposited here in this house, some stores, some clothes. You can take them.*

House — *please live in this — the shore is hot.*

Rabbits — *the rabbits are in abundance on island.*

Water — *take the small way who conduct in N.O (or NW) along side the sea. You shall find a basin of hot water when low water.*

Profit the flood and make brackish — is better instant.

Fresh water — *in height on mountains N.O. is a small wooden [?] which gives you indications to come up by pingouins way — when you are near this wood, you shall find a way which shall conduct you to three basins of fresh water which is very good.*

Fish — *great abundance.*

Lobster — *ditto.*

I don't desire that those instructions serve you. [This seems to mean he wishes it will not be necessary.]

If a vessel sail in the Sud put a piece of clothes, white and he shall come take you.

Capitaine Angele Eliza
Translations
1st here lies Anthony Timothy Boucret deceased the 19th Feb 1903

2nd here lies Henry Medon deceaced the 6th of the 10th month 1886.

Here lies Octavius Potin deceased the 25th December 1903.

Rêve (dream) this was the fishing schooner to which three of these men belonged, and belonged to Réunion.

The 10th of Oct 1904 Ralph Fleurie, freighter or owner (of the said ship) having an artificial wreath inscribed to our Father.

Here lies Joseph Emilien Irasha deceased 9th January 1901.

No. 1 hut bore a notice nailed to one of the rafters inside which read as follows:

Salerie Fleurie a fermes moisées sapin construite en Novembre 1904. (Rêve)

There was also a letter box full of rubbish marked Lettres Fleurie, 1903, 1904, 1905, 1906. A rock outside the hut was completely covered with inscriptions, a lot of which were illegible but one or two of which I could:

Moussepen 1883 Mâtelot. H Bégué second 1902 and 1903. Capitaine 1906. Pelle Fournier, Emile Mazarin Denovarez from Grenoble Cautou de Sassenage department de l'Isère (county of) 1844. Also the name Gordon and the other side of the rock in white paint SS Kent.

Translations continued

Trainsit of Venus from the 5th January to the 5th of Feb 1885 which read as follows:

Passage of Venus over the sun observatory of the French party 9th Dec 1874.

———————⧓◆⧓———————

[Journal continues:]

And hooks, a little tea, some candles and matches. These also are mentioned in one of the letters I found. There were also two bottles of whisky. In the bottom of one of the boats was the notice of provision and clothing left by the man-of-war Eure in 1893. This I had shifted to the hut where the provisions are stowed and which I have called No. 3. Two of the letters I found alluded to 12 barrels of provisions being there and two empty. I found 7 full barrels and two empty ones in No. 3 hut which, with the 3 empty ones already mentioned in No. 1 hut, makes up the twelve.

The hut, as before mentioned, is open to the sky and the barrels are in a rotten condition but the provisions are stowed in tins inside them so are probably still quite good.

In No. 4 hut were 3 boats bottom up which appeared to be in excellent condition.

There are 6 graves. 4 belonging to the Rêve schooner together with crosses and inscriptions and surrounded by and old ship's cable to as a nailing.

These read as follows:

Ci-git Bouveret Antoine Timothé decide le 19 Février 1903.

Ici repose Henri Medou décidé le 6 X 1886 (this man could not have belonged to the Rêve)

Ci-git. Octave Potin décidé le 25 December 1903 & Rêve le 10 x lre 1904 Raoul Fleurie Armateur du Rêve.

This last one also had a stone cross bearing the inscription 'Raoul Fleurie Dec 1904' and a wreath of artificial flowers inscribed 'à notre père'.

The other two graves were some little distance off the other side of a hill. One was surmounted by a cross which read as follows, 'ci-git Iracha Joseph Emilien décidé le 9 Janvier 1901'. And on the other the post was still standing but the cross arm has fallen and was illegible.

The observation spot is on the northern arm of the rocky spit which we landed on. It is marked by a small brick and mortar cube on which is painted 'Coup de Vénus due 5 Janvier au 5 Fevrier 1885' but it is almost obliterated and very hard to read. Bolted to this is a slab of granite on which is engraved 'Passage de Vénus sur le soleil observatoire de la mission Francaise 9 Dec MXCCCLXXIV. Lat 38.42.51S Long 75.11.0E'. The Longitude is that from Paris which is equivalent to 77.31.9E of Greenwich. I would point out that the Longitude of North Entrance on the plan of St Paul's is 77.31.15. Sights taken for the rating of chronometers gave the Long as 77.36.0E when the ship was 2 N23E true of Ninepin Rock.

3pm returned on board and [the] ship proceeded at half speed for Amsterdam Island. St Paul's is overrun with rabbits and some wild goats were also seen.

The Basin is full of fish, some bream and crayfish were caught. I found one hot spring about ¼ to the westward of No.1 hut. There were a few seals on the South side of the entrance.

Burned searchlight.

Sun 24 April

2am stopped engines.

4.10 am proceeded half speed for Amsterdam Island and steamed up the East coast of it. There was a heavy NEly swell and landing was quite out of the question owing to the surf that was breaking on the rocks. Observed what we took to be a flagstaff lying on the ground close to the landing place. We steamed around the North side of the island and when off that coast experienced a SSE (true) set of 1 knot per hour.

Near the little beach on the North side of the island we observed what looked like the remains of a hut. When off the NW point turned and at noon stopped engines and allowed ship to drift. During the afternoon ship drifted SE true at a speed of 1 per hour and during the two day watches SSE at a similar speed. During the middle watch, however, the ship drifted SE again.

The island is crowded with cattle which could be clearly seen from the ship. We must have seen several hundred of them and they all appeared exceptionally large and fine animals. When steaming round the East and North coasts the ship was 1 to 1½ miles from the shore.

TRANSLATION OF A LETTER WRITTEN IN FRENCH BY THE SKIPPER OF THE ANGELE ELIZE fishing schooner:

To the Commander in ship of the French East Indies Naval Station, St Paul 30ᵗʰ April 1893.

To Mr the Commander of the ship of state who will pass the first

Mr Commander

Extenuated and ill, as a result of a blow of wind of the 25ᵗʰ March, blow of wind wiped at sea and lasting five days I entered into the basin with little tide on the 8ᵗʰ of April. I was no longer able to hold the sea and my second was not received. All my linen being in a pitiable state, not being able to warm myself, I had extracted from one of the barrels two shirts, wood, two drawers and two blankets. Not being able to keep rice on the stomach I had taken fifty biscuit cakes for soup to me made for me. As soon as I arrive at Bourbon I shall have the honour to write to Mr the Commander in Chief of the Naval division of the Indian Ocean and I shall bring to his knowledge what I have written here. I leave lines, hooks, and instructions for ship-wrecked ones. Kindly I receive Mr the Commander my salutations respectful of your servant (respectfully your servant) Bertuilly

Captain of the schooner Angele Elize of the port of Saint Pierre Réunion

Sund 22 May

2.25 afe to NExN. First block of search completed and commenced the second one. Strong Wly gale with very heavy hail squalls. Lookout in crow's-nest all day.

7 afe to NNE. Found two rivets in deck sheared off owing to excessive straining.

Position at noon Lat 48.45S Long 89.56E. Course and distance made good. Indirect 195. average speed 8.1 knots. Burned searchlight.

JUNE
Mon 6

Strong breeze and moderate head sea. Lookout in crow's-nest all day.

7.15 afe to sw. position at noon lat 46.22S long 95.8E. Course and distance made good. South 76. average speed 3.2 knots. Afe to SWxS. we frequently observed that between the Lat on 49 and 50S large masses of kelp were to be seen floating around, but owing to the heavy seas and strong winds experienced during the zig zag we had been unable to determine the direction and strength of the current which brought this kelp so far East. On June the 5th for the first time we saw kelp as far North as 45 showing the northern tendency of the current whilst the ship's position speaks for the strength of the easterly tendency. On June 6th the ship ought to have made good as S6W course with the wind and sea dead ahead, as it was she made a south course and if it had not been for this current she ought to have made an average speed from 4 to 5 knots instead of 3.2. I am of the opinion that this current is the same as we experienced on our way to and from Heard Island and up to date this is the only real current experienced since we commenced the zig-zag. We have been frequently set to the Eastward but the winds we have met with have been extremely violent and a ship in our present trim (the mean draft being about 12 feet) is greatly affected by wind and sea, more so than by current.

We have observed that after a gale of short duration when the ship has been driven to the Eastward, we had no difficulty in making good the ground lost, but after an exceptionally violent gale or one of long duration, an Easterly set is caused and we have had to steer almost due West to get back to th meridian up or down which we are steaming and that our speed has been considerably reduced. It has also several times happened that when shaping course North or South a set of 2 or 3 or even 4 has been allowed for and that in spite of moderate Nly or NWly winds. The ship has got to the Westward of the desired position showing that the Easterly set if it exists at all is negligible. After the first three or four lines of the block movement has been allowed for but only wind and sea and the straightness of the lines during the few days of fine weather that we have had shows that no stream of current exists (except the one previously mentioned). I am therefore of the opinion that the current in these waters are solely due to the winds and that during the summer months when light winds are more prevalent a ship would not be set to the Eastward by currently except after gales.

The Capt of the Wakefield, with whom I have discussed this subject at great length, is also of the same opinion.

On June 5th a bottle containing a paper on which was written the ship's position and a request to the finder to make known the fact of its having been found and the date and place when picked up, was thrown overboard for the purpose of ascertaining whether any current exists and this has also been done on several occasions since the commencement of the block.

5pm afe to SW. Burned searchlight.

Days out of Melbourne the journal stops, but Seymour includes a copy of a letter he was to write to the Melbourne Search Committee as he was required to make a report on the search and his findings, if any. The long gaps illustrate the tedium of the zig-zag as there was simply nothing to see and report apart from weather and position. Here is his letter:

SS Wakefield
Melbourne
Sir,
I have the honour to hand in my report on the proceedings of SS Wakefield during her search for the missing Waratah.

Nothing whatever has been seen or heard of the missing liner, nor has any wreckage been discovered on any of the islands visited, nor later on the block.

The report gives full details of the search and a meteorological register accompanies it. All the bearings and courses except the course made good daily and the directions of currents experienced are by compass unless otherwise stated.

The barometric observations are from an Omeroid Barometer by Hutchinson and Jackson Sunderland as it was found the mercurial barometer jumped too much for accurate records to be registered.

Lookouts were stationed in the crows nest every day or on the bridge if excessive rolling rendered it unsafe to go aloft and the searchlight was burned every night for 5 minutes every 15.

The islands named have been visited and searched and the block of [the] search has been faithfully carried out from the 79th meridian to the 98th meridian of East Longitude. A full explanation of the loss of the surf boat on Marion Island will be found in the report.

The potatoes supplied for the passengers of the Waratah if met with were found to be bad at Prince Edward Island and were consequently thrown overboard. The remainder of the stores are intact and in good condition. We have experienced very bad weather throughout the search and it is through this the ship was so long detained at the islands but of this you have been informed through by letter to the Port Captain at Durban from Kerguelen. I would point out in consequence of the cold weather that the crew of the Wakefield have all been compelled to purchase extra clothing and also that the four naval ratings have all spoiled their clothes with boat work, salt water etc.

Finally Sir, I would have you believe that the search has been thoroughly if insufficiently carried out and that no efforts have been spared to find traces of the missing vessel. Also that all my wishes relative to the search have been put into execution by the Captain and Officers of the ship.
I have the honour Sir to be
Your Obedient Servant
Hobart Seymour
Lieut. R.N.

To the President
The Waratah Search Committee.

the report. The potatoes supplied for the passengers of the
Waratah if met with were found to be bad at Prince Edward Isld
& were consequently thrown overboard The remainder of the stores are
intact & in good condition. We have experienced very bad weather
throughout the search & it is through this the ship was so long detained
at the Islands but of this you have been informed through my letter
to the Port Capt at Durban from Kerguelen I would point out
in consequence of the cold weather that the crew of the Wakefield
have all been compelled to purchase extra clothing & also that the
four naval ratings have all spoiled their clothes with boat work
salt water etc Finally Sir I would have you believe that the
search has been thoroughly if insufficiently carried out & that
no efforts have been spared to find traces of the missing crew
also that all my wishes relative to the search have been put into
execution by the Capt & Officers of the ship.

　　　　　I have the honour Sir to be
　　　　　Your Obedient Servant
　　　　　Hobart Seymour
To the President　　　　Lieut R N
The Waratah search Committee

Second page of Lieutenant Seymour's original letter to the Melbourne Search
Committee. (Courtesy of B. Putt)

WALTER SMITH

During Walter's account he mentions the discovery of another reef, named 'Seymour Reef' – obviously after the lieutenant – yet Seymour himself does not make note of it. Mr Bryan Thynne, Curator of Hydrography at Greenwich Maritime Museum, has kindly investigated the location of Seymour Reef on charts and whilst we believe he may have a fair idea of its position, we are at a loss as to why it was not noted for future charts.

The programme for entertainment in this section was almost certainly produced by the naval party as it was kept with the naval journals. It is a wonderful reminder of how they managed to keep their sense of humour in dreaming up this wonderful little pro-gramme. One frankly wonders at their resilience.

Walter's mention of Jacky Fisher refers to Admiral of the Fleet John Arbuthnot 'Jacky' Fisher, 1st Baron Fisher of Kilverstone, known for his massive reforms and for cutting down on unnecessary surplus. He briefly retired in 1910 for a few years but was recalled.

They were on Marion Island Sunday to Friday as *Wakefield* could not collect on Wednesday as arranged due to weather. It was to be six weeks before Walter had a night without crow's-nest duty and at anchor.

From Walter P Smith, Yeoman of Signals, S.S. Wakefield At Sea

Date: Sat 26.2.10

My Dear Parents,

I will now endeavour to relate of few of my exploits during the last 6 weeks and as time rolls along I will let you know what's going on onboard Ocean Tramp No2.

To start with we were asked if we were willing to proceed on another 3 months search for the Waratah *and naturally we said Yes for nobody likes to go halfway through with a job of that sort whether there's anything to come out of it or not. This happened about the 2nd week in January and as* Hermes *was leaving for a month at St Helena on Jan 19th we hustled round for sea-boots, oilskins and soap and bacca, in fact anything that we thought we should want and the Paymaster says 'What money do you want and what shall I do with your money while you're away and us thinking we were going straight round to Durban to join* Wakefield *and go to sea in a day or two, says 'Give us a couple of quid to get on with and the keep the remaining till we come back, so he gives me 2 £10s of them. As* Hermes *was sailing they sent us to* Pandora. *We had a grand time aboard there, they seemed to think we were a kind of Heroes and wouldn't let us do any work at all consequently we put in plenty of shore time in Simonstown and having some money and only a short time to stay, we had rather a good time but still had no news of S.S.* Wakefield *arriving at Durban and we had done a week in* Pandora *when she had to sail, so they placed us ashore altogether on compensation at the Sanatorium and that was great, but we began to wonder how much longer we would have to wait and at the same time began to realise that it would be June or July before we met our old friend 'Pay Bob' again so we eased down to slow speed to wait orders. Of course the orders we were expecting were 'to proceed to Durban by train' (which is a splendid 3 days ride through the country) but they were not having any just then and the Captain of the Dockyard being in command of the Port during the absence of flagship thought he would study one of Jacky Fisher's economy schemes and as HMS* Odin

Programme of entertainment by the naval party.
(Courtesy of B. Putt)

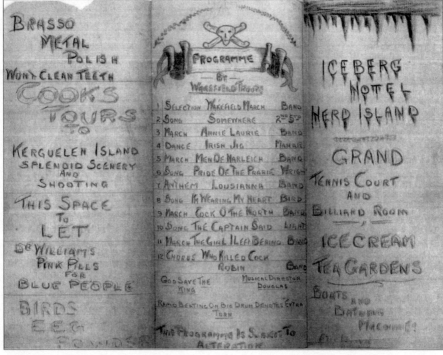

(a soap box of the smallest order) was calling at Durban on her way to Bombay he allowed us to take passage round in her and on the 2nd Feb we went aboard and sailed immediately we got aboard. Note the economy 'we were allowed 7/6 per day for 5 of us at Sanatorium and we used to do very well on it (as we were used to Beg, Borrow or Steal all our vegetables and fruit from a Boer Farm over the hill). Well the morning we joined Odin it cost them 35/- for a wagon and 8 bullocks to bring our baggage down the hill for a start and after a dirty, wet, rolling rotten 4 days trip we drifted into Durham to find no Wakefield yet. That was on Sunday, but to save more money they wouldn't discharge us to the shore so kept us there until Tuesday p.m. and then as Odin was to sail at daylight Wednesday they sent us to the Seamen's Institute, that's one of those places where a Merchant Seaman is looked after when he's out of a ship, but where he never goes when he's got one. Well we booked up there for 4/- a day that was 1 pound for the 5 of us and we stayed there 9 days, till at last in comes the long looked for Wakefield and we were very glad to get aboard her and found that everybody aboard were Britishers, North Country and Scotchmen, and we have got a champion cabin – it is the apprentices berth proper but we have got it for this trip, it's on the bridge deck amongst the officers and nothing at all to do with the crew. Cracked chums with the cook and steward and left Durban yesterday with very little to complain about. Of course you know that when you volunteer for a turnout of this sort its no picnic party you're on, in fact it's more like a wedding in as much as you take it for better or worse and if it turns out too bad there is only one way out of it and if you take that way it's cold, but if it's at all stickable you say the same as the married man does 'it's fine' and 'the best day's work I've ever done and so on' and that's roughly what we're doing, you know it could be a bit better and it's a good job its no worse, but time's young yet and as I ramble on with this epistle I shall be able to let you know what gains, changes etc. and in a day or two's time when we get further South and start the lookout in the crow's-nest I'll let you know the state of the Pole (I mean our foremast not the South Pole).

I forgot to tell you, we have not got the same Lieutenant this time but a young fellow named Seymour from Hermes. He is a very nice fellow but a big failing he's got is seasickness and that's right in this old skipper's barrow for you see to make up for his non-appearance on deck at sea he has told the Old Boy he can use us for anything he likes and at present that is from the time we left, we are working Wheels and lookouts whilst his own ABs are washing down and doing odd jobs but I don't think it will last long as we have got the searchlight and masthead to do in a day or two and then we shall drop Wheels and lookouts. We are steering dead South now for the Crozet Islands, not started zigging and zagging again yet but there's plenty of time to finish this off as this is only the 1st day out so for the present I'll pack up and see how the bunk fits me once more.

Wednesday 2.3.10 Forenoon

Packed up on Saturday forenoon and on Sat evening it began to blow a bit and by way of enter-tainment the Wakefield gave an exhibition of rolling and pitching but it wasn't to be for ever and by Sunday a.m. twas fine again and the wind behind us so we bumped along all kiff doing roughly about 200 miles a day. On Monday they took us off Wheels and started the lookouts from the crow's-nest and working the searchlight by night and today Wednesday it was my first 2 hours up there from 6 to 8 and I turned out to find that the wind had gone ahead and we were in the roaring forties without a doubt and I can tell you it struck a bit cold for a start but it's all over now, had breakfast and shan't be long before I try the bunk for a few more points. I have got to rearrange blankets etc. as we go south and it's different to last trip, you see we zig zagged last time and this time we're making a straight dive and going headlong into cold weather.

Well we ran out of fresh meat yesterday and started salt pork and pea soup and by what I can hear of it we are in for quite a gorge of salt stuff as they have very little tinned meat aboard and up to the present we don't look like faring so well as we did in Sabine, but can't grumble yet, there is about a dozen sheep aboard so I suppose we shall have a change now and then although up to now the sheep have lived down the main hold on top of the coal and I'm not much of a 'Vet' but I shouldn't think they would thrive much on nobs of coal will they.

Oh I forgot to tell you this ship belongs to Harrison Dixon Co, they are a crowd who are always on the top line for these chartered jobs by what I can make of it. You know, a sort of Amalgamated Society of Pawnbrokers who run things on as fine lines as possible, for instance the Sabine carried 12 ABs and 15 Firemen, this ship which is larger altogether carries 6 and 8 respectively so that she took on no extra hands for this trip and its a bit thick for them having to hump coal up and down from the hold all day and strike it down the bunkers. But that's nothing to do with the Naval brigade so I don't see why we should growl. I expect George knows the firm she belongs to. By the way I hope George has got going again by now. Oh I must tell you that the day before we left Durban we received a month's mail from Hermes and was glad to hear you were all kiff and I hope to hear the same on arrival at Melbourne. I got a letter from Jim Montgomery 'Capetown' [sic] asking me if I was his cousin and if my mother's name was Kate and if I had any relations in Newcastle N.S.W. and a lot of other stuff. So I dropped him a line and told him Yes, I was the bloke he was looking for, but that he didn't stand much of a chance of seeing me before July but hoped to see him then, you see I think he wrote me at last just as a kind of Blind, as he knew I was in Sabine and the papers said the same five were in Wakefield and as we're going Australia way thought praps might see someone and they would think it strange not having met. Of course I may be wrong but I don't know. Anyhow it's not my fault we've not met and if everything's all gay when I meet him it will be alright and if not, Well, 'nuff said'. I was also very pleased with 'Nell's' long letter. How did she manage it and who is this Post Master's son she mentioned. I don't think I know him. I thought Billy Looze was the nearest approach to Postmaster down that way, but again I suppose I don't know everything eh Nell.

We are making our way to Prince Edward's Island now and expect to arrive tomorrow and Lieut. Seymour has quite an elaborate programme made out for us landing and making a thorough search of these Islands. He has a tent, cooking apparatus, Rifles, ammunition and all sorts for a 2 or 3 days camping out job so lookout for some thrilling exploits on the pages to come. That yarn of Nelson's tussel [sic] with a polar bear won't be in it and Shakelton's [sic] S. Pole yarn won't touch it, but by what we saw of the islands last time they don't seem very inviting for a Picnic, but I suppose we shall stick it and as it will be all over by the time you hear about it, it won't matter much what it's like will it, but what a skylark it would be if we found any of the Waratah camping there too, that meeting as per Bognor Observer would be all kiff wouldn't it? And after all there's faint hopes. I don't think weather will stop us making a proper job of it this time as they intend to wait if it's too bad and no matter how long we take over it.

Here we go again, still keep on keeping on and on the whole it's not too bad although I've got a fine old yarn to spin this time and here goes. We arrived at Prince Edward Island on March 4th and after steaming round it looking for a decent spot to land we lowered the boats (by the way this said boat was an old surf-boat they purchased in Durban and if Lt Seymour is right they paid 50 pounds for her but there's better boats hauled up in the road in Bognor I'm sure and you wouldn't like to shell out 50 quid for them would you?). Anyhow we lowered her and Lt Seymour, The Doctor (a civilian) and 2 of us landed after a struggle as it was a very rocky coast and our 50 pound bus got her first lumping (for some time) for it shook a lot of putty and white lead out of the wounds and scars she had received in previous engagements and as it was too rough to beach her the others had to take her off to the ship, who was still underweigh, and hoist her and in doing so she got another clout and chippy had to patch her up while us four went in different directions searching the island and a fine job it was too. Of course there is nobody living on the island and as far as we could see, nobody dead. There was any amount of Seals, Penguins and Albatrosses which we amused ourselves by knocking about and chasing into the water just for satisfaction, for I can assure [you] I was not in the best of humours after getting wet thro up to the waist on landing, but as I've said before we're not to reason why we're but to do and do again and so in sea boots and oilskin suit over a wet serge suit I wended my way along the shore at least along the top of the cliff for it was impossible to get along the shore and after getting as far as I could, that was allowing myself time to get back before dark and only having daylight and a bit of sun to tell the time by (for you know I never owned many watches) I turned back and when I got to the cave where the corned beef sandwiches were I found the others had been back sometime and so after seeing a couple of sandwiches off made a signal for a boat and made another bold bid for the Wakefield, having gained no information whatsoever of any wreckage. Well we got aboard all kiff and stayed off the island that night and steamed round it again next morning and pointed out to the Lieutenant and Skipper how far each party had gone along the shore and they seemed very well satisfied with the performance, at any rate I was, for I had aches and pains everywhere, but as per usual kept smiling and we proceeded to Marion Island.

Now Marion Island is a bigger one than P E Is and not far away so we got there on Saturday afternoon and as the Lieutenant had an elaborate scheme laid down for thoroughly searching it, we landed on Sat afternoon to look out for a snug corner for the tent and great was our surprise to find that a Norwegian sealing steamer had been wrecked ashore there some time or other and with the stuff out of her they had built huts to live in and turned it into a proper sealing Depot. There were tins of biscuits, barrels of flour, oatmeal, tins of beef, lamps, oil and any amount of useful gear, so after passing our opinions etc. we called it Ours as there was no sign of its being inhabited lately and we put off to the ship again and on Sunday morning Lieut, Doctor and 3 of us landed, intending to stay till Wednesday a.m. and of course taking enough necessities for that time, taking into consideration that there was some stuff already there. We took an oil stove fitted for cooking, some coal (there was stoves there), oil, bread, butter, beef, sugar, tea, milk, in fact everything we thought we should want for 3 days camping out, but found out as time went on how much we HAD NOT BROUGHT with us. We had seaboots, oilskins, big coats/blanket each and as an additional blanket took our hammocks, but as the place was dirty we left our beds and anything we had any respect for aboard and as it's too deep and dangerous off these Islands the ship cannot anchor but had to get away under the lee of Prince Edward Is and was to call for us Wednesday morning, but it wasn't to be. When we got inshore there was a heavy surf running and we had the Devil of a job to beach the boat. In fact [we] were all wet through before we managed it and then we started to get the gear out and haul the boat up and that was more than 3 Bluejackets, a Lieutenant and a civilian Doctor could do, so the Boss surmised we'd have to haul her off and anchor her to save her bumping her bottom out and of course this meant one hand to let go the anchor and swim ashore again or stay there and die so as we were all wet through already it didn't matter much who went and so the biggest bloke among us 3, an AB named Light, native of Selsey, hopped in and we shoved her out with the backwash and he let go the anchor while we stood by in case he got cramp but it went off all gay and the boat looked good for riding it out, so we started humping the furniture up to the 'Hotel' and after a long time we had a fire underway and tried to dry some clothes and get something down our necks.

Well we had appointed the AB as cook and he got to work in that direction while us two bunting tossers unpacked and tried to make things a bit ship-shape and put the officers beds (they brought

A contemporary view
of Marion Island.
(Courtesy of B. Putt)

*their beds, couldn't face bare boards, not in this life) in a small hut next to ours and by the time
we were finished that cookey had some spuds done and we set about lunch consisting of Boiled
potatoes and tinned beef on plates, with bread and butter as a sweet, or what we call Afterwards,
but as cookey had apologised and being pushed for time we passed it over for once and he promised
us a good feed for dinner 7pm (Quality hours please). Well, this over we dished up and were just
sitting round the camp fire smoking and someone came in with the terrible news that our yacht had
dragged her anchor and was on the beach, or rocks to be precise, so down we goes to battle with the
briny once more.*

    *Well we found her just on and just off a couple of nice little rocks and we had to manhandle her
and get her clear then haul her up as high as we possibly could then put the painter (which was
far and way the strongest and best party of the boat and her fittings) round a big rock and secure
her there. But her stern was not yet clear of the water and as the wind was from seaward there was
a few heavy seas lifting her every now and again aft, but we wedged her up as best we could and
trusted to provy for a while as the tide was going out and made tracks back to 'The land we live in'
and got along with the dinner. This caused us to open our fresh water 'breaker' and we found that
they had put the water into a dirty stinking breaker so had to throw it away and go in search of
fresh water, which we were lucky enough to find not too far away, but plenty far enough considering
the weather conditions and state of the ground.*

    *Then we had tea, more corned beef and spuds and bread and butter, with more apologies from
Cooky and more promises of better food tomorrow. So we resumed our previous positions round the
fire and watched our clothes dry once more till about 8 or 9 pm. Then the Lieut. says, well could you
go your tot now and of course we said we'd try and force it so put the kettle on and made hot water
and with a bit of sugar made a Rum Hot, just here a small difficulty arose for the other Yeoman was
a T.T. and aboard the ship where we draw the 5 tots and take it to the cabin it was easy for yer 'umble
to take his and my own but ashore here it was now different and of course the 'Bloke' didn't have to
know the game, so just as he was pouring 'em out I says to 'Phil' are you going to have yours now
'Fil' or hang on as usual and he tumbled and says oh don't put any water in mine yet Sir, I'll have
it last thing before turning in so as I can sleep better and that went off all kiff, every night the same
Walter having one with the officers and seeing the other off after they'd turned in. Now came the
turning point in business, we put on all the clothes we had dry and camped down in front of the fire
which we had banked up to last the night, with overcoats, seaboots, and S Westers on, but there was*

dozens of mice running over us and it took some time for us to fall off properly and when we did the fire did likewise and we woke up but it being still dark and thinking the others were asleep each of us laid quiet till 4.45 a.m. at which time we had put an old alarm clock we had found on to go off when that time came and the alarm went off we all got up saying 'thank God' and then found out we'd all been awake best part of the night but kept quiet for the same reason.

17th March Forenoon. Amy, many happy returns of 17th

Then we got the breakfast underway, one hand making Burguw or porridge another cooking hot water for tea and dishing up last night's <u>Supper things</u> (sounds alright don't it). Well when the officers awoke it smelt too cold for them to wash in cold water so we had to cancel the tea water for a time so as they could wash and us thinking we wouldn't be done had a wash in the dishing up water so that we all had Hotters and then breakfast consisting of the usual Chicago Beef, spuds

S.—1320 c. (Established—May, 1900.) (Revised—March, 1904.)

NAVAL SIGNAL.

FROM	TO	DATE
17		TIME

wet through before we managed it & then we started to get the gear out & haul the boat up & that was more than 3 Bluejackets, a Lieutenant & a civilian doctor could do, so the Boss surmised we'd have to haul her off & anchor her to save her bumping her bottom out & of course this meant 1 hand to let go the ☐ & swim ashore again. For stay there & die so as we were all wet through already, it didn't matter much who went & so the biggest bloke among us, an AB named Light, native of Selsey hopped in & we shoved her out with the backwash & he let go the ☐ while we stood by in case he got cramp but it went off all gay & the boat looked good for riding it out, so we started humping the furniture up to the "<u>Hotel</u>" & after a long time we had a fire underway & tried to dry some clothes & get something down our necks.

M. 1704/1900.
Sta. 318/04.
Sta. 1765/07.
476c G & S 3416 [9667] 8/07m

Page 17 of Walter's journal. (Author's collection)

S.—1320 c. (Established—May, 1900.)
            (Revised—March, 1904.)

NAVAL SIGNAL.

FROM	To	DATE
_21_		TIME

before turning in so as I can sleep better & that
went off all Riff, every night the same Walter
having one with the officers & seeing the other
off after they'd turned in. Now came the turning
in business, we put on all the clothes we had
dry & camped down in front of the fire which
we had banked up to last the night, with
overcoats seaboots & 3 Westers on, but there was
dozens of mice running over us & it took
some time for us to fall off properly & when
we did the fire did likewise & we woke
up but it being still dark & thinking the
others were asleep each of us laid quiet till
4.45 AM at which time we had put an old
alarm clock we had found on to go off &
when that time came & the alarm went
off we all got up saying "Thank God" & then
found out we'd all been awake best part
of the night but kept quiet for the same reason.

M. 1704/1900.
Sta. 318/04.
Sta. 1765/07.

476c G & S 3416 [9667] 8/07ss

Page 21 of Walter's journal. (Author's collection)

and oatmeal with more bread and butter and less apologies. Then we split up again, the Lieut and Dr going away searching in one direction and us two the other leaving cooky to prepare the lunch which we were to have on our return just before dark. So down goes Phil and me and had a few more pulls at the 50 poundsworth on the rocks and then did a few miles of mountaineering.

Well we didn't get far before it came on to pour with rain and hail and we plodded along mile after mile till it began to get foggy and we turned our noses once more in the direction of 'The Old House at Home' and had just got back and shifted into the clothes which was a bit dryer than the others when in comes the Lieut and Dr, offering up prayers of different sorts, well we told them where we had been and gave them our deepest sympathy and then got to work on a good tuck in of Pea soup, corned beef spuds and rice and prunes and cooky sat there waiting for any complaints but there was none and then the Doctor put himself on the sick list with skinned feet (he'd not been used to seaboots and bogland I don't think). Then we humped our bodies down and had another go at the bane of our existence, but couldn't get her up any higher and the sea seemed to be having a little more mercy on her, at any rate it was certainly letting her live a little longer for the money and we goes back for the night. Well Monday night went much the same as Sunday night only colder and to give the mice all the floor to play on we hung up our hammocks but the cold got into us just as quick and we were further away from the stove and the usual chorus went up with the alarm in the morning and the same routine as regards washing in the dishing up water etc went off and had a change for break-fast, Corned Beef, Rice and Curry with Spuds, apologies and promises, then the morning visit to half hundreds worth which was not improving at all and the Lieut and Dr laid up disgusted at the previous day, but us two got over a few more miles in the opposite direction and after getting wet through to the skin we sat down and had a sandwich and having been awake nearly all the night before I nearly fell asleep and my chum seeing me bobbing and some birds hovering over us thought he'd get a little way away from me and see what they'd do if I was asleep, but it was too cold to sleep and he told me that one vulture of some sort was getting close up to me when I moved and the bird flew. You see his idea was to chase him away after he had nipped me. I suppose by throwing a stone at him and no doubt hitting me, but it didn't come off and we made our way back to Home Sweet Home with nothing at all to report except a big fresh water lake in between the hills that hadn't previously been discovered. Well we had some more dry clothes, soup, corned beef, peas, curry and anything the cook could lay hands on and then the usual routine pull up the boat, spin a yarn and turn in.

Well, Wednesday morning arrived and it was blowing a gale of wind rainy and foggy and not the faintest chance of the ship coming anywhere near the Island and even if she had come we could not possibly have launched the yacht for there was a very heavy sea running, so we went exploring and found 2 or 3 more things in tins and found them all pretty good, a tin of treacle, some lard and coffee and Cooky made sponge cakes à la bath bricks and we got outside of them as we had no more bread and ran out of sugar and milk but used the treacle in place of sugar, then found we had come to the last of the rum bottles and after reading the burial service over we turned in as usual all standing, after looking once more at the remaining parts of our craft on the beach and coming to the conclusion that the 50 pound looked shaky and another night to go.

Dad Many Happy Returns of the 19th I think that is your birthday.

Date 19th March Forenoon

Wednesday night went off much the same as the others but less sleep owing to the very small sleeping draft we had but had to go down and have a look at 'what they paid the money for' at daylight and it was still blowing and the stern post of the boat had opened out about 2 inches from the planks and the leak was from right aft up to the after thwarts and so could do nothing but go and tell the Lieut.

that our hopes of a trip off in her looked very doubtful and when he saw her he agreed, but there was no need for a panic yet as the ship would not venture within signal distance and we had not run out of provisions (thanks to what the sealers left behind) so we had breakfast and set to work chopping up spars for a fire as we had no more coal and the oil stove didn't warm the shanty. After that I got hold of a pot of paint (white) and started operating on the front of the Black with the following ----- 'Visited by Naval party, searching for S.S. Waratah, in S.S. Wakefield' then our names and the date and took a photo of it with the party in front but I hear that the party have not come out very well but the visiting card is alright and you shall have one from Melbourne. Then we went down the beach with rifles and worried seals and penguins for pastime and took a couple more photos but I don't know how they came out, but if they're any good you'll have them. Then we cruised about and began to realise what it would be like to be stranded on an uninhabited Island and the chow runs out, but we were only playing pretends as the Kid says, for we had hopes and plenty of 'em and when we got back we found more corned beef, curry and rice, prunes and pea soup. So quite forgot all about being stranded etc. By this time the wind and sea were inclined to give us a chance and just before dark we heard the ship's siren blowing off the Island but it was impossible for us to get aboard that night so they made a siren signal to say they would call tomorrow morning and then proceeded under the lee again. I said they made a signal and so they did but we couldn't hear it or see the steam and I didn't know what it was till after we got aboard. Well then came the last night, which was very sleepless owing to the sleeping draft being a thing of the past, but before turning in I concocted a letter on a big sheet of paper addressed to the inhabitants of the sealers' hut, Fogtown, Marion Is. thanking them for the use of the place and giving them our deepest sympathy in return for the flour, oatmeal and stuff we had commandeered. Of course I don't suppose the same people who left it there will go there again as it's not a place a fellow would want to spend a lifetime, but if they do they'll know who helped them along with it. Well, Friday morning came and the wind had dropped but still a heavy swell running outside and we made up our minds to face the music, but when we saw our 'Basket' boat it made us think again and then we saw the Wakefield coming closer so made a signal asking for a ship's boat as ours would not stand a rub and they told us a boat was coming now. Well, they came in and gave us a hand to launch ours and the idea was for a couple of us to go off in the Basketwork 50£ boat and keep her bailed out in tow of the other boat and as I was one of those two I thought to take off all the unnecessary clobber and seaboots and shoved them under the stern sheets, but we had not been in the water 5 minutes when she was full up and thinking of the Bankbook and other things dear to me we gave her a miss and climbed into the other boat after getting what gear we could out of the wreck then as we couldn't tow her any further the Chief Mate cut the painter and away she went and on arrival onboard, after another bit of life on the ocean wave, I found that in the final gallop I had only rescued one of my seaboots and the other, with a nice penguin skin and a sealskin I had found in the brine ashore, had gone down with the Half Hundred poundsworth. So that now I've only got 1 boot to grease. But it might have been worse as that's about all that was lost and the boot belonged to the Navy and has been logged 'Lost by accident' so that I shall not have to pay for it and can borrow a pair off the Stoker for the remainder of the trip so after all it wasn't so bad and we made our way to 'The 12 Apostles' a group of rocks which [we] didn't land at but steamed round them close enough to see if there was any wreckage but had the usual amount of luck. Found nothing and after doing that we proceeded to Hogg Is. one of the Crozets group and arrived there on Monday 14th and the Lieut. and one Hand landed while we steamed round the other side where they could not walk, and went in to bring them off again before dark with nothing to report and no huts for camping out and we were not sorry as the ground was very marshy and no good for the tent, well we laid off Hogg Is all night and landed the Lieut and another Hand next morning and steamed round again bringing them

The iceberg reminded Walter of the Royal Norfolk Hotel, Bognor. (Courtesy of the Royal Norfolk Hotel)

off again before dark as it came over very foggy. Of course now we were using a ship's boat and a lot better boat to handle. There was dozens of seals and sea elephants here, also some provisions that were placed there in 1882 and the tins were rusted through and no good at all. Perhaps they will renew the supply after Seymour sends in his report for 28 years is about as long as a tin of meat or biscuits will keep I should think …We then steamed round Penguin Is and then proceeded to Possession Is where we arrived yesterday 18th and today Dad's birthday (I think) we are battling about off the Is. too rough to land or anchor. This is the place we called at first on the trip in Sabine *and it was much the same weather then, if it goes down I suppose we shall be able to see the board we put up last time and put up another, but as it is getting near dinner time and I'm up to date with the yarn I think I'll pack up and let you know some more as the time rolls on. By the way I see I am making this much longer than the other one, but I suppose you'll find time to read it. We are still living pretty good and have nothing to complain about and when we leave here we go down to Kerguelen Islands and after that begin to crawl to the Northward and Eastward and it will get warmer and I can assure you we can do with it.*

Oh I forgot to tell you that the evening we left Marion Is we passed our first iceberg, it looked like the Norfolk Hotel fitted with a spire and smelt cold, but the skipper gave it a wide berth and I don't know that I wanted to go very close to it and on the way to Possession Is we sighted our first sail since leaving Durban, she was a Yankee Whaler, we asked her if she'd seen any wreckage and got the usual reply, 'no', and after wishing them a pleasant passage we got along a bit further and eventually landed on Possession Is. on Monday am. Lieut Symour and 1 hand going up inland and the others hanging round the beach exploring.

There was a hut put up by a shipwrecked crew of a ship called Catherine *(hope there's no more Catherines wrecked yet) and it appears that the Norwegian that was wrecked at Marion Is. had just been here and landed provisions and then went to Marion Is. and got smashed up herself, pretty rough luck that isn't it, but it's an ill wind that blows nobody any good, for it's through them being wrecked and building the hut and having the provisions there that we fared so well ashore on Marion Is. Well we landed every day and searched the Island, found the* Sabine's *Visiting card still standing but someone (sealers I suppose) had taken the letter away and then we put up* Wakefield's *card alongside it and in the afternoon we took the Steward ashore he took our photos laying down in front of the 2 boards and it came out fine, the names of ships, dates and everything and you shall have one as soon as possible. The Captain of Sabine will be glad of that for they seemed to have doubts as to us going there and that will settle it. Then we got aboard and once more said Ta Ta to the Crozet Islands and this time I suppose will be the final.*

Then we steamed round East Is. which is a very high rock straight up and down and impossible to land, but saw no signs of wreckage, so proceeded on 23rd March on our way to Kerguelen Is and yesterday 25th Good Friday we had salt fish for breakfast and wished Horace many happy returns of the day, had a nap and carried on with the usual crow's-nest lookouts and searchlight at night. That finished our first month out of Durban and up to the present the ship has not been able to anchor, but I think if the weather is fine we shall anchor at Kerguelen as it is rather a large island and will take us a week to search. With a fair run of luck we shall be there tomorrow, Easter Sunday, and do our Bank Holiday Monday on the island looking for wreckage and flaking out seals etc. for consolation. The hopes of finding anything of Waratah are getting shaky now altho the search is being kept up day and night just the same and as I've got the afternoons I must dry up and hop into the bunk.

We arrived at Kerguelen Is on Easter Sunday and it was too rough to land or anchor so remained underway and today Easter Monday we are still rolling about off the Is. waiting for the wind and sea to drop. It looks very bleak ashore and the hills are covered in snow and fog and no signs of any huts so I expect we shall come off to the ship every night to sleep, same as we did at the Crozets, hope so anyhow, for it wouldn't take much of the camping out business to shove us in the sick list with [?] and a few other complaints which we don't want yet a while. I expect we shall be quite a week or 10 days doing this group as its one big Is. and about 8 small ones and we can't make a start in this weather, but will let you know more at the days go by. We were going down to Heard and McDonald group in the same Latitude as the Horn but owing to the weather they are letting them off and we are not at all sorry and I don't think she could possibly have drifted down there.

Sunday 3rd April Forenoon

I packed up writing on Easter Monday and thought of Amy and Ern on the Tuesday (7 years eh). On Wednesday the weather dropped a bit and we landed the Lieut and 1 hand climbing up over the hill to try and get down the other side where it was too rough to go in the boat, but they could not manage it and as it was coming over dirty and a thick fog they returned and we came back to the ship and put to sea again as its no catch hanging about too close to these islands in such funny weather. Well Thursday and Friday we were knocking about at sea waiting for a chance to inspect that part of the island and on Saturday at 6 a.m. after having the middle watch on the searchlight our 'Boss' got tired of waiting and with a big overcoat, muffler etc. he says man the boat and we landed him after a struggle with the briny breezes. We could not beach the boat as it was all rocks so had to lay off till he came back about 9 am. and we started again for the ship which was about 2 or 3 miles away but would have got a lot closer if the bloke had waited but he wouldn't and when we got clear of the land we were in a gale of wind and he didn't know what to do for the best, we could see him go white then green and yellow and we were managing the boat with our oars for we couldn't get anything from the officer who by this time was in what they call a Blue Junk and had pulled off his big coat in case of a swim, well eventually the ship came near enough for them to give us a line and no sooner were we alongside than he nipped up the ladder and we hooked her on and hoisted and had breakfast, shifted dry clothes and turned in thinking that we'd been as near Davy Jones' locker as ever I wish to be and hoping that we never have the luck to get in another lop with the same Bloke in the boat.

And now it's Sunday again and we are at the other end of the Is. and its still blowing a gale of wind and we can't land, so that we've done a week round here and done practically nothing in the

way of searching but praps we shall manage to get ashore tomorrow. There is some talk of this Is. being inhabited but up to now we can't see the faintest sign of anyone there but will let you know more about it when I find out. Shall be very glad when we get further North for it's bitter cold at the masthead and continually hailing or snowing and the crow's-nest is only a barrel, so that we can't walk round much and so you can bet one is rather pleased to see his relief coming up after 2 hours there. And now I must follow the laws of nature by getting the head down and thinking of the Sundays I have not done in these parts and the ones I've got to do in better parts later on.
(2s + 1½d return)

Now it's April 8th and we are doing another day in the same little basin we were in yesterday when I wrote your unexpected letter. It snowed hard all last night and the decks were covered when we turned out this morning, but I must tell you about the last 12 days or else it won't read proper and I must get it up to date tonight as this is the only bit of this scribbling that has not been done at sea and it's quite strange laying still and not having to hang on to the ink bottle with the left hand. Well it was Sunday when I knocked off and now it's Friday night. On Monday we went round to another part of the Is. called Royal Sound and had a change of weather this time it was a larger breed of snow, the flakes being as big as 2 bob pieces, there was a lighthouse here put up by some whalers but nobody looking after it at present, I suppose they only light up when they have whaler[s] out at night which is not very often, they do pretty well, all their work in daytime and anchor at night. Well we laid off that night and on Tuesday morning sighted a small Norwegian steamer called Jeanne D'Arc but she had seen no signs of wreckage. We then made tracks to Hillsborough Bay and on the way sighted another small whaler and ask her the usual question and got the usual reply. They told us where we could anchor but our Skipper wasn't having any, so kept to sea for better weather and on Wednesday saw another small whaler (they all belong to the same company) and got the same reply to our usual question. Well it had bettered a bit and we landed and had a climb round in search of a provision depot but after about 5 hours found nothing of this supposed cave so returned to the ship and were congratulating ourselves on getting back <u>dry</u> when just as we got alongside they opened up the exhaust and nearly filled our boat up and of course washing us down lovely and we didn't growl at all <u>Not Much</u>.

Well as you must know by now that a wet shirt is not a very unusual event on a ban-yan like this and therefore it passes off much the same as any other <u>meal</u> and is soon forgotten and as long as it's not the same water every time we know we must be getting along with the trip. Then came Thursday and we were seeking pastures new when we fell in with a small whaler and went up close enough to hail her but found she had a French Skipper and as an Englishman's French doesn't sound very well through a megaphone or speaking trumpet, we lowered our boat and the Lieutenant and myself went aboard and he had a yarn in the Wee-Wee lingo and I was keeping up a continual argument by semaphore with the other yeoman who was with the Skipper of this ship, and after a lot of parley-voo (how's that for French) we took the man from Gay Paris land aboard here and he took us up through a very narrow passage to the cosy little place already mentioned and there we found another steamer called Mangora. She is a kind of Depot or Flagship of the whalers and we took the French Skipper aboard there and then he took us ashore and showed us where the provisions were stowed for shipwrecked mariners, so you see it is a long way from where it was supposed to be by our charts and had we been in want of anything and had not fell across the whalers we should never had found them, so you see the 'Entente Cordial' came in handy again. After that we got back to the ship with nothing worse than wet feet and bottoms of trousers (quite a record) then it was we got the news that one of the boats was going back to civilisa-

tion today and would take a mail so dashed off one to you and one to the Messmates in Hermes and then turned in to enjoy the 1st all night in and the 1st night at anchor for this trip and we left Durban six weeks ago today.

Turned out this morning after a grand sleep, no noise of the engines thumping and no rolly motion to contend with and had a good feed of salt fish (our favourite feed in this ship), then had a regular spring cleaning in the Old House at Home and not having anything better to do, had the hair cut and whiskers trimmed up and if you could see me now you'd say I looked quite respectable. This afternoon the lads went ashore with guns to shoot rabbits (there's thousands of them here) but they are too well educated to stand still and be shot and the party returned with the large amount of 3, so I don't think we shall get very fat on rabbit pie. And now I'm up to date once more and I suppose we shall make tracks to another part of the same island tomorrow and start on the second half of this 3 months cruise. Another all night in the bunk tonight with no engines going and no rolling from hither-thither.

Sat 15th April Forenoon

Well it's now the middle of April and we are steaming round another part of Kerguelen Is. but I have a week to make up to keep the yarn going so here goes. We left Gazelle Basin at 6.30 a.m. on Saturday 9th and thought we were going to another part of the same Is. but when we got outside and found the weather favourable they made up their minds to make a run for the Heard and McDonald Islands about 280 miles further South, and away we went down to still colder climes arriving at Heard on Monday 11th and found it nothing but a high rock covered from the top to the waters edge in Ice and Snow and it was still blowing a gale of wind as we steamed round it. In the afternoon the wind increased and we stood off towards McDonald but it was not good enough to hang about off these islands as we had already discovered an uncharted reef and gave it the name of 'Wakefield Reef' and then as it was dark and having no particular wish to find any more in the dark we cleared out of that district and shaped our course back to Kerguelen which we sighted on Wednesday pm. Also found another reef not on the chart and called it 'Seymour Reef' (if we find many more it will run one each and don't be surprised to hear of one called 'Smitheys Heap' or something like that). We layed off all night and went into Royal Sound on Thursday and anchored again (2nd time this trip). We landed after dinner and found about a dozen graves of seamen who had died there years ago some of them dated 1840 up to about 1860. They appeared to be Yanks, whalers I suppose. Found no other signs of wreckage or habitation and returned to ship and had another nice quiet All Night in the bunk. Next morning it was too rough to land and we had to steam slow ahead to prevent her dragging anchor, we remained aboard all day and had another all night in and as we had dragged a little during the night and it was blowing hard we got underway again and I relieved the crow's-nest at 8am. in a heavy fall of snow and after doing 1 hour up there the Skipper called me down as it had finished snowing and we were only just crawling up and down waiting for the wind to drop and there was no necessity to keep a man aloft, so down I came and here I am struggling with very cold hands to keep you up to date. It's not far off dinner time now and if things don't alter I shall get between the blankets again p.m. I suppose we shall get clear of this island in a day or two and make our way North to St Paul's Is and Amsterdam. Then we have got to zig-zag to Melbourne and then I'll post this off to you and hope to be able to spin a more pleasant yarn when we are in the mailboat taking passage back to the Cape to wait paying off orders in Hermes.

Wed 20.4.10 Forenoon

Here we are again still bouncing about on the briny but am very pleased to say finished with Kerguelen Is. after 2 weeks and a day in proper rotten weather and doing no good at all. The Skipper and our Lieutenant had a bit of a barny on Monday. We had as I've just said been climbing round this lump of earth over 3 weeks and not a sign of any wreckage and in a very good position to make some ourselves very often, and the Skipper was, like everyone else, fed up with it and the Lieutenant wanted to anchor for another night and land again in the morning but the Capt didn't reckon it was good enough and after a lot of rangling [sic] they concluded they would get clear of the land before dark and away we went on Monday night bound for St Paul's Is. and today, Wed, it is a lovely fine spring morning and the wind in our favour and we are all very glad the Skipper got the best of the argument, for it was absolutely useless from a 'Searching for Waratah' point of view to remain there another night and run the risk of finding the beach ourselves. There was half a dozen whalers huts ashore and I rather think he wanted to go exploring or Curio hunting, as we had already been aboard the sealers or whalers and ascertained there was no news and had landed in a Doz. other parts of the same island and found nothing but those graves I've already told you about. Well now we've only got 2 more islands to visit and they should be pretty easy work and fine weather and then start on the Hurdy-Gurdy passage to Melbourne. We are running out of spuds, bacca, and matches and the Lieut. says he doesn't think the Rum will hang out so things look like getting worse before better. But I suppose we must keep smiling and I suppose we shall come out of it as per usual.

Friday 22 April Evening

Here begineth the 2nd half hundredth page of this yarn and its Friday 22nd April and we've just stopped engines off St Paul's Is in glorious weather. We have had 2 days of it now getting warmer every time you go on deck and I can tell you we are all very pleased to be able to crawl out of our shells and have a good wash, for I've been wearing a flannel and 3 jerseys for the last 7 weeks (not the same flannel all the time) and only taking them off to wash when it was hot water which wasn't very often, but while we are here and Amsterdam we shall be able to dig ourselves out and put 'em' on again for the Zig-zag which is to occupy about 59 days, going down as far as 53 degrees South again so that's going to be a bit lively again, but as I've said before what's the odds about where we go or what we do as long as we get through with it and it will all be finished by the time this is posted and by the time you get it I shall be back to the Cape of Hopes etc. again and ready for anything in the way of a small present that they like to shove along. I don't really know who I mean by 'They' but you must allow a fellow to ramble off the path a little when he's skulling round the world on a racket like we've been for nearly 9 months. You'd hardly believe the silly things us four Matlows talk about after the day dreams up in the crow's-nest. The different times we have found the Waratah and the good times we're going to get when we take her into Melbourne and all such stuff as that, it's a good job nobody else hears us or they would think we're on a fair road for Coney Hatch with what's called the missing liner tap. But I think it's only temporary and I'll try to shake it off in the Mailboat passage we are going to have from Australia to Capetown [sic] Praps. (By the way that Mailboat Passage is another one of the day dreams we get very often, don't know how it will pan out.)

And now as it's a fine night and we have only one more place to tick off the programme and then a couple of months at sea, seeing nothing, I'll try and force another page just for pastime. Well I suppose 50 years ago you were wondering what you'd wear on Tuesday 26th April, 'A cream chiffon taffeta' trimmed with elitrope [?] or 'squashed strawberries' or was it a navy serge dress off Dad's slop list. Any old how I'd like to be somewhere near you on Tuesday and if I was in a civilised part of the world I would certainly have sported a cable, but under the circs this is about all

I can do and hope that you'll make up your minds for a Diamond Jubilee, its only 10 more years you know it's 10 years now since we went to Scarbro together and that's not long is it now. And before that we shall all be pensioners Dad. Well now I'll pack up for tonight and let you know more tomorrow after we have landed.

Well on Sat forenoon we manned the boat and had a good 4 or 5 mile pull to the island and to finish up we had to run for about ½ (half) mile on top of a surf and it was grand, like shooting the shoot at a fair. Landed and found our letter left by Sabine still there so took it off to be forwarded as proof that she called there. Then the Lieut and 1 Hand went over the hill whilst we went round the beach but found nothing and after luncheon on corned beef sandwiches went fishing and caught some very nice Bream (I think they were) also 3 or 4 crayfish (like lobsters) and later on in the afternoon returned to the ship. When the Cook saw we had a lot of fish he saw that he'd have to cook them and started growling right away, but the Skipper told him to get on with them and he did but when they were cooked we found that everyone else had fish for tea and the Bluejackets corned beef so of course had to investigate the case, which naturally went very close to a punching match but it passed off with only words but Cookie and me ain't been on the best of terms ever since but that doesn't matter much for there is not a man in the ship who can get on with him and only his age saves him from being jammed into his own ash bucket. Well then on Sunday we went over to Amsterdam Is. but there was too much swell on the shore for us to land, so layed off and on Monday it was the same and although there is a lot of Cattle, put there for shipboard crews, we would not manage to land and to get any and as we've got to do this zig-zagging we shoved along on Monday 25th April.

(Ditty)
We see cattle on Amsterdam, Amsterdam, Amsterdam
If it hadn't been for breakers,
We might have had steakers,
At Amsterdam
How's that for [a] parody on ..... [?]

Mother and Dad. Hearty congratulations on your Golden Wedding 26th April 1910.
So that on Tuesday 26th April, 50 years after you both said 'you would' or 'I Will', we were started on the 58 days Ziz-Zag and by now which is May 13th we are getting along with the 2nd half of the cold runs to the Southard and shall soon be on the run North to Australia. You see it's roughly like this I'm not much at drawing.

Something about like that, each one of the runs up and down are 300 miles and those from east to west 40 miles. We come down to 50 degrees South each time and up to 40 degrees with 40 mile to East every time. Now I don't know if you'll understand that but it's my idea of what we're doing and if I get a better copy when it's all over I'll send it. Anyhow I shan't get a worse one I know. And again, as long as it's all over when you get this, what does it matter.

I might as well tell you that today is the best day, in fact the only fine day we have had since we started and don't suppose it will last long.

Monday June 6th

You will see by the date that it's over a month ago since I handled a pen and then there wasn't much news, and now there's less. for we have been zig-zagging all the time and had nothing but one long spell of cold, wet, rough, foggy weather and the prevailing wind is a Westerly one and us running North and South have had it on the Beam both going South and coming back again every time and being very light and high out of water I can tell you we have had a fine time of it rolling round all the way. We are still on the zig-zag altho everyone is fairly fed up with it as it seems so useless now and we have not even sighted another ship all the way.

The latest is that we get on the straight for Melbourne about the 14th inst and arrive on about 25th. That will give us 4 months to the day away from civilisation and by the time we get back to the Cape we shall have been over 6 months away from Hermes and the 2 year commission will be horribly mutilated by then won't it. I am looking forward to a good mail on arrival [in] Melbourne and a pleasure trip back to Capetown but don't know anything yet, as our orders will be waiting for us at Melbourne. And now as everything is on the shake and there is nothing more to talk about I shall pack up and put another 4 hours in the bunk and let you have a few more lines the next fine day when I hope to be able to say we are on the straight run for the finishing point.

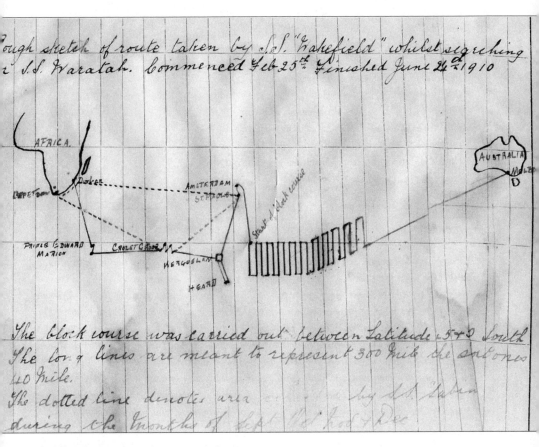

Walter's hand-drawn map. (Author's collection)

Rough sketch of route taken by SS Wakefield while searching for SS Waratah commenced Feb 25th. Finished June 24th 1910.

Note the block course was carried out between latitude 45 and 50 south.

The long lines are meant to represent 300 miles; the short ones 40 miles.

The dotted line denotes area searched by SS Sabine during the months of Sept, Oct, Nov and Dec.

June 15th

Hurrah, on the 12th June we finished the round of jollification known as the zig-zag and got into the straight for Melbourne and that Westerly wind that had been on our beam for a couple of months must have known that if it continued to blow from that quarter it would do us a bit of good and not feeling at all that way inclined it took up a position in the North East so as to be Dead ahead and there it looks like staying. But never mind, we are punching through it and with the usual amount of luck we shall roll into Melbourne about tomorrow week Thursday 23rd. Now I'm going to put in the distances from one lump of rock to the other but of course I can't say how many more thousand miles we did running round them and clearing away to see at night or in bad weather, as we only anchored twice and then only for a few hours each time.

Distances

Durban	to	Prince Edward Is.	1064 miles
P Edward	to	Marion	12
Marion	to	12 Apostles	583
12 Apostles	to	Hogg	14
Hogg	to	Penguin	15
Penguin	to	Possession	48
Possession	to	East	18
East	to	Christmas Harbour	714
Christmas Harbour	to	Hillsborough Bay	80
Hillsborough Bay	to	Royal Sound	79
Royal Sound	to	Heard Is.	270
Heard Is	to	Royal Gd.	270
Royal Gd	to	St Paul's Is.	720
St Paul's Is.	to	Amsterdam Is.	50
Amsterdam Is.	to	Melbourne	7390

Of course you will understand that's the bare distance direct from Is. to Is. and not the search round and that the big bite on the end is the zig-zag or keep on keeping on spasm.

Well I'll try and force another page for practice. We are living chiefly on curry and rice and salt beef with an occasional surprise packet thrown in such as rice and prunes or a tin of bloaters. The pass word with the Steward is 'Run out'. But what's the matter, how often do we have to hang out for a week or two on the thoughts of that first feed shop and why can't we do it again. I shall send this by the 1st Mail after we get in and if we stay there any longer I'll write again but if not will let you have another from the Cape. That sounds as though it's all over don't it. Anyhow it soon will be and we ain't dead yet. And now I'll pack up again and wrestle with the dinner, haven't seen it yet so don't know his weight but I'll take chances and let you have some more of this stuff later.

It's now the Wednesday before the Friday on which we are down to appear at our destination and by the look of things in general its about time too, for we have run out of this and run out of that, in fact the only thing that doesn't appear to be 'running out' is the ship herself and she's absolutely 'crawling in'. We haven't sighted another ship yet and I am beginning to think we are the only one left. We read a lot about a Comet striking the Earth and wiping it out before we left and if that's happened I'm going to appoint myself Governor of Australia on arrival. In any case I'll bet I govern the first steak and eggs I can manage to lay hands on. We ran out of Rum on Sunday last which was the only redeeming feature of the day. Salt beef is finished and we are journeying along on Rice Curry and tinned stuff of the poorest order. But we can stick it for another 2 days. The weather is a lot warmer altho the wind still manages to keep ahead. We have all been busy in our watches below lately washing clothes and blankets which had got in an awful state on this trip. But everything is all ready now for that Mailboat passage back to South Africa and if it comes off I shall have a much pleasanter yarn to spin in about another month's time. Of course I shall send this 1st opportunity and if we stay in Melbourne any time will write again the following week, but if we leave it will be about 3 or 4 weeks trip and then you'll get another and I think I can almost promise you that I shan't volunteer for any more long trips in a Merchant ship where they try their best to make 3 months provisions hang out for 6 months. Am anxiously waiting to get your mail on Friday 24 June.

Just after I packed up writing we had to stop engines on account of something going wrong with the condenser but were alright again inside of 3 hours and carried on with the trip to Melbourne and at about 3 pm on Friday we got the Pilot and two newspaper reporters onboard and the first thing they told us was King Edward was Dead about 6 weeks and there was no news of Waratah and of course we had no news of her. Well we anchored off Melbourne about 7pm and went into Dock on Saturday morning and then reported ourselves by wire to Sydney and then came the biggest shock I've ever had. The C in C cabled our orders for the 2 Yeoman Sigs to proceed to England and the other 3 and 1 Lieutenant return to Hermes in 1st boat going, so that on Wed we got aboard the Royal Mail steamer Ormery bound for Tilbury Docks London and of course we are carrying the English mail with us and will be home on Sat 6th Aug. That's not a bad stroke of luck is it, to get home in the middle of summer instead of the dead of winter. Many thanks for all the letters but the funny part of it was that the only letter adrift was the Registered Letter but after a lot of trouble at the GPO they paid me on a duplicate form as they had the advice letter but trace of the real thing and then just at the last thing before leaving Wakefield I got this from some offices nothing to do with GPO so as I had got the money on Tuesday and no time to go to the P.O. I am keeping it intact and bringing it back.

26 July pm

Twelve months today Waratah left Durban and I left Portsaid this morning for Naples where we should arrive on Friday. We have had a pretty fair passage so far and the remainder should be all plain sailing. We got into a sneezer coming through the Australian Bight and it was terribly hot in Red Sea and Canal but we mixed it up with the Wakefield weather and have got through with it all kiff and all going well shall be at Plymouth on Saturday Aug 6th. We are booked right thro to London but shall try and disembark at Plymouth so as to get on to Pompey and report myself and up to Bognor same night. Otherwise it will mean going down from London to Pomps on Sunday and that's no good. I've done quite enough Sunday travelling this year to last me a time.

I sent a P.C. from Suez as I believe that will reach you a day or two before this and I wanted to break the news to you as soon as possible, and would have written a long letter or sent this but I didn't think there was an earlier opportunity of posting than Naples and when I did find out I only had time for a P.C. but this will keep you going for a day or two and the following Sunday you ought to hear my old chin wagging at No 7 Argyle. And now I think I've said about enough for 1 letter Don't You and with my best to all the family and friends and hoping to see you in a week's time after receiving this I conclude and believe me to always remain your loving and affectionate son Walt.

CAPTAIN PUTT

Captain Putt was en route with his cargo ship SS *Wakefield* to South Africa and onwards, unaware of the adventure which was about to unfold as he received orders to continue to another port where his charter ship had been secured for the second search for the SS *Waratah*. His diary is meticulously kept and he adds lovely details, such as their experience of Christmas Day:

Sat Dec 25 1909
a.m. Christmas Day proceeding down Irish Channel.
  0.25 am South Rock Light Vessel abeam dist 1 mile. Strong breeze and clear weather. Sea rough ahead.
  6.45 am Rockabill Lt abeam distance 14 miles.
  8am Bailey Light abeam 9.55 Codling Lt Vessel abeam.
  Noon Fresh breeze and fine clear weather. Had turkey for dinner, not much appetite. Probably sea sick?

[It is strange to note that on his passage across he makes note of signalling a ship named *Wakool*, which of course was also a Blue Anchor Line ship.]

7pm signalled SS Kamerni *[?] of Hamburg also* Wakool *of London.*
  Position at noon 26.16N 15.48W course S21W Distance 221 miles.

Captain Putt records the details of his trip across and we can begin there before heading off to the islands once more.

Thurs 27th
1.50 am St Johns Lt abeam distant 3 miles.
  Moderate breeze and overcast slight southerly swell.
10.10 am Port Shepston Lt house abeam dis 2 miles.
  Strong current against us for the 24 hours.
  2.35 pm Alival Shoal Light house abeam dis 1 mile.
  6.25 pm Arrived off Durban received orders from Pilot to proceed Delagoa Bay. Also a letter saying we were chartered to search for Waratah.
  6.40pm proceeded full ahead. Fresh breeze think rain. 9.50 took cast of lead. Bottom 45 fths fine sand. Midnight cast lead. Bottom 40 fths.
  Patn Lat 30.32S Long 30.38E Course various dis 202 miles.

Captain Putt had to discharge cargo and there were problems due to not having enough wagons. This caused delays and they often had to work through the night; on 4 February one dock worker was killed and another seriously injured whilst unloading.
  Four sailors and two firemen were also down with malaria and Putt headed off to Durban on Tuesday 15th stating he was very pleased to be at sea again!
  Only on Friday 1 April did he voice any negative feelings regarding their orders and the expectations put upon them and even then his comments were very mild.

Thur 17 February

Am light winds and fine clear weather.

7am started discharging out of 3 holds.

Lieutenant Seymour and five naval ratings from the HMS Hermes *joined the ship this day (these are to search the islands we may visit).*

Three men still sick and off duty and being attended by Doctor.

7pm finished cargo for the day.

Calm and fine clear weather.

Fri 18 February

Am moderate and Ely wind and clear.

9.30am resumed the discharging.

Very busy taking on board provisions bedding etc. for Waratah *if found.*

Carpenters, fitters etc working on board preparing ship for search.

Two of our crew sent to hospital.

Fitters at work all night erecting dynamo in Engine Room.

Sat 19 Feb

am strong SWly wind and dull.

Crew fitting up crow's-nest, taking on board surf boat and stores. Fitters and carpenters still at work on the Dynamo and search light. Noon shifted to another berth.

8pm finished work for the day.

Tues 22 Feb

am dull cloudy weather.

2.30 am owing to heavy swell outside caused ship to range badly breaking three mooring wires and a rope, all hands on deck re-mooring.

7am all fresh water on board 216 tons.

Crew preparing ship for sea.

Noon had to hire three large coir ropes from the harbour board to hold ship in berth owing to heavy range.

2pm Electricians and other shore workmen finished.

9pm tried the dynamo and searchlight, everything in working order.

Thu 24 Feb

am moderate Easterly wind and clear.

Steamer sill awaiting orders from London. Also the Victorian Government from Melbourne.

The Waratah *was lost on 27 July 1909 from Durban to Cape Town.*

7pm received cable from owners to be ready to sail at short notice (so expect soon to be off).

pm fresh breeze and clear weather.

Crew list of the SS Wakefield *when leaving Durban in search of the Lund liner SS* Waratah:

F.W. Putt	Master
T. Ryan	1st Officer
D. McNeil	2nd Officer
H. Wright	3rd Officer
J. Purse	Carpenter
J. Clarke	Boatswain
W. Fisker	Steward
W. Parsons	Eng Steward
W. Miles	Cook
W. Nicholson	A.B.
M. Wright	A.B.
D. McLeod	A.B.
W. Henderson	A.B. and Lamps
J. McCurdy	A.B.
P. McCollum	A.B.
J. Grozier	O.S.
J. Heller	O.S.
T. Dixon	Apprentice
P. Raisin	Apprentice
A. Davie	1st Engineer
A. Bathgate	2nd Engineer
A. Banks	3rd Engineer
G. Hall	4th Engineer
R.B. Brown	Surgeon
W. Douglas	Donkeyman
D. McBride	Fireman
J. Mahar	Fireman
H. McArthur	Fireman
T. Walker	Fireman
H. Hicks	Fireman
W. Jackson	Fireman

From HMS Hermes *stationed off the Cape of Good Hope:*

H.W. Seymour	R.N. Lieutenant
W. Smith	Leading Seaman
A. Phillips	Signalman
C. Bird	Leading Seaman
W. Light	Leading Seaman
J. Paull	Electrician

Fri 25 Feb

Am fresh SW wind and clear weather.

This being the third vessel to search for the Waratah *and Crew 119, passengers 92.*

9am received cable to proceed on search.

11am Pilot and tug arrived unmoored and proceeded out of harbour.

11.10 discharged Pilot and away full speed for a long dreary cruise in the Southern Indian Ocean and Islands.

Draft on leaving forward 13.0 Afe 20.6.

Pm fresh breeze and squally sea moderate.

Sat 5 March

A fresh gale and terrific hail squalls.

9.30 proceeded full speed for Marion Island.

11.30 eased engines and steamed along the coast looking for suitable place to land.

11.15 sent the boat away 4pm returning having found some fishermen's huts, proceeded back to Prince Edward Island for the night.

Position at noon Lat 46 47S Long 37 51 E course various, dist 25 miles.

Sun 6 March

5am full speed for Marion Is 9.15 sent search party away then steamed around the island two mile off but saw no wreckage 3pm finished the sail around the island and went to the lee side of Prince Edward for the night.

Position at noon Lat 46 58S Long 37 40E course various, distance 68 miles.

Mon 7 March

Am vessel dodging under the lee of the island.

Noon fresh breeze and commencing to rain sky looking bad and threatening.

3pm half speed towards the island strong breeze and misty rain sea rising.

6pm put to sea for the night thick dirty weather wind likely to change suddenly, midnight wind shifting rapidly with rough sea and dirty weather.

Position at noon Lat 46 43S Long 38 4E course various, distance 44 miles.

Tues 8 March

Am strong breeze and drizzling rain vessel drifting off the land.

Noon steamed slow towards the land.

6pm full speed ahead blowing hard.

7.20 stopped close under lee of island.

Fresh gale and misty rain rough sea outside of island.

Vessel dodging off and on all nigh, at time island not visible although quite close.

Positon at noon Lat 46.40S Long 38 8E course various, distance 45 miles.

Wed 9 March

Am moderate gale and misty rain with terrific squalls.

9am proceeded for Marion Island to take off search party. 10 am vessel racing and pitching fearfully, blowing whole gale and mountainous seas.

10.15am turned back for Prince Edward Is 11.40 under the lee of the land. Whole gale blowing terrific squalls and thick blinding rain.

Vessel dodging off and on weather looking very dirty and thick fog steamed slow to sea

Midnight vessel hove to high mountainous sea running fierce snow and hail squalls.

Position at noon Lat 46.37S Long 38.3E course various, distance 60 miles.

Thurs 10 March

a.m. whole gale and heavy sea. Fierce squalls. 7.50am close to the island. Severe storm and mountainous seas, thick misty rain hiding land from view. Vessel steaming full being unable to keep her head to the sea. Noon whole gale with terrific squally. During the latter part of the afternoon weather moderated somewhat, shaped course for Marion Island to take off search party. 5.10pm arrived blew steam whistle to attract attention but got no reply and too rough to launch the boat. Returned to Edward Island for the night. Marion Is having too many reefs to dodge under during the night.

Position at noon Lat 46 37S Long 38 3E course various, dist 65 miles.

Fri 11 March

a.m fine weather 5a.m left again for Marion island. 6.40 arrived and stopped, blew the whistle but saw no-one. 6.50 observed a man on the hill signalling this was to send boat ashore, surf boat damaged, sent away the lifeboat at once but found the surf boat was passed all repairing so all hands returned in the ship's boat, Lieutenant reported having searched South East and north coasts and found no trace of anything, impossible to search west coast owing to the high mountain. 12.40pm proceeded full ahead. Very pleased that we were leaving that vicinity. Sighted large iceberg 5 miles to the South of Island (smelling quite warm?).

Position at noon Lat 46 49E course various, dist 40 miles.

Mon 14 March

a.m fresh breeze moderate sea sky overcast.

Lookout in crows nest from daylight.

11.15am spoke Amercian Barque Alice Knowles, *a whaler, had seen nothing of any wreckage or the* Waratah. *Thanked them and proceeded, experienced strong, northerly current. 1.30pm sighted the Twelve Apostles islands. 5pm rounded close to the Apostles but saw nothing, steered for Hog Island. 6pm arrived close to the island and turned round to dodge for the night steaming slow from the land, sky overcast.*

Searchlight going from dark.

Position at noon Lat 45 47S Long 49 40E course N77E distance 170 miles.

Tues 15 March

a.m engines working at various speeds to hold position.

Moderate breeze and thick misty rain. NW swell lookout in crow's-nest from daylight, moderate gale and cloudy. Steaming up and down East coast of island looking for suitable place to land but too much surf everywhere. 10am set in thick fog. Steamed slow to sea. Noon fresh gale and thick fog. 4pm took cast of lead, bottom at 90 fths turned ship around. Fog lifted for a few minutes sighted a reef about a mile astern. Steamed full speed for sea. Stopped engines at 5.30pm ship drifting all night. Searchlight going from dark.

Position by D.R. Lat 46.8S Long 50.16E course various, dist 80 miles.

Wed 16 March

a.m weather cleared. 8.30am lowered no 2 boat and landed search party. Boat returning on board vessel steaming slowly off and on. 3.30pm despatched boat for searchers 4.10pm. All on board having searched all North and East coast and saw no trace of anything. Found provisions depot totally destroyed and everything rotted beyond recognition. Saw large quantities of sea elephants and albatross and a few King Penguins, no fish of any description. 4pm stopped and allowed ship to drift to the eastward for the night.

Searchlight going from dark, moderate breeze and rain.

Position at noon Lat 46.8S Long 50.16E. course various dist 40 miles.

Thu 17 March

am engines stopped and drifting to eastward. 4.10am full speed for Hog Island.

7.45 stopped close to landing place and sent away search party, boats returned on board. Ship proceeds full speed to steam around island. 11.20 off SW Cap set in thick fog. Turned around and came back having seen nothing. 2.40 boat and party on board. Lieutenant reported having walked around SE cap and south coast and saw nothing. 2.45 full speed down round SE cape to where we stopped before, thus completing the circle. Proceeded full speed for Penguin Islands. 3pm passed Heroine Reef, two rocks, four feet above water.

4.30 close to Penguin Island, steamed round but saw nothing, set course for Possession Island patches of thick fog and rain. Searchlight going from dark.

Position at noon Lat 46.31S Long 50 14E course various distance 35 miles.

Mon 21 March

a.m wind moderating drifting off East coast of Island. 8.15am weather fine but fog around the horizon. Steamed in close and landed party to explore island. 11am boat returned while Lieutenant and men search the coast. 3.45pm sent boat away for the explorers. Lieut reports having found the provision depot in a dilapidated condition and swarming with rats but provisions in tins in apparently good condition. Travelled around the coast to Ship Cove and saw nothing.

5.30pm steamed slow off the land and lay dodging all night. Light breeze and cloudy with smooth sea.

Searchlight at work from dark until daylight.

Position at noon. Lat 46.21S Long 57.49E courses various dist 20 miles.

Wed 23 March

a.m thick fog engines slow. Ship's head off the land. 8am wind shifted and weather cleared. Steamed in close and sent away the boat and party at 840 and landed them in Ship Cove. 1.15 sent boat away again and all on board at 2.45 steamed full ahead and set course for Kerguelen Land (very pleased to think there was another lot finished). Lieut. reports having travelled round to SW Cape and saw no sign or trace of anything only notice board left by the SS Sabine – last searching ship and we left one of ours beside it. Strong breeze with high following sea. Weather clear.

Search light on from dark as usual.

Position at noon Lat 46.28S Long 51.50E course various. Dist 30 miles.

Fri 25 GOOD FRIDAY

Am moderate gale and high following sea and cloudy.
Lookout in crow's-nest from daylight.

Captain Putt with albatross.
(Courtesy of B. Putt)

Captain Putt with the chief
officer and a penguin. (Courtesy
of B. Putt)

For breakfast this day, hot cross buns for all hands. They were alright considering the weather.
p.m no change in the weather. Searchlight on as usual.
Position at noon by DR sun being obscured.
Lat 47.20S Long 60.42E course S81E distance 198 miles.

Sat 26

Am fresh breeze and overcast moderate sea.
Lookout in crow's-nest from daylight.
Noon similar wind and weather.
Searchlight form dark to daylight.
Position at noon Lat 47.55S Long 65.15E course S81E dist 184 miles.

Sun 27 EASTER SUNDAY

8.15 am sighted Roland Is ahead and Bligh's Cap on port bow.

Noon arrived off Christmas Harbour (funny place on Easter Sunday).

Blowing whole gale and squalls of sleet too much sea to launch a boat on to land. Much snow on the hills.

Position at noon Lat 48.37S long 69.1E course S74E dist 157 miles.

Monday 28 EASTER MONDAY

[pic 7e-7]a.m whole gale with heavy sleet and rain squally.

8am hail and snow squally wind blowing with hurricane force, high swell from the NW.

Noon weather still the same. Engines working to hold position impossible to land.

Pm heavy gale with terrific blinding snow and hail squally. Searchlight at work as usual.

Position at noon Lat 48.40S long 69.5E course various dist 30.

Tuesday 29 Easter Tuesday

a.m heavy gale and terrific snow squalls heavy swell coming round the island.

Lookout in crow's-nest from daylight.

9am whilst standing in the wheelhouse doorway and vessel rolling in trough of sea, gave a heavy lurch sending me head first on to the spokes of the wheel, cutting my chin badly. Doctor putting in five stitches.

p.m no change of weather still blowing a gale and high sea

Searchlight on from dark.

Position at noon by bearings Lat 48. 41 S long 69.6E vessel dodging 10 miles.

Wed 30

a.m strong gale with squalls. 11.15 steamed in to Foul Hawse Bay and as gale was abating launched the boat Lieut and six men. Proceeded ashore with difficulty and landed alongside of rocks, owing to the violent squalls in Christmas Harbour, landing was impossible there. 3.50 sent boat ashore for the search party. 4.20 all on board. Thick fog set in steamed slow to sea clear of the land. Lieu reports having walked round cliffs to Christmas Harbour but could not get down to beach. After two and half hours walk and as the fog was settling over the mountains they had to hurry back. I was very pleased to see them on board, if they had been left that night they would have frozen to death.

Position at noon Lat 48.41S Long 69.5E course various distance 45 miles.

Thu 31

2am stopped engines and allowed vessel to drift. 4.10am full speed back for Christmas Harbour. 6am wind increasing and coming to rain. Weather looking bad. Barometer falling rapidly and no shelter in any of the bays. At 6.15 turned around and steamed to sea. Wind rapidly increasing and mountainous sea getting up.

8am wind almost hurricane force and mountainous sea. Vessel pitching and labouring heavily and shipping heavy seas. Secured everything on the deck.

Noon storm continue with tremendous sea and thick rain. Found several rivets leaking in the hold due to heavy straining, steaming full ahead to keep ship head on to the sea. Searchlight going from dark but very little use.

Position by DR Lat 48.34S Long 69.40E course various 85 miles.

Fri 1 April

Am weather moderating somewhat. 3.30 half speed engines.

8am strong gale with heavy sea and fierce hail and snow squalls. Vessel pitching and racing heavily. Lookout in crow's-nest from daylight.

2.40pm reduced speed close to Christmas Harbour but unable to land on account of high sea and frequent hail and snow squalls.

3.30 stopped engines and let ship drift, waiting an opportunity to land, this being one of the places we had to visit and of course had to obey orders never mind the consequences?

Working engines at various speed during the night to hold position. Searchlight at work as usual.

Position by bearings of land Lat 48.29S long 69.12E course various dist 90 miles.

Sat 2 April

6.15am being close to Christmas Harbour sent away the boat, Lieut. Chief Officer and four men. Searched the beach hurriedly, found nothing of Waratah. Saw flagstaff left by French warship Eure in 1893. left board with our name and date. 8.40 all on board and steamed away to sea, dirty weather coming on very glad to get away from the reefs.

Position 6.30pm by stars Lat 48.41S long 70.19E heavy gale, searchlight as usual 15 miles.

Monday 4 April

a.m fresh breeze squally. 6am steamed nearer the land for shelter. 9.15 hailed the Norwegian steamer Joan de Arc but they had not seen any wreckage around the islands. Lookout in crow's-nest all day. Noon strong gale and high sea with blinding snow squalls. Proceeded up Royal Sound half speed as far as Long Island surveying the coast as we went but saw no sign of anything or anyone near the Lighthouse (which is unattended). 3pm snow squalls more frequent turned and put to sea for the night out of danger. Strong gale to storm with snow squalls, reduced speed and steamed slow about 6 miles off the coast. Fresh gale and continuous snow. Searchlight at work all night.

Position at noon Lat 49 22S Long 70.36E course various dist 50.

Tues 5 April

Am fresh breeze and cloudy with high choppy sea.

4.10am full speed ahead, making for Hillsboro Bay whilst weather looked favourable. Fresh gale and high head sea with clear weather the high land being covered with snow nearly to the water's edge. Noon rounded close to Kent Rocks.

2pm spoke to small steam whaler Éclair of Christiania. He saw nothing of any wreckage around the coast. There being too much wind and sea to launch a boat or to land. 4pm turned around and steamed out of the Bay to sea for safety. Strong wind and heavy squalls of wind and snow coming from the surrounding hills. Searchlight on from dark.

Position at noon Lat 49.8S Long 69.52E course various distance 82.

Wed 6 April

Am moderate breeze and clear weather. Snow squalls less frequent.

5am full speed ahead for the Bay. 8.30 having arrived inside the reef lowered boat and sent search party ashore in Kirk Harbour.

Noon wind freshening 2pm commenced to blow and looking bad with falling barometer. Search returned on board having searched all round Kirk Harbour but saw nothing. Proceeded full speed to sea out of danger. Strong gale and high rising sea with thick rain. 5.50 being then clear of the land put engines slow and dodged off the coast. Strong gale raining weather looking ugly and threatening. Searchlight as usual.

Position by bearings of land Lat 49. 13S long 69.47E course various dist 55.

Thu 7 April

a.m overcast with snow squall, sea moderate.

4.15 full sped ahead and shaped course for Hillsboro Bay (once more).

10.10 a small Norwegian whaler came close to and stopped, launcher our boat and got pilot out of her to take us into Gazelle Basin, the passage being very narrow and intricate. Scarce room for ship to pass between the high cliffs. Very safe when once inside.

1pm anchored in Gazelle Basin in muddy bottom with 45 fths cable.

2pm despatched search party ashore who returned again at 4.30. found provision depot but most of provisions gone.

8pm fresh breeze and snowing let go second anchor with 20fths cable.

Position at noon Lat 49.14S Long 69.47E course various distance 75 miles.

Friday 8 April

Lying in Gazelle Basin and had good nights rest which was needful. This harbour is practically sheltered from all winds having high hills all around. The only safe anchorage in the whole of Kerguelen Land. Here we found the SS Mongora a depot ship. The whale caught by the smaller whaler are towed in here and blubber melted down on board the large boat and at the end of the season she takes it to Durban S Africa where it is shipped to Europe. Search party ashore all day. Having searched the greatest part of the Peninsula but saw nothing, only a few rabbits which were killed and we had for supper, a very welcome change. Fine night with snow.

Position at anchor Lat 49.18S Long 69.42E course various dist 5 miles.

Mon 11 April

a.m moderate gale and high sea.

7.30am sighted land on port bow (Heard Island). Steamed along western shore of island the land being covered with snow the southern end of the high land being a glacier whereas the other end of the island is a volcano and in action as we could see smoke issuing from the crater.

10am discovered uncharted reef (which we named the 'Wakefield') breaking heavily about four miles off the coast and extending to the land. Our intention being to steam around and up the eastern side but at noon weather changed and looked bad decided to start for the McDonald Island (which we never saw, it only being a small rock). At time of passing it blowing a heavy gale and snow blinding everything. Searchlight on from dark.

Position farther south, Heard Is. Lat 53. 14S Long 73.57E course various, dist 153 miles.

Wed 13 April

Am strong gale with high sea, heavy hail squalls vessel rolling and straining heavily. Lookout in crow's-nest from daylight.

2.30pm sighted uncharted reef breaking heavily south of the Bernadet Islands. Altered course and passed quite close to ascertain its position. Steaming along south coast of Kerguelen but saw nothing. Moderate gale and high sea speed reduced. All night awaiting daylight to round the end of island and enter Royal Sound.

Fresh breeze with frequent snow and hail squalls.

Searchlight at work from dark.

Position at noon Lat 50.18S Long 68.56E course N31W dist 155.

Thu 14 April

a.m strong breeze with frequent snow squalls.

4am Cape Challenger abeam altered course. 5.40 full speed ahead. Lookout in crow's-nest from daylight.

8.40 entered Royal Sound and searching the North shore but saw nothing. Lead kept going continuously.

Noon close to Long Island. Intending to visit the whaling settlement but owing to the appearance of the weather, turned round and came back to Cat Island and landed search party. 2.30 they returned having seen nothing. Steamed into Island Harbour and let go anchor in 10fthms water with 45fthms cable, landed search party on Grave Island walked all round it and saw nothing. 5.40 returned to the ship.

Position at noon Lat 43.31S Long 70.3E. (Royal Sound) course various dist 108 miles.

Fri 15 April

9am wind freshening and wind backing to the eastward. Let go the second anchor.

l.15 vessel started to drag her anchors. Hove up and steamed further up the bay and anchored again with 60 and 45fths on each.

Unable to land search party owing to the state of weather.

Whole gale blowing with heavy snow and hail squalls.

7pm veered out more cable on each anchor.

Snow falling continuously the whole night and freezing.

Position at noon L 49.28S Long 70.19E. course various dist 14 miles.

Sat 16 April

a.m whole gale with terrific snow and hail squalls. 1.15 vessel started to drag. Hove up anchors and proceeded full speed to sea. 8am whole gale and blinding snow squalls. Ship dodging off lower Long Island. P.m the conditions unchanged, proceeded outside Sound to dodge for the night. Heavy hail and snow squalls. Searchlight on from dark.

Position noon Lat 49.28S Long 70.19E course various dist 14 miles

Sun 17 April

5.30am full speed ahead lookout in crow's-nest all day.

11.20 arrived off Balfour Rocks, it being too late to reach the settlement before dark. Slowed engines and dodged off the Sound.

Position at noon Lat 49.30S Long 70.33E course various dist 80 miles.

Mon 18 April

a.m steaming slow.

4am headed for Royal Sound full speed.

4.15 thich [sic] fog, eased engines. 5.25 fog lifted, resumed course and speed.

Lookout in crow's-nest from daylight. Stopped forty minutes for fog. Lead going continuously.

Noon gentle breeze sky overcast.

2pm arrived within 2 mile of whaling settlement but not sufficient time to go further and get out clear of the reefs before dark and as barometer was falling rapidly and every appearance of bad weather, turned back. 4.35 St House on Long Island abeam.

6pm abreast of Balfour Rocks, set course for St Paul's island having finished the search on Kerguelen. Strong gale and high following sea with thick rain.

Position at noon Lat 49.31S Long 70.3E course various dist 62.

Thu 21 April

a.m fresh gale and high beam sea, rolling and straining heavily and shipping much water Lookout in crow's-nest from daylight.

Weather much warmer than we have been getting lately.

Searchlight going form dark as usual.

Position at noon lat 42.35S long 75.21E course various dis 160 miles.

Fri 22 April

a.m moderate head wind and swell fine weather.

Lookout in crow's-nest from daylight.

Noon fresh breeze and cloudy, sea smooth.

2pm sighted St Paul's Island right ahead.

6.25pm stopped engines 6 miles south of island and let the ship drift until daylight, gentle breeze and fine weather.

Searchlight on all night as usual.

Position at noon Lat 39 32S Long 76.50E course N21E dist 195 miles.

Sat 23 April

4.10 am full speed ahead for the island. 8am proceeding up to Crater Harbour. 8.30 am boat with search party sent away, vessel drifting.

2.40pm search party on board. Saw no trace on anything concerning Waratah. *Found letters left by SS Sabine, also some in French. Left for Amsterdam Island.*

Position at Noon Lat 38.40 S Long 77.38E. course various dist 70 miles.

Sun 24 April

2am stopped engines. Daylight proceeded slow along east side of island. Heavy surf on the rocks rendering landing impossible. Observed large quantity of cattle on the island. P.m vessel drifting, awaiting finer weather to land.

Position at noon Lat 37.50S Long 77.39E course N2E dist 63 miles.

Mon 25 April

3.40am half speed ahead towards island. 5.30 full speed. Lookout in crow's-nest from daylight.

8am proceeding slow, fresh north wind and overcast, high confused swell, close to south side of island. Heavy surf breaking everywhere on the rocks. Landing impossible. After going round the island slow and made sure no one existed on it, proceeded south full speed (and we all wanted a bullock very badly and plenty there for the asking, but I expect tough). This finishes the islands.

Noon light breeze and fine clear weather.

Kerguelen Island in good weather. The remains of the German observation station. (Courtesy of Hans Helfenbein)

A contemporary view of Heard Island, close to the uncharted reef they named 'Wakefield Reef'. (Courtesy of B. Putt)

Searchlight on from dark as usual.

Position at noon Lat 38 15S Long 77.37E course various dist 40 miles.

Sun 1 May

a.m heavy storm and mountainous. 5am kept ship head to the sea.

Lookout on the bridge, not safe to send men aloft. vessel rolling.

Pm weather moderating slightly. Searchlight as usual.

7.30 by star Lat 45.0S.

Position at noon Lat 45.24S Long 79.49E course N10W dist 97 miles.

Wed 4 May

a.m fresh breeze and irregular sea, vessel rolling.

Lookout in crow's-nest from daylight.

Noon. Moderate breeze and clear weather. High following sea.

4.30pm sighted sailing ship on Port beam about 20 miles off.

Steering East. 5.40pm flashed ship's name by searchlight and asked to be reported by sailing ship but got no response.

7.25 Lat by star 46.54S.

Gentle breeze and moderate swell clear weather.

Searchlight at work from dark.

Position at noon Lat 47.54S Long 82.9E course various dist 187.

A contemporary view of St Paul's Island. (Courtesy of B. Putt)

Fri 6 May

a.m altered course to keep head to sea. Vessel making 2 pts leeway.

Strong gale and tremendous sea. Heavy snow and hail squalls. Vessel pitching and racing violently. Lookout being kept on bridge.

noon whole gale to storm and mountainous sea vessel thumping heavily, not able to keep head up to storm, falling off to SW and making all leeway. Set main trysail to keep her up to the sea. Pm storm still raging and mountainous seas.

Searchlight on from dark.

Position at noon Lat 47. 12 S Long 83.23E course various dist 148 miles.

Sat 14 May

a.m fresh gale and squally heavy head sea. Pitching and rolling heavy.

Lookout being kept on the bridge.

Noon heavy gale, vessel not steering.

4pm set main trysail to try and keep ship head to sea but no use. Vessel only lying in the trough of the sea and drifting.

Searchlight as usual.

Position at noon Lat 47.17S Long 86.6E course N4W dist 126.

Sun 15 Whit Sunday

a.m strong breeze and squally continuous heavy rain.

Lookout in crow's-nest from daylight. Noon moderate beam sea.

2pm sighted a sailing ship 10 miles Port bow steering East.

Searchlight as usual. Position at noon Lat 45.46S Long 86.28E course N10E distance 93 miles.

Mon 16 Whitsun Monday bank holiday

a.m heavy rain and lightning, wind and sea increasing.

Lookout in crow's-nest from daylight.

8am whole gale with frequent heavy squalls, set all sail.

Noon gale moderating squalls less and sea going down.

2pm sighted steamer's smoke ahead going to the eastward.

Pm moderate breeze and cloudy. Heavy westerly swell.

Searchlight on from dark.

Position at noon Lat 46.1S Long 86.57E course various dist 153.

Tues 17 May

a.m wind and sea increasing and heavy rain.

8am moderate to fresh gale and squally, beam sea.

Lookout in the crow's-nest from daylight.

Noon, wind shifted to SSE with hurricane force and rain.

Pm heavy storm and mountainous sea, ship not able to keep head up to it. Vessel thumping heavily.

Searchlight on from dark.

Position at noon Lat 48.46S Long 87.12E course S4E dist 165.

Wed 18 May

a.m fresh breeze and clear high confused sea.

Lookout in crow's-nest from daylight.

8am strong increasing wind and high sea.

Noon fresh gale and high cross seas. Vessel rolling and pitching.

4pm strong easterly gale and continuous showers of snow and sleet.

9pm heavy squally blew main trysail to pieces.

Searchlight on from dark.

Midnight heavy storm and mountainous seas.

Position DR Lat 49.54S Long 88.00E course various dist 121 miles.

The block course continues with weather Lat and Long until Monday 13 June.

Mon 13 June

Finished the block and shaped course for Melbourne.

Heavy gale and high dangerous cross sea, vessel rolling very heavy and straining. Heavy rain continuously.

Lookout in crow's-nest from daylight.

8am moderate gale and thick misty rain.

Noon no change in the weather.

4pm strong NW wind and high confused sea.

Searchlight on from dark.

Midnight fresh breeze and overcast misty.

Position at noon DR Lat 47. 30S Long 101.24E course N88E dist 128.

Thu 23 June

a.m fresh breeze and showery. Rough beam sea, vessel rolling heavily.

Lookout in crow's-nest from daylight.

8am moderate beam wind and sea weather showery.

Noon light winds and moderate sea, fine and clear.

4pm strong breeze and squally choppy beam sea.

7.15pm sighted Cape Nelson Light, fresh breeze and smooth sea.

Heavy rain showers.

9.15 Cape Nelson Light abeam distance 11 miles. Flashed ship's name with searchlight.

Position at noon Lat 38.46S Long 140.15E course N82E dist 178 miles.

Fri 24 June

a.m moderate breeze and clear. Sea smooth. 7.55 Cape Ottway light house abeam, hoisted ship's numbers.

Noon breeze and clear, sea smooth.

2.35pm stopped at Port Phillip Heads for Pilot.

2.40 pm proceeded full ahead. The first news we had of King Edward's death and lots besides after being away out of the world for four months.

6.30pm arrived off Williamstown and anchored with 45 fthms cable on starboard anchor. Very thankful to find ourselves safely there after travelling 15,027 miles on a fruitless search having seen nothing in the way of wreckage belonging to the SS Waratah. Draft on arrival For'd d5.0 aft 13.0.

Position noon Lat 38.34S Long 144.13E course various dist 194 miles to Melbourne 58.

A contemporary view of Heard Island. (Courtesy of B. Putt)

Sat 25 June

7.30 am proceeded up the river Yarra.

8.40am in dry dock. Found vessel's bottom covered with shell and long grass and top sides looking bare and rusty.

10am went ashore to enter the ship. Afterwards had luncheon with the Mayor of Melbourne and members of the Waratah Search Committee.

In the evening saw all the friends and slept ashore. Nice change.

Sun 26 June

This day the vessel was visited by hundreds of people, the dock gates being left open for the occasion. Came on board for a little while in the morning and found everything alright and spent the remainder of the day ashore and also slept the night ashore.

Mon 27 June

Vessel being scraped and painted with one coat this day.

11am meeting of the committee until noon. Saw the charts and left the report for them to read.

Paid off the Surgeon and done other business.

Large number of people visiting the ship.

Called at F Hill's place of business but he had gone home, spent the evening at J Cheffer's house, also met W Cole and J Luckham.

Slept ashore at W Adam's.

Tues 28 June

Vessel being painted second coat.

Discharging the Waratah's stores, men taking adrift the dynamo and searchlight and sending the same ashore.

Had luncheon on board Huddart Parker's new mail and passenger, SS Zealandia, just out from home. Lovely ship and quite a swell affair, everything of the best. The afternoon pretty busy at the office.

4pm called on F Hill and went with him down to Frankston, found the family all well. Very nice house and grounds but long way from business.

Wed 29 June

7a.m left the house heavy rain. Drove to the station in small pony trap, rather uncomfortable. I pitied the pony.

9am arrived in town went on board and found everything alright. Still discharging the stores and men taking adrift the electric fittings. Went to the office had lunch with F Hill. In the afternoon had another meeting with the committee. In the evening went to W Cole's house. Came back and spent the night at Will's.

Thur 30 June

Vessel still in dry dock.

8am let the water in the dock and floated her alongside to take out the heavy stores and put ashore the Dynamo.

11am final meeting of the committee at the Lord Mayor's Parlour in the Town Hall. Met quite a number of M.P.s. Lot of speech making were quite satisfied with what we had done and gave letter to that effect.

Very busy getting ready for sea.

3.20pm let go moorings and hove out of dock. 3.43 whilst swinging into the Basin, fouled the stern tug with the propeller breaking off three blades, hauled ship to wharf and then cabled owners of damage.

Fri 1 July

7.30 am left the wharf and proceeded to Dry Dock assisted by Tugs Racer *and* Alacrity, *not being able to work main engines.*

8am entered the dock.

11am ship rested on the blocks. Men at work on broken propeller. Received instructions from office to give the ship another coat of paint whilst was done. Wrote letters to the owner of the tug holding them responsible, received one from them for damage we done to the tug, all business left in the hands of agents, would also have to pay for picking up the broken blades from the river.

Everything on the ship.

Sat 2

a.m fresh breeze and clear.

7.30 new propeller on in place.

8.30 ship afloat, everything waiting for the shaft to be coupled up.

11.20 moved out of dock and swung into Basin. At noon proceeded down the river. 3.40pm discharged Pilot at Port Phillip Heads and proceeded towards Newcastle N.S.W.

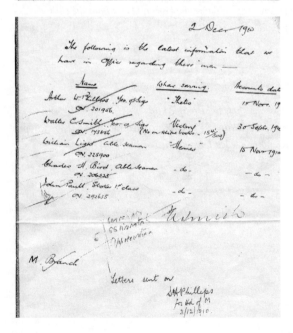

Draft letters of appreciation from the Admiralty in thanks for the efforts made by those involved in the *Wakefield* search. (By kind permission of the national archives reference ADM 1/8038)

This page and opposite Draft letters of appreciation from the Admiralty in thanks for the efforts made by those involved in the *Wakefield* search. (By kind permission of the national archives reference ADM 1/8038)

William Light, Able Seaman
O.N. 225900.

Charles H. Bird, Able Seaman
O.N. 206523

and John Paull, Stoker 1st Class
O.N. 292635.

Sir,

× - 4

to [Arthur W. Phillips, Yeoman
  Walter C. Smith, Yeoman
of Signals, O.N. 201956,] who
of Signals. O.N. 173856.
accompanied Lieutenant Seymour

in the "Wakefield" & who is understood

to be now serving in [H.M.S. "Thetis"
                       the R.N. Barracks
                       at Portsmouth]

I am, etc.

A similar letter has
been sent to the C in C
Portsmouth, with regard to
Walter C. Smith. Yeoman of
Signals, & to the Vice Admiral
Com'dg the 3rd & 4th Div'ns Home Fleet
with regard to Arthur W.
Phillips, Yeoman of Signals, both
of these Petty Officers having
returned home direct from Melbourne

The V.A. 3rd & 4th Divs
H.F
duplicate to C.O.
HMS. Nock

The C in C,
Portsmouth
(as altered in red)

Sir,

With reference to your submissions
of the 10th and 13th August, N.os 333
& 334 /54 B / III, I am etc to acquaint
you that an expression of their
appreciation of the manner in which
the search for the missing s.s "Waratah" was carried out
has been conveyed to Lieutenant Hobert
N.T.R. Seymour R.N. & to the Petty officers & men who accompanied
him.

I am, etc.

COPIED FOR SIG...URE
5|12|09

The C in C,
Cape.

CHAPTER 8

CONSPIRACY THEORIES AND THE BOARD OF TRADE INQUIRY

The Board of Trade Inquiry lasted around two weeks and took place at Caxton Hall, London. It was presided over by Mr John Dickinson, police court magistrate, who was assisted by a team of nautical advisors ultimately answerable to Winston Churchill, at that time President of the Board of Trade. They began their mammoth task on 15 December 1910 in the wake of massive publicity and conjecture. This ranged from doubts as to the ship's seaworthiness to the paranormal and was to produce a tally of conflicting evidence throughout. At one point a woman giving evidence shouted out that a certain man had told his friends the ship was unseaworthy, whilst he stood and refuted that he found nothing to complain about at all. It was an emotional and exhausting investigation, calling on witnesses from all over the world to offer their opinions and experiences. Mr Claude Sawyer was to become a major player on this tragic stage with his knowledge of shipping and background of travel, fuelled by his eerie premonitions, yet even Mr Sawyer's evidence was not as straightforward as it first appeared. The booking office in Sydney was quick to respond to newspaper articles released about his disembarkation, pointing out that his stories could have been constructed in an effort to get off the ship early and that he might have meant to get off at Durban all along, otherwise why wait a week in Durban for another ship to Cape Town when there was available space on an earlier one?

One attendee at the Inquiry declared that it was a strange state of affairs when the argument about the events of that night overhsadowed the fact that it was human lives being discussed, so extensive was the talk of legalities and blame. The ladies sitting in their mourning clothes were a stark reminder of what the Inquiry was really about and what the focus should be upon. It was not that it was impersonal, but the Inquiry's goal was to sift through the mountain of evidence to get to the point where they could offer up an intelligent picture of what really happened on that stormy night off the South African coast.

The fact that nothing has ever been found has inspired many theories, both at the time and over the intervening years. The lack of firm evidence is partly what prompted those organising the searches to continue, buoyed up by the hope that if there was no wreckage, she could well be drifting and, with sufficient food and desalination facilities, could have sustained those on board for a substantial time.

Ships adrift have long been a problem from a practical point of view and a great deal of effort has always been made to remove them from shipping lanes. This was of far more importance when the drifting ships were of wooden construction, simply float-ing within the busy trade runs until they were forced away by the elements, as whilst they remained they were a very real hazard to other vessels. Eventually there was to be legislation to ensure that vessels would go out and retrieve abandoned ships and thereby keep shipping lanes clear.

This was not the reason for searching for the *Waratah*, however; it was believed she had either sunk or was adrift and as no one had reported an incident with a drifting steam ship we must assume no other ships aside from the designated search vessels had encountered her. Moreover, steel ships were more likely to sink and less likely to remain as a block in the way of other vessels.

As the *Waratah* was registered 100 A1 at Lloyd's it strongly suggests that when she was launched she was considered as safe as any ship with that rating and deemed fit for the mighty seas she would undoubtedly encounter. However, it transpired that although roughly planned to emulate her sister-ship *Geelong*, there were significant differences between the two. It appears that disputes between the builders and the owners had broken out regarding the *Waratah*'s design, the builders agitated by some of the decisions and feeling their advice may have been overlooked.

In any case, whilst Mr Lund was waiting for his ship to arrive at Cape Town, he seemed confident that she would appear and showed no sign of fearing any other outcome. He had declared that the weather was bad off the coast and that if some of the machinery had been disabled it could take some days to repair, particularly if it was a steam pipe, so she was probably just drifting.

Another theory pointed out that she had gone aground by Kangaroo Island off Adelaide on her maiden voyage, which may have weakened her rudder and only manifested as a problem in the storm which undoubtedly raged the night she went missing; it might easily have severed something and rendered her unmanageable. However, one would have presumed that would have been picked up at her survey. Mr Samuel Trott (father of crew member Fred Trott) gave evidence at the Inquiry on day eight, stating that he had been a crew member alongside his son on the maiden voyage. He spoke about the incident at Kangaroo Island, outlining how it took six hours before the ship was afloat. Had there been any breakdown there would have been no way of repairing the damage whatever the weather and those on board would have known that their only hope of rescue was to be seen by another vessel.

It had been said that there were no drills but certainly Claude Sawyer mentioned a drill when he was identifying the lifeboat he was assigned to, and the officer who was in charge of it, so one may assume lifeboat drills were carried out although it was recorded that none took place on the maiden voyage. It was also mentioned that in a storm the lifeboats may have been lashed down and thereby rendered useless in an emergency. This would seem to be a very bizarre thing to do to: to remove access to lifesaving equipment in a time of heightened danger. There appears to be no record of fire drills on either voyage.

Whilst on the subject of lifeboats, it is interesting that mention was made about the dreadful condition of those on the maiden voyage. It had been commented that they did not look seaworthy – yet this was only her second voyage. One would have thought that the owners would have been out to impress and it would have been a remarkable economy to supply vital pieces of equipment below standard and visibly worn and old. They had been cleared as safe by Captain Clarke before leaving for her second voyage, although arguments still rumbled about the maiden voyage.

During the Inquiry at Caxton Hall it was stated that the *Waratah*'s was not an experimental design and that her depth and proportions were as good as, if not better than, many of her peers. Evidence was given that her seven watertight compartments and extra enclosed bridge space gave her extra freeboard which helped buoyancy and confirmed that the captain had ordered 250 tons of coal stowed on the spar deck, obviously with the same amount on each side (this was not on the bridge deck as had been suggested). The suggestion that this storm constituted her first big beam sea was strongly contradicted; it was stated that it would in fact have been a head sea and that a problem which might have been encountered was in the trough of the sea, without any 'way on' when another wave hit. It did not of course answer the question of wreckage other than drift in the current.

It was also noted at the Inquiry that Captain Ilbery had commented about events and animals on board, yet maintained a silence about the performance of his new ship. This raised a number of questions, as he had mentioned her 'tenderness' and she clearly had some issues as she was to receive minor updates, including water ballast, it having been evident on the maiden voyage that there was a list. Later, the list was to transfer to the other side but this too was fixed before her fateful voyage. Her voyage from Albany, however, on the return leg of the maiden voyage, caused a great deal of anxiety amongst her seasoned travellers, but these passengers were reassured by various officers in spite of their own fears. In fact more than one crew member wanted to leave the ship and not return to her, and indeed one man did so, choosing to remain unpaid. Officers were not permitted to just leave a ship and were contracted to complete any voyage they took on, yet still it was noted that some had considered this extreme course of action. This was most unusual; men hopped on and off ships all the time, but rarely out of fear for the ship's stability and hardly ever officers. But once again there were conflicting reports, as Mr Dew, the pilot from Melbourne, declared there was absolutely no listing which would not be in line with the way the wind was blowing and he certainly had no concerns about the ship's behaviour. Neither did Captain John Rainnie, port captain and captain of the *Richard King*, the tug which had taken her out of Durban.

It was reported at the Inquiry that Professor Bragg (Professor of Physics at the University of Leeds), who travelled with his wife, two sons and daughter on the maiden trip between Adelaide and London, was reassured, after voicing his concerns, by the chief engineer, who declared that the ship was 'safe as a church'. Most of the original officers had signed up for the second voyage, indicating there were two very different schools of thought regarding the whole issue of the ship's stability and top-heaviness, with both sides equally adamant that their views were right. What was happening to cause such heated debate among passengers and crew alike? Was panic creating problems where there were none?

It is a point of interest to note that *Waratah* was the fifth ship to carry that name and they all but one foundered.

On her voyage from the shipyard in Scotland to London, her rolling and reluctance to recover from those rolls had already been noticed and yet the only comments made by her captain were that she was not 'stiff' enough in his opinion, and even this only came out later. She had been passed by Lloyd's and the emigration authorities, who oversaw the safety of passenger ships used for emigration, and who were keen to endorse her as a trading ship on that route.

It was reported that the chief officer had trouble loading the cargo and another stability issue involved the fact that she could not be moved around harbour without ballast. Still, this did not seem to have caused alarm as this was the case with many ships; they are built to carry great loads and are actually easier to manoeuvre with weight on them.

On board there had been discussions between crew members and passengers regarding her list and rolling and it was reported that the dining room had to make allowances for the list by adding devices to level the tables out to keep everything in place during dining.

But the Inquiry reveals that for every negative comment there was a positive one. It was often the officers who were uncomfortable with the ship's behaviour and Mr Hemy, the second officer, was apparently very anxious about the trip down from the Clyde to London – this did not bode well for a man who was signed up to work aboard the ship in the most treacherous of waters. However, Hemy's nervous attitude is merely heresay, as he was destined to go the way of the others in disappearing on that fateful July night.

Chief Officer Owen was possibly the most vociferous in condemning the *Waratah's* behaviour. In one discussion a passenger, Mr Mason, said to him, 'If I were you, I'd get out of this ship, she'll be making a big hole in the water one of these days', to which Owen replied 'I'm afraid she will'. Owen also reportedly advised a seaman looking for a berth on board the steamer not to join the boat on any account, 'because this ship, in my opinion, must prove a coffin for all hands one of these days.' It is remarkable that he should have been advised in this manner. It is possible that Owen was trying to dissuade this man for some other reason, but these were strong words and in hindsight an uncanny prediction.

Edward Dischler was due to do the round trip as an able seaman in the *Waratah* and was taken on in London. There was talk among the seamen that the ship would not make Las Palmas because she was not safe and that none of the first trip sailors would sign up with her again, whilst further rumours claimed that the captain and chief officer wanted to leave her. This negativity must have had an effect on Dischler, because he was to become one of the fortunate ones. He claimed that a compass in one of the boats was broken and he had been told there were no more and that they did not have fire drill. He spoke of portholes being closed due to rolling and a general feeling that the ship was not recovering herself. Dischler tried to leave at Melbourne and stated his reasons to the captain, who refused to pay him off but was sorry to lose him. Dischler wavered at the thought of not being paid but was so sure of his decision that he left at Sydney, finding someone to replace him. We do not have his replacement's name but it may be inferred that the captain paid Dischler off as a result.

So many strange stories emerged from the Inquiry. There was talk of pianos moving across the saloon and of passengers sustaining injuries, but for every negative comment there was a positive one, such as the report from Mr Charles Richard Campbell-Lloyd who travelled on board the ship from Cape Town to Sydney and was so impressed with the captain and his diligence that he wrote a handsome testimonial upon reaching Melbourne.

Second Officer Hemy had supposedly remarked that he felt that the *Waratah* had a deck too many; for an officer to be saying such a thing would not inspire confidence, but this conversation was reported by a shipping tally clerk at Sydney who had spoken to Hemy whilst tallying meat. Whether he was referring to her unsteadiness is not recorded. What was reported in a newspaper was a comment by the chief engineer's sister-in-law, Mrs Maude Hodder, who assured them that a third deck was added at the last minute and could account for her being top-heavy. She also added that it had been arranged to make a run in record time and that was the reason for the extra coal on the spar deck. That may well have been the case but there was talk of an unscheduled re-coaling on the first trip and it would have necessitated carrying more coal henceforth.

Another interesting report came from a man from Bournemouth, England, who said that whilst visiting South Africa he had met inhabitants of Willowvale who claimed the loss of the *Waratah* had been witnessed by a white trader along that coast. This gentleman went to meet the trader who told him that he had seen a large steamer inshore that night and went for his night glasses but by the time he returned it had disappeared. At this time he had known nothing of the missing liner. He had in his possession a piece of wood with the letters 'WAR' carved upon it. He claimed that sharks would account for the lack of bodies but if the ship had been lost so close to shore surely wreckage would be seen by the ships actively looking for it?

A man called Harry Hulse wrote to the newspapers in response to articles about the white trader as he was involved with the searches along that coastline. He introduced himself as being connected with the Cape Mounted Riflemen, who had made a detailed search of the Transkei Native Reserve from St Johns to the mouth of the Xora River and said that all the traders along that coast had been interrogated and nothing was reported or produced as being from the steamer. He said that he had lived along that stretch of coast for a good many years and that he had never heard anything about a trader witness.

Barclay & Co. were not called into question over their ship-building skills as such, having as they did an exemplary record in ship-building safety, but there were clearly disagreements between the owners and the builders. It was claimed in one report that there was no stowage plan and yet these plans were available. It is unclear why that would be remarked upon.

Then there was the matter of the coal at Durban and how it was stowed, or rather not stowed. Although it appears no cargo was taken on board at Durban, and only around thirty-four passengers, the ship had to bunker and it was reported that she had coal on her bridge deck. Whilst that was refuted, it appears to be true that she had coal stowed on her spar deck.

Mr Robert Mackenzie was superintendent of Cotts & Co., the ship's agents in Durban. He was on board until she left and the only other person to leave the ship alive was the pilot. During Mr Mackenzie's time on board he was in conversation with the officers and was under the impression that the bilge pumps were not working. To add to that, the untrimmed coal on her decks would produce an added difficulty. He recounted his story to a journalist, his opinion being that the ship was slow to recover. This would present a particular problem for this ship as her design meant there were fewer scuppers to release the water taken on board. It was his belief that if she took on a powerful wave, the water would not have time to drain before a second wave crashed onto the decks; to add to his conviction, a 42ft-long hatch would not have been able to withstand the impact and would snap with the force, filling the ship in seconds. But this theory would still not answer the question of why no wreckage was found, bearing in mind that derricks, boats, oars, lifebuoys, boats' masts and items such as hatch covers would put up no resistance to a full force of water.

Echoing the overall theme of the Inquiry, Mackenzie's belief was contradicted by naval architect Mr Robert Steele, who declared that after making a painstaking study of all of *Waratah's* design and figures, it was his opinion that the elements would not have got the better of her at all.

Other theories have been postulated and the freak wave phenomenon is a much researched one. It is often reported that waves of up to 20m in height are not uncommon along the coastline in question and many ships have been hit by these huge walls of water. It is perhaps possible that if the *Waratah* corkscrewed into a sea at speed, the looser items on board and the weaker hatches might not have been washed away, plunging down with the ship. It does not explain how smaller and more vulnerable ships have survived these freak waves. These waves were identified specifically by Professor Mallory of Cape Town and his studies revealed that there were elements which made them appear in a particularly localised area.[1] Indeed his research led to ships being advised to avoid this area in certain conditions and to remain within a precise corridor of sea. The Algulhas current, combined with severe gales and the presence of the continental shelf, all contribute to the build-up of treacherous seas, particularly during a south-westerly force when conditions align for these freak waves to build up momentum.

Another potential problem for the *Waratah* was the lead she was carrying. There was evidence that in certain conditions the friction created by the lead moving might summon enough heat for it to begin to melt and then cause her to turn turtle as it shifted. She had 1,300 tons of lead in two forms, lead and leady concentrate. Today there are rules about the transportation of lead, but when this lead was taken on board at Adelaide there was little if any awareness of the dangers of this cargo. Difficulties caused by the lead would still not explain the lack of wreckage.

There was also talk of methane – how it builds up from dead matter and is prevented from getting out by a protective layer. When the layer is removed the methane can escape and the gas is drawn up before it returns to the sea, pulling down with it whatever might be in the way. This phenomenon would seem to be capable of taking down huge weights and the ship would have had no way of taking evasive action. An occurrence such as this, of course, would have rendered wireless useless.

On the *Waratah*'s maiden voyage there had been a fire that had taken three hours to extinguish. There is always the possibility that on this second voyage there had been an explosion caused by the combination of coal dust and fire. However, it would have had to have been a massive explosion due to the size of the ship and again one would tend to think it would shower debris, leaving tell-tale wreckage.

Piracy is another possibility, but quite why that would occur would be a mystery in itself. There were certainly people of some financial standing on board but no one seemed to consider this option following her loss, so we have to assume this is merely another idea which, whilst it cannot be disproved, is perhaps unlikely.

There is a school of thought which suggests that maybe *Waratah* temporarily recovered the use of disabled engines and took herself away from the search areas in an attempt to head back somewhere. Although she may have been sighted, she was travelling over a very large expanse of sea. Even if she had sent up flares, in high seas and with the engines in tickover, it would be challenging to find her. The accounts from the *Sabine* and *Wakefield* describe just that – how for days, even weeks, they saw nothing at all in the way of other shipping, and it would have been exactly the same for the *Waratah*.

The drift theory, of course, is what the journals featured in this book are based upon. She was believed to have been unsinkable and, bearing in mind that smaller ships had weathered the storm that night with little or minimal damage, the *Waratah* should have fared very well. The *Waikato* had been successfully retrieved after months at sea and it was hoped the same would happen with the missing *Waratah*. Our four first-hand accounts in the diaries and journals paint a gruelling picture of the searches. The men started out with great optimism, visiting uninhabited islands and searching for wreckage during what became a lengthy, and physically and mentally trying ordeal with only the belief that they might actually succeed to drive them on.

If she resides beneath the sea then Emlyn Brown has spent many years searching there and so far it has left us as bewildered as before – surely making the *Waratah* the most searched-for ship in history.

There are a couple of unconfirmed stories which may be of interest, one concerning a deckchair washed up off Coffee Bay – roughly in the area the ship would probably be had she sunk – with the name of a passenger and SS *Waratah* written upon it. No other objects were found and it was suggested this one was brought there by the current, and yet this deckchair supposedly survived. There is a dearth of further evidence on the deckchair, as with the lifebuoy in New Zealand. Its presence would not support a drift theory due to the area in which it was discovered. Furthermore, it would be remarkable to assume that nothing could have been accidentally knocked overboard when there were so many lively children on the ship!

Bizarrely, in August 1909 a man in a severely confused state of mind was found on the shore in South Africa only able to say 'Waratah' and 'big wave'. He was too confused to say any more and it is just possible that this man was actually a survivor. He was put in an institution where he remained, dismissed as mentally ill. He may have held the key to the fates of many, but was not to be helped in a way which would offer any insight to anyone.

The vastly conflicting evidence makes it clear how impossible a task the Inquiry was faced with. At every turn they were confronted with contradictions. The government dock official at Adelaide, one Charles Johnstone, stated that the captain of the *Waratah* had spoken highly of the ship and that he (Johnstone) had examined her boats which were in perfect order. The stevedores also declared her a stout ship, saying that she was upright at all times. John McDiarmid (the pilot) inclined to a feeling that she was behaving unusually, whereas his fellow pilot said she steered beautifully.

Mr Copeland K. Etheridge of London wrote to the papers to say that he had dealt with Captain Ilbery for over twenty years. He had helped him load even bad cargoes and had seen him running the trials for the *Waratah*, and was convinced that there would be no issue of instability under such a commander; had he felt the ship was 'crank' then he had the ballast to use which would have steadied her. He confirmed that the ship was insulated and explained that this meant that her weight was distributed evenly up and over the decks, making her even more seaworthy when in ballast trim. He added that her heavy refrigeration units were positioned at an even safer level than in many other ships. His theory was that one of her connecting rods was carried away, resulting in a flooded engine room and damaged engines. He hoped that as coal would not be used for engines there would be sufficient to ensure the refrigeration to keep the food fresh and that they would all be able to eat well, drink fresh water and at least remain fairly healthy on her drift out of the shipping routes. There was also a large supply of wine, which would have been gratefully devoured no doubt!

One man wrote that he had gone out on the *Waratah*'s maiden voyage and was plagued by the same fears as Claude Sawyer, writing in his diary 'still rolling badly, nearly turtle'. His original plan was to return on her next (fateful) voyage but he changed his ticket at some monetary loss. It was interesting that on his eventual return, on board the SS *Manuka*, he spotted another passenger from the maiden journey on *Waratah* when *Manuka* was coming in to Auckland, the other passenger standing on shore at the time and shouting to him, 'Has that *Waratah* upset yet?'

Other opinions saw her as dropping down to the bottom of the ocean like a stone, or that the forceful Agulhas Current had taken her far out of reach, too far south to be encountered by the sailing ships on the sailer routes. One gentleman described how all captains have a feeling of anxiety about this coast in winter and how once he had to jettison cargo in order to regain stability in a ship; they had also been carried far away from their Dead Reckoning position. He thought the *Waratah* would be drifting with the current eastwards at 37 or 38 degrees. Of course, all sailors will disagree over the drift path. The steamer *Bannockburn* from New York to New Zealand had to re-coal at Albany, having had her coal washed out of the ship by a ferocious storm which they declared had nearly the same disastrous effect he was sure was the fate of the poor liner.

However, what proved most remarkable were the findings of the Court. They did not lay any blame at the door of the builders, owners or officers, but neither did they claim to have come to any resolution whatsoever over the *Waratah*'s fate. Experts and witnesses were locked in opposing views and even after the most detailed of hearings they were no nearer a definitive answer than we are today.

The court offered its sympathy to those affected by the disaster and nodded to the doubtfulness of some evidence, which, considering it was mostly in total disaccord, must have been a challenging task to endure. The court wanted it to be known that they had fulfilled the necessarily thorough investigation and that they felt this should set the minds of those involved at rest. They saw no reasonable doubt that, whatever the cause, all those on board the *Waratah* had met their deaths at sea shortly after leaving Durban. Its statement 'The Court regarded it as the *kindest* course to emphasise this view in the strongest manner' was extraordinary; it was seen as the kindest finding, though not necessarily a truthful one. In a case such as this one, any finding was inevitably conjecture.

Perhaps after all it was not the kindest finding for the Blue Anchor Line who, whilst they were not blamed, did suffer as a result. Mr Lund was now elderly and his dreams – from the sail loft on the Thames to owning a large fleet – were indelibly marred. The Blue Anchor Line sold to P&O for £275,000 and that put P&O into its new branch line – the start of their emigration business.

Notes

1   Mallory, J.K. 'Abnormal waves in the south-east coast of South Africa', Int. Hydrog. Rev., vol. 51, pp99-129, 1974. Kindly identified by Paul C. Liu, Oceanographer with NOAA.

CHAPTER 9

THE DEEP SEA SEARCHES

Clive Cussler.

Emlyn in a helicopter looking for signs of the wreck. (Courtesy of Emlyn Brown)

In more recent times, the enigma of the whereabouts of the *Waratah* has continued to intrigue and captivate people. None were more captivated than dive specialist Emlyn Brown. Emlyn found an ally and investor in author Clive Cussler among other philanthropists and together they attempted to solve the mystery. Here Emyln Brown shares his experiences.

Emlyn Brown's Story

For my darling mother who passed away quietly
while I penned this. Thank you for your beauty my lovely.
To my dad, who lost his will to live, may the light shine
upon you my darling dad.

As with all young boys, we became inspired and motivated by our wild imaginations and those of others. Mine was always overactive. Listening to the radio in my parents' bed when they were out dancing, my brothers and I would listen to adventure stories while staring into the speaker grill and imagining that people were somewhere in the radio. I would go a step further and open old radios up to see for myself. I needed to know just how radios worked, and why. Thus a hobby in electronics was born. I restored an old 1940s PYE radiogram just like the one my parents had to full working order and always listened to it when at my desk. Keeping in time to the music, I would use my mother's knitting needles as drumsticks and drum away on greaseproof paper placed over the dining room chair seats, and use brass ornaments as symbols.

By the age of twelve I had my own workshop in the backyard crammed with old radios and salvaged electronic parts. I would lock myself away for hours on end building electronic things that went bzzzzz and ting ting. I can recall an amplifier I was making went *BANG!* when the power supply polarity was reversed. One learns almost immediately never to do things like that again. Unbeknown to me I was amassing a working knowledge of things electronic and beginning to understand the rudimentaries of the subject.

I was by no means brilliant, as mathematics was and always had been a mysterious subject to me. But nothing prevented me from reading up on everything I wanted to know. My Uncle Eddie and friends were all hobbyists so the exchange of knowledge and experience was a constant flow between us. These were very fulfilling days in my youth.

I always liked ships, too. I was fascinated when my dad took me to see a shipwreck off the Moullie Point lighthouse in 1967 at the age of twelve. The *Safamarine* freighter was hard up on the rocks and her stern had broken. The huge seas rammed and buffeted the ship. One could clearly hear the tearing sound of metal and the dead-weighted thump of the sea as it pounded the ship with tremendous force.

Air Force helicopters were busy rescuing crew and landing them nearby to where my dad and I stood. It was a ringside seat to an impressionable dramatic event in a young boy's life. I did wonder how it was possible for a ship to run aground so close to shore when there was such a big sea to sail in.

Years later I read a book on the *Andria Doria* and the *Stockholm* and I realised that if it was possible for two passenger ships to collide with each other on an open sea, there was every possibility of a ship running aground under an intoxicated ship's master while everyone else was sleeping when they should have been on watch. It is of the utmost importance to remain ever alert at sea.

I completed my junior and high schooling with career plans to become a civil engineer. This was a natural course of events as they were building a bridge in front of my parents' house and so I decided I wanted to build one too. We still had conscription in South Africa in the seventies, and naturally I chose the South African Navy. I love all the navies of the world. No warship arrives in Cape Town without a visit from me. They are becoming more frequent with piracy off Somalia and naval exercises, with the South African Navy having acquired new ships and submarines. I wanted to join the submarine base but my interest waned.

It was now time to say goodbye to my close family and leave the house in Mowbray, Cape Town, where I was born to sail the high seas and see the world. Well at least I thought that this was supposed to happen. Sanctions against South Africa at the time prevented our ships from visiting foreign countries, except on very rare occasions like the Cape to Rio yacht race. In those years the politics of the country were as obstructive as they are now, considering the political scandal surrounding the acquisition of the new ships and submarines. I completed my basic training at Saldanha Bay and was drafted to the Wingfield Technical College to undergo training in engineering.

So it appeared that my dream of being an engineer was being realised, although I was interested in becoming a civil engineer and not a marine engineer, or artificer as the navy called it. Learning the theory of engines and how they worked was a lot different to actually being in the engine room of a warship getting ready to go to sea – as I was to find out with my fellow rating when ordered to open up the gear room.

The gear room is a compartment with two large gearboxes coupled to the port and starboard propeller shafts. The fuel in the form of super-heated steam is piped through from the boiler room into the reduction gearboxes at extreme high pressure. A concentrated jet of steam would be enough to slice a man in two with laser precision or cook you to the bone. My fellow rating and I opened up all the wrong steam valves for all the wrong reasons. Soon we simply vanished in a thick fog, having no idea what to do next. The logical step of closing the valves we had incorrectly opened eluded us as we were unable to find them again. Needless to say my fellow rating was assigned to watch the donkey boiler and I volunteered to become a messman preparing breakfast and lunch in the warrant officers' mess for a while just to cool off.

Evading all other seaman duties for weeks on end, I would dash off to the radio shack on shore and missed a mustering on deck with disciplinery consequences. It became increasingly difficult. On leave days I slipped over to the radio shack where two of my friends were training as electronic technicians. One of them, the Admiral's son Robin, was and still is a brilliant technician and I would end up years later working with him as a lighting technician at the Baxter Theatre.

Navy Open Day at Simonstown is always a draw for me but I find the changes in the infrastructure and lack of commitment from young people to join the service disturbing.

Whilst on engine room duty one evening I noticed a novel by Pretorian author Geoffrey Jenkins called *Scend of the Sea* and for the first time read about the SS *Waratah*. It struck me that it would make a great film. I had no idea where the thought came from but I believed it would make an even greater film if the actual wreck of the *Waratah* could be found. The *Titanic* held enormous interest for me and I was spellbound by Dr Robert Ballard's September 1985 discovery of the ship and eventual submarine dive with Alvin when they filmed this most supreme and spectacular of all shipwrecks. The salvage of gold from HMS *Edinburgh* in the Barents Sea with Keith Jessop and his team was equally captivating for me.

Sixteen years later in January 2001 I conducted my very own submarine exploration of the wreck of the *Oceanos* off Coffee Bay and became part of that exciting group of undersea explorers. To explore a deep-water shipwreck in a submarine is to experience first hand the stories one has read with such thrills. Diving to a deep-water wreck in a submarine is rarely accomplished and yet here we were. The vast technicality and costly undertakings with towed surveillance camera systems, side scan sonar arrays and remote-operated vehicles became an obsession for me, also firing up my love of engineering. I devoured vast amounts of technical magazines on everything and anything to do with deep sea exploration and shipwreck discovery. With hindsight, the ability to understand this vast and highly specialised subject was to stand me in good stead as I was able to hold a conversation with quiet confidence. Knowledge alone is not power, but financial freedom and knowledge was the ultimate combination when making my dreams come true.

Fast-forwarding a little, James Cameron's feature film on the *Titanic* used the wreck footage itself. I realised then that my thoughts about a *Waratah* film were not as far-fetched as some people around me had thought. However, getting to the point of being part of an elite group of deep-water explorers, involved with filmmakers and television interviewers on both local and foreign networks, would not come until years later.

By 1985 I had already met Clive Cussler, author of the bestselling novel *Raise the Titanic*. I continued with a passion which drew me to like-minded people; in later years I met the chairman of a British company who was to make it possible for me to bring the Delta submarine in from the USA to dive on the wreck of the SS *Waratah*.

With my navy service over in 1977 and facing an uncertain future, I secured a position as an assistant radio technician through a friend of my brother, training in specialised two-way radio communication equipment. It was a vast electrification project for the Saldanha Sishen railway line, some 800km along the west coast into the Northern Cape; it was a great adventure.

We worked on replacing radio sets in the middle of the night, climbing terrifying heights up radio towers to install antennas to relay communication over mountainous regions. Our mobile workshop was crammed with electronic test equipment and spare radio sets. It was around this time that my interest in photography and shooting film began to emerge.

I was armed with my Kodak Instamatic and a second-hand 16mm Bolex movie camera having shot two rolls of film with a display of ebullience. Two weeks later, setting up the projector before a canteen of highly expectant fellow team mates, about fifteen frames of film were correctly exposed. The rest was a blinding white-out reflected from the screen that lit up the canteen. All this was met with raised eyebrows and jibes which lasted for weeks! As with incorrect polarity of the amplifier, you soon learn never to guess an exposure setting and to use a light meter instead. Only experience will allow you that latitude. I never repeated this again when I was a cameraman shooting television insert material, so it proved a valuable lesson.

Never far from my mind was Geoffrey Jenkins' novel. I still believed a film on the *Waratah* (one that was correctly exposed) was a good idea. But I would have to find the shipwreck first. After I had left the Sishen project I had a variety of jobs. By nature I constantly want to explore and grow and I knew that settling into a mundane job was not enough and I would become frustrated. Later, searching for the *Waratah*, I was to learn the lesson my father and others were trying to teach me, one of patience.

I always felt that I was able to handle things on a bigger scale with lots of responsibility, with engaging thought processes in the planning and execution process, but found the mundane tasks tedious. The strategy was my strength and I loved to see it coming to life.

Whilst working as a cameraman and theatre lighting technician in 1982, I decided to research the loss of the SS *Waratah* and became deeply involved in uncovering stories of the people, articles and in fact anything I could find which would help with what I knew would be an important part of my life.

Geoffrey Jenkins' novel was a fictional account of the *Waratah* and the lost S.A. Airlines Vickers Viscount aircraft, weaving the mysteries together, yet I felt needed to know the facts surrounding the sinking of the ship. The lost passenger aircraft also held interest for me, but I attended to that a little later. Uncovering facts on a ship which simply vanished somewhere off the Wild Coast in 1909 was a gargantuan task but with the assistance of helpful librarians who helped uncover archives, I found a wealth of information using various resources to piece together the story of that night in July 1909. I was also referred to a merchant naval historian with whom I would share hypotheses, but I needed facts, documents and accounts. I needed history because you can only ever understand anything if you understand its history and I needed, if possible, an X on a chart whilst understanding how I arrived there. I was headstrong and resolute and I needed a pattern of events to unfold because if someone was going to bankroll the project I needed to tell them a story of sorts and it had to be a convincing one.

One naval historian's 'theory' as to the last resting place of the ship was soon to be tested with my first 1983 *Waratah* expedition, surrounded by much fanfare and publicity. By May 1983 I had gathered enough facts surrounding the last possible resting place of the ship to at least point me in the right direction. This mainly came in the form of a side scan sonar report of 1977 by the CSIR (Council for Scientific and Industrial Research). Our historian friend was convinced the ship was in shallow water to the south of East London. He also knew someone who would finance the search, Tony Ashworth, a flamboyant gentleman who had just arrived back from a most 'successful' expedition to the Pacific having found Amelia Earhart's aircraft with author Oliver Knaggs. He was adept at attracting media attention; they were intrigued with his glamorous lifestyle. A series of meetings followed in Cape Town with much of the dialogue undertaken by our esteemed merchant navy authority. As he poured more wine over lunch, the backer explained that he had a contact for a ship and all the gear and diving equipment for a spectacular search geared for success.

But the search was not going to be in the area I had reason to believe the ship was in. My own pre-expedition publicity was well covered in the local newspapers, which was absolutely deserved, but they soaked up the enormity of this search, which was going after the 9,300-ton vessel with three ships, an aircraft, underwater cameras and detectors with three divers. The media, never allowing the facts to spoil a good story, printed it.

This initial expedition was to be my training ground and stand me in good stead for the next twenty years, being my introduction to diving and a mysterious instrument shaped like a missile called a side scan sonar. It was also where I was to learn that without a global positioning system (GPS), towing a side scan sonar was a useless exercise.

Towing a side scan sonar is like mowing the lawn. A wide sonar scan from both sides of the instrument's transducers sweeps the ocean floor from a certain height above the sea bed. The sonar signal pulses very rapidly and saturates any anomaly like a shipwreck in its path with acoustic sound waves. The reflection or return signal is relayed back to the sonar control unit on the ship which decodes the signal, displaying one half of the anomaly on a monitor or print out. The survey ship is turned around and the other half of the anomaly is scanned. Once all the necessary scanned information has been surveyed and stored, the post production analysis pieces together the two halves and we then have a full image of a shipwreck, aircraft or whatever one has been looking for on the sea bed. Digital sonar units are highly sophisticated systems with high frequency port and starboard sonar transducers producing full colour images of such clarity they look like aerial photographs. In summary, it's like holding a torch high above your head in a dark room and shining the torch beam onto an object placed on the floor from a slight angle. One illuminated side would be the port side acoustic signal. Shining from the other side would be the starboard side of the acoustic signal. When the two halves are joined one has a completed image of the object. In my future surveys we used the most advanced side scan sonar systems with a highly trained operator and surveyor, Dr Peter Ramsay.

This expedition was massively important and filming it was essential. My Polish friend Troy and his new Canon 16mm movie camera came along and needless to say I filmed anything and everything, shooting thousands of feet of film and remembering hard-earned lessons. Viewing that film twenty-five years later is a reminder of such blatant daring and fearless ambition; a wonderful time to be part of such an adventure. Troy shared my fascination in film and we pooled our interests on the 1983 expedition, taking it in turns to record sound and shoot film.

Captain Peter Wilmot was to captain the *Kunene*. A complex, tall, thin, grey-bearded man with a speech impediment caused by a diving accident, Peter had a healthy mistrust of the press. But he liked me and our friendship lasted for twenty years. He was

Filming it all. (Courtesy of Emlyn Brown)

a technical genius with a vast knowledge of electronics, ships and diving and we had many discussions as he joined me in my determined enthusiasm. In 2008 I was shocked to read of Peter's death in the obituaries of the local newspaper. Peter had been on my mind for some time and I was due to call him up to have a meal at Panama Jacks and catch up on things. I never did and regret it now.

The *Kunene* sailed ahead to the port of East London with all the diving equipment and the side scan sonar. My friend Troy and I with diver and crew member Kallie would leave Cape Town by truck with helium cylinders for the mix gas dive.

The journey to East London by road was a long one. Fatigue nearly saw us crash into a barrier, with the gas cylinders thrown around violently in the back of the truck. I can remember an instant when I referred to Peter Wilmot as a skipper and was corrected with lightning speed by him; he made it clear that a skipper was someone who was in charge of a fishing boat. I was confused because the *Kunene* was an ex-fishing boat and with him at the helm that made him the skipper. I chose not to voice that!

Our backer and a friend were to join the May 1983 expedition and we all boarded within a day or two of each other. Diving equipment was tested out in the harbour, press photographers were chased away by you know who, while Kallie sorted out accommodation in the confined interior of the ex-fishing boat. Admittedly it was all very exciting for me and I had no idea what to expect – apart from dreadful food, which made Ashworth speechless.

Interestingly enough, at the time of this expedition Jack Grimm, a Texas oil tycoon, was attempting his third costly expedition to locate the *Titanic*. I could see myself in all those books I had read about other shipwreck hunts, Mel Fisher's search for the *Atocha*, *Pieces of Eight*, National Geographic's *Undersea Treasures* to name a few.

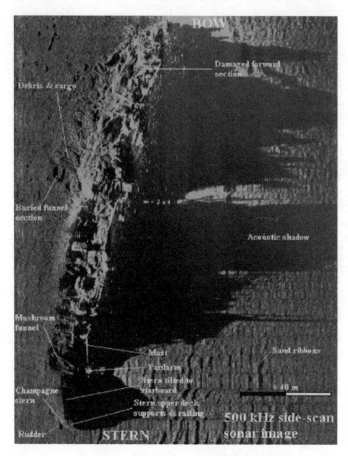

Side scan sonar
image of shipwreck.
(Courtesy of Emlyn
Brown)

We cast off around 1600hrs and sailed south towards Kasyers beach where our merchant naval historian, Peter Humphries, had convinced us the *Waratah* was to be found.
My previous survey report of 1977 remained in my sleeping quarters as it had been
dismissed and, although I felt my theory was valid, the evidence of Humphries was
preferred at the time.

   Kunene arrived in the area in the early morning and the side scan sonar was deployed
and towed around for much of the day. By late afternoon a thermal trace on the sonar
showed a broken line rising slightly. Contact had been made with something on
the ocean floor. A few more passes showed the same rising line but less broken up.
Ashworth's eyes went wide with anticipation, as did mine. One cannot help getting
caught up in the moment. The rising line on the trace indicated a mound opposed to a
hard anomaly. The line was not broken up or serrated as it would have been if the sonar
signal had been reflected from a hard surface.

   There was only one way of finding out what that sonar trace was and Peter signalled
to the crew to prepare the diving equipment. Ashworth was convinced this was the
Waratah. Peter was reserved in his opinion, knowing all too well that the press would be
all over him like a rash for such a statement and he would become the laughing stock of
the local marine and diving industry.

The only statement Peter did share was that he had dived on a mound of sand. According to Ashworth the *Waratah* was under that mound of sand. With Humphries equally satisfied, all that was now needed was to pump the sand and get to the wreck. When these statements were released in the press all sorts of experienced people from the diving industry came forward with comments about the enormity and cost of such an excavation. They were right.

To pump a mound of sand without knowing what to expect would have been an expensive and monumental task. A sub-bottom sonar profile would have gone a long way in knowing what one could expect under that mound of sand. But we had no such instrument onboard. Press releases after the May 1983 expedition were less than complimentary, causing friction between the parties, particularly when I declared that I was going to go ahead with a new operation focused to the north of East London. What followed was a public battle in the press and a regrettable time for us all.

Ashworth had also made claims that the South African Airways Rietbok aircraft had been located. This passenger plane crashed into the sea off Kaysers beach under mysterious circumstances in 1967.

Peter Humphries also faded away a little but watched all my future attempts from the sidelines. For me, at least, I had many rolls of 16mm film capturing an historical event in my life. Two years would pass before I was to meet someone who would change everything. In the interim I continued to intensify my research and gathered some startling new information as to the *Waratah's* possible whereabouts. Particularly of note was a meeting with Brigadier Roos. He was a former military attaché to Portugal, Officer Commanding of the *Cape Town Castle* and an absolute gentleman. He and his wife were an absolute tonic.

Brigadier Roos. (Courtesy of Emlyn Brown)

Lieutenant
Roos.
(Courtesy
of Emlyn
Brown)

Brigadier Roos had found a map which had been lost for many years and impor-
tantly on that map was an X. The story was beyond fascination. Brigadier Roos' father
was Lieutenant D.J. Roos, a South African Air Force pilot. In 1925 Lieutenant Roos was
flying the D.H. 9 aircraft in the first experimental air mail service between Durban and
Cape Town along the east coast. This service was to connect with the Union Castle mail
steamers bound for the United Kingdom.

Whilst flying between the Xora and Bashee River mouth he had noticed a wreck
lying on the ocean floor. He had not thought much of it but made mention of this
observation to naval officer Commander Woodhouse, who had played an important
part in a South African coastal survey and was somewhat puzzled, for there were no
known wrecks in the area. From Lieutenant Roos' description, he thought it may be
the wreck of the *Waratah*. Five years had passed before the *Star* newspaper came into
the picture and charted an aircraft for a search. Lieutenant Roos was to pilot the aircraft
accompanied by a young reporter, Lindsay Smith. Lieutenant Roos drew a map of the
area and a flight path to guide their search. The wreck was approximately 4 miles off the
coast between the Bashee and Xora rivers, but more towards the Xora River.

Dogged by bad weather and engine trouble, nothing was accomplished on this
search. Shortly afterwards Lieutenant Roos was killed in a car accident. The map was
lost and Lindsay Smith's copy had also been mislaid. In all, both maps had been lost for
forty-two years. In 1973 Brigadier Roos was going through an old family album when
he found a map. According to the him, it appeared to be Lindsay Smith's authentic
copy of Lieutenant Roos' original map. On reading this story in a newspaper cutting I
tracked Brigadier Roos down and could tell from the number in the telephone book
that he lived close by. I could have easily walked from my home in Mowbray to his in
Claremont.

We arranged a meeting and he showed me the map, which had been placed inside
an old family album full of war-related photographs. So not only did I have my X on
a map, I had an historical account of its placing and was now sitting with Lieutenant
Roos' son in his living room talking about it.

Right Mouth
of the Xora
River.
(Courtesy
of Emlyn
Brown)

Below Edward
Joe Conquer
seated in the
front row, fifth
from the left
in the airforce
uniform.
(Courtesy
of Emlyn
Brown)

That was not all, there was something even more extraordinary I had pieced together. I had obtained the military record of a Cape Mounted Rifleman, Edward Joe Conquer. He had been stationed on the Wild Coast in the early part of the 1900s. On 28 July 1909 the soldiers had been ordered to carry out live shell practise at the Xora River mouth with signalling exercises with a heliograph.

As it was clouded the exercise was suspended until the sun re-appeared, as a heliograph requires the sun to reflect the mirrored signal. On 28 July, sixteen years earlier than Lieutenant Roos' aerial sighting, Conquer was stationed on the knoll on the right bank of the Xora River with signaller H. Adshead. He noted the following through the eyepiece of his telescope: a large ship proceeding very slowly in a south-westerly direction and making very heavy weather. Conquer's record notes the following:

I watched this vessel through a telescope and can still see her in my mind's eye. She was a ship of considerable tonnage with a single funnel. Two masts and a black hull, the upper works were painted yellow. I gave the telescope to Adshead who remarked that the ship was having a very rough passage. I watched the ship crawling along and saw her roll to starboard and then before she could right herself a following wave rolled over her and I saw her no more. I told Adshead she had gone under. 'No,' he said, 'she has run into a squall.' But there was neither squall, mist, nor drizzle to be seen. I reported what I had seen to camp by semaphore. The message was acknowledged by signallers Hulsberg and Armstrong. I handed in my report also telling the Orderly Sergeant what I had seen. He told me 'not to chance my arm' or some such words of disbelief, and so the matter passed from my hands.

About three days later the East London Dispatch arrived in the camp and the main page carried big headlines of the non arrival of the *Waratah*. For me I thought this was an extraordinary observation. This was no theory by Edward Joe Conquer, this was an observation witnessed not only by Adshead, but by other soldiers as well. His description of the ship was correct.

There was no complex pondering by Conquer, who had an impeccable military record and rose to Colonel in the South African Air Force. I met Conquer's second wife in Pretoria and there was sufficient testimony to his character to satisfy me that he was not seeking any attention. How was Conquer able to describe the ship in such detail? He had no idea the *Waratah* even existed, let alone give a full and accurate description of the ship's livery.

Colonel Joe Conquer actually met with Lieutenant Roos many years later and discussed their sightings with each other. It also turned out that Brigadier Roos' wife was a childhood friend of Geoffrey Jenkins.

There was more excitement to follow in the form of a side scan sonar report undertaken by the CSIR onboard the MV *Meiring Naude*, a research and survey ship I was to place under charter in 1989.

The 1977 survey report was handed to me at a symposium at the University of Cape Town. The survey report contained information of a shipwreck located off the Xora River mouth in 375ft of water (117m). The side scan was not an intense sonar investigation but most certainly confirmed an elongated anomaly on the ocean floor that was without doubt a shipwreck. On the face of it, it appeared to all accounts that what Edward Joe Conquer had witnessed in 1909 and what Lieutenant Roos had observed from the air was now confirmed in the 1977 CSIR report. I felt it was evidence enough to warrant a full investigation as it would have been unthinkable to ignore such evidence, albeit circumstantial.

These events, spanning some sixty-eight years, had always been the very basic ingredient for my search and the basis to sell the project on to find the finance to carry out further investigation. Now it was a matter of meeting the right people who shared my vision and passion for the project.

In 1985 my mother alerted me to the fact that American author Clive Cussler had appeared on a television programme. He was in South Africa on a book tour and promotion and was heading for Cape Town. I remembered the name because I had ordered a book through my book club by him called *Vixen o3*. This was the book which introduced me to the National Underwater and Marine Agency, or NUMA as it was known. Never in my wildest dreams would I have ever thought that I would appear as a character in Clive's novel *Trojan Odyssey* some twenty-two years later and run my own NUMA organisation since 1990, under which all of my marine operations were undertaken.

The *Waratah* adventure was also recorded in Cussler's *The Sea Hunters 11*. Despite not knowing where he would be staying while in Cape Town, instinct told me he would stay at the Mount Nelson Hotel. I phoned to check and indeed my instinct was proved correct; he would be staying at the hotel and arriving later that evening. I duly left a message and was surprised when he did in fact return the call. Here I was in the hallway of my parents' home talking to Clive Cussler as if he was a frequent caller. Nobody was going to believe this!

'Mr Cussler, I hear you may be interested in finding the *Waratah*? I have considerable research material into this ship and am looking for someone to fund the search.'

I attended Clive's lecture at the Music College that evening and afterwards I took him back to the hotel in my little Fiat. We were to spend hours in the lounge pouring over my research and reaching a conclusion about Conquer, Lieutenant Roos and the 1977 side scan sonar survey. I had no idea what sort of money I was to ask for because I had no idea how to cost out such an undertaking, so I thought a few thousand would be enough. The planned survey off the Xora and Bashee rivers was to cost a lot more than I had originally anticipated.

But Clive rose to the occasion and my files are still filled with the letters that passed between us as we worked towards finding a survey company to carry out the survey off the east coast. We eventually found a company called Sistema.

In the meantime, sonar expert Gary Kozak had much doubt that the 1977 side scan sonar image was that of the *Waratah*. Nevertheless we forged ahead and the primary design of the survey was to be based on the facts at hand. In the interim I had gathered other supporting information of other sightings in and around the Xora and Bashee rivers of a steamship in trouble.

In 1987 two attempts were made to survey a large area between the two rivers. The first was from a ski-boat crammed with generators, survey equipment and crew. Shore stations were set up along the coast at three different locations. The master unit, set up high on the ski-boat *Purdey II*, would lock into the three shore stations and provide the survey with the much-needed navigation.

We were stationed at Coffee Bay and had to steam south to the search area. I was convinced at times that the boat was going to roll over like I imagined the *Waratah* had. It was very low in the water. We were to have many problems out at sea in the next few days. Known as nulling, we would lose the microwave signal between the shore and boat's master station, which made keeping an accurate running plot impossible. To deploy a towfish (sonar unit) and depressor to keep the fish underwater was a mission. Even worse was to hand winch some 300m of heavy cable out of the sea with a boat bouncing around like a cork. Not to mention seasickness. If this was adventure on the high sea looking for a shipwreck, then all those books I had been reading were lying!

Although we got a sonar trace of a wreck – the same one as the 1977 recorded wreck – it was not much more than that. The survey merely confirmed the 1977 wreck which

Gathering essentials. (Courtesy of Emlyn Brown)

Emlyn in *Waratah* shirt. (Courtesy of Emlyn Brown)

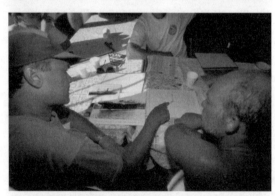

Planning vital detail. (Courtesy of Emlyn Brown)

Planning the expedition. (Courtesy of Emlyn Brown)

to all accounts was a by far more detailed sonar graph than this survey achieved. The survey was to be abandoned and a few months later a survey ship of opportunity was in the area and placed under short-term charter operating out of Port Elizabeth.

This survey was not quite as eventful as I had hoped. The search by now had been expanded to some 80 square miles of ocean floor. The *Reunion* sailed for the survey site with some new crew members, was crammed with sonar equipment and a satellite navigational system. Aubrey Price, a geologist, was survey party chief and we became good friends for years. Again, strong currents and equipment problems played a pivotal role in preventing accessing good-enough sonar images of the wreck. No other wreck was found in this huge survey site. Only the original 1977 wreck showed up. So this process of eliminating narrowed the odds considerably for me.

With hindsight I wish there had been more than one option open to me. The dimensions and tonnage of the wreck on the sonar did tally with that of the *Waratah* so there were these little surges of confidence, yet it had proved a frustrating process so far. Equipment failure and the ever powerful Agulhas Current created problems with getting the towfish down sufficiently to get improved images of the wreck . The *Purdey II* ski-boat survey vessel would have been fine on a lake, but was inadequate crammed with gear four miles off the Wild Coast.

I took a long hard look at my search for the *Waratah*. Should I give it all up? Perhaps I should return to electronics or make a career as a cameraman or producer. M★ Net television was starting up in South Africa as the first pay channel. They needed technical staff with lightning speed and I got a job at their Cape Town offices in the old Kodak building off the M5. M★ Net was an abbreviation for Media Network and made up of shareholders from the media industry, namely newspaper groups and heavyweight magazine publishers. Among them was the *Star* newspaper and sister newspaper *Cape Argus*.

I researched the structure of the company, its directors, PRs and chief executive producers. I had hatched a plan which I thought would work and be beneficial to both parties. I had the material ready to go out on air, combined with media coverage to drive the whole project and create publicity and draw more viewers away from other television channels. Basically I could provide an exclusive if the company cash-flowed my project. We just needed a deal.

If the *Star* newspaper had sponsored Lieutenant Roos to search for the ship by air, why would they not sponsor a search for the ship fifty-nine years later with a ship? We would film the event for a new television magazine programme, *Carte Blanche*, and let the newspapers and magazines cover the expedition. The mix was perfect. My proposal was galvanised into action and before long I was on a plane to Randburg headquarters for a meeting with the executive producer and public relations officer Kate Monoghan, who was truly dynamic in cementing it all together. I was whisked off to the *Star* newspaper's editor-in-chief's office and sub-editors gathered around as I spread out photographs. They bought into the adventure and directives were given to producers, editors and journalist to cover the story and begin pre-publicity on the project. My job was to get an expedition underway. The television coverage was going to be flighted within weeks, so there was a mass of work ahead for all involved. It was a very exciting time. We were now going to lower a camera onto the wreck and reveal the phantom ship exclusively on television. I would be heading the operation, so the eyes of the media were upon me and I had a lot of promises to keep. The departure date was set for 12 May 1989. We chartered the RV *Meiring Naude*, the same survey ship used in 1977 during the CSIR survey which produced the only reasonable sonar graph of the wreck to date.

A black and white camera was assembled onto an aluminium framework with an umbilical to the surface ship feeding into a monitor set up in the control room. The camera was lowered over the side and trailed the bottom for a brief moment revealing the sea bed. Now it was just a matter of the camera imaging the wreck itself. Then the monitor went blank. The camera was hauled back to the surface and we saw that the entire aluminium framework had collapsed with the umbilical wrapped around the frail-looking framework. The inadequate frame was no match for the powerful currents we were dealing with out there. One or two further attempts were only in vain. What on earth was I going to say with such focus on the project? Rob Cooke the producer simply told me to tell it as it was: 'We have a problem with this strong Agulhas Current, and the camera frame simply collapsed.' The programme went out on the broadcast date and I was nervous because I was not sure what to expect from the public and how they would react.

Happily I had no need to worry as fierce interest in the hunt for the *Waratah* had gripped the public's imagination. My brief from the top was to double my efforts in my attempt to identify the wreck and make my recommendations as soon as possible or public interest would begin to wane. Captain Peter Wilmot had watched from the sidelines as had Peter Humphries. Wilmot called me and invited me down to his new support ship *Deep Salvage I*. He had a proposal for me – a new, space age motorised diving bell had been built and he wanted to convince me to use it to identify the wreck. It was truly a very impressive high-tech diving bell with powerful thrusters to manoeu-

The diving bell. (Courtesy of Emlyn Brown)

vre the bell around whilst internal and external cameras would film the wreck. The huge aluminium horse shoe buoyancy collar added a NASA effect. It was to also prove a major problem, as the buoyancy collar created a massive resistance in the current and the bell resisted sinking underwater. The bell was to be tethered to the ship and two-way communications ensured that commands between Peter and the bell operator on the deck were carried out. One of the problems with identifying the wreck was that at the time there was no suitable ROV or submarine in the country to carry out positive identification of the wreck. To carry out a full saturation closed bell dive would require a dynamic positioning support ship to keep station while over the wreck.

These are extremely expensive operations, and unless you have a ship full of gold bullion, like Keith Gessop had with HMS *Edinburgh*, the cost would be prohibitive. Normally such deep-water recovery operations are made up of a consortium of interested parties with shareholding in the project's rewards. In the meantime my options were limited and to import a remote-operated vehicle (ROV) would also be an expensive item. I decided to run with the bell as it was the best option available and I needed to get back on track as the media needed material.

A competition was launched in the newspapers. A large graphic appeared with a grid of the coastline and the two rivers Xora and Bashee. The graphic extended into the Indian Ocean and participants had to place an X on the grid where they thought the *Waratah* to be. The first prize was a voyage for two to Mauritius onboard the 7,554-ton liner *Oceanos*. Each participant paid R10 and submitted their entry forms. It was an easy competition and most certainly stimulated public interest as now the public were directly involved.

Ironically three years later the *Oceanos* sank off Coffee Bay and a massive rescue took place removing the 361 passengers and 184 crew from the ship before she went down bow first. The *Oceanos* settled a mere 16km north east of the area I was operating in.

Deep Salvage I departed from Cape Town amid huge publicity. Naturally Peter kept his face out of the spotlight but was clearly thrilled to be on a project once more. The navigation had also improved. The voyage would take two days and journalist John Yeld was assigned to cover the project with Rob Cooke back onboard covering the event for television. It was an excellent voyage with equally excellent food. Clearly the menu had improved from the days of the *Kunene*. The sea was flat calm and the beauty of the Wild Coast as seen from the ship was as magnificent as ever in its beauty.

On the face of it the omen was good but it was brief and the weather changed. *Deep Salvage I* rolled and pitched. Huge rollers crashed their way onto the aft deck while the ship strained at the anchors. It was frightening at times. Peter decided to keep station but if it got any worse he would head for the safe haven of a bay which he had marked off on the chart. The weather eventually abated with wind and current having dropped considerably. With this window of opportunity the order was given to prepare the bell to dive while the ship was positioned over the wreck. The wind can whip up into a frenzy on that coast, then drop to a calm breeze hours later.

Peter was the only one suitably experienced to operate the bell from within. The bell was deployed and was down for about less than 10 minutes when the order was given to bring the bell back to the surface. As Peter opened the hatch there was a dull thud followed with a column of blue smoke emanating from within. It was nothing to be concerned with as Peter had smoked almost a pack of Camel in the bell and with the scrubber not cleaning the air properly, he decided to surface before being asphyxiated! It was the first time the bell was going this deep and I still think that Peter got a fright that day and smoked himself into a thick mist similar to the one we had created in the gear room.

The bell was deployed the following day but this time the current was roaring at a full 6 knots. The huge buoyancy collar created a big resistance on the bell and it would not go under the water. It was at a full 45-degree angle and straining on the tether. If the tether cable snapped, the bell would have been carried away with Peter inside and we would have to up anchor and go fetch him with him off at a speed, which would have been terrifying. We abandoned it and waited for the conditions to settle.

The next deployment of the bell, bell run number three, was in a slack moment with the current and the bell went all the way down to the wreck. Peter reported he could see the wreck and the video cameras were switched on. He was very close to it and remarked about the huge size of the wreck. He then signalled to bring him back to the surface as the power supply for the electronics had overheated and his instruments were going to fail. In any event it was in bad design to have everything operating off one power supply with no backup or without splitting the circuits up so that if anything went wrong, it would not be necessary to abort the entire mission.

The video footage was not particularly revealing but there were images of the wreck; however no identifiable feature could be discerned. My time with the charter was now up and I was unable to extend the budget so we sailed for Port Elizabeth and Rob Cook and I drove back to Cape Town discussing the final version of the story going to air within a week.

With all credit to the media I was not crucified and the public were more sympathetic than ever. I think the adventure of it all was more important than the *Waratah* itself somehow. As Clive said in his book *Sea Hunters II*, I was not yet ready to give up against the odds of a Vegas Keno game.

Two years later in 1991 I was back over the wreck with *Deep Salvage I*, this time with the submarine *Jago*, owned and operated by Professor Hans Fricke, the first person to film living coelacanths in the Indian Ocean. He had returned to South Africa with major sponsorship to film more coelacanths. *Deep Salvage I* was a ship of opportunity, and when the opportunity arose an agreement was worked out and we headed for the wreck site whilst the ship was in the vicinity. It would be a ten-day mission. But the *Jago* was never launched. Strong currents simply shut down the operation and once again I was on my way home.

Between 1995 and 1997 two attempts with professional technical diving crews were attempted. They were huge operations, with divers from around the country being selected to dive 117m to identify the wreck. Rehan Bouwer was the official diving officer and the set-up itself was highly technical. Photo journalist Patrick Wagner was appointed by *Getaway* magazine and we set up at the Xora River mouth. A large military tent became our dining hall and planning room. A medical supervisor and accomplished technical diver joined the team along with over twenty-five back-up divers and crew.

There was no room for error. Any problems at that depth would result in death. Pre-dive planning was crucial and re-checking of equipment was second nature. Mixed gas decompression tables were going to be pushed to the very edge of the envelope. It would take three minutes to reach the sea bed with only twelve minutes bottom time for the diver to identify the wreck.

Not only was the descent into 117m (375ft) of Indian Ocean intimidating, the two-hour drift decompression in that current was to carry the divers kilometres down the coast. We knew when the divers were in decompression stage as a red inflatable tube would be sent to the surface and the support boats would track the diver. Back-up divers would then go down to the decompressing diver with back-up air and to check his physical condition. The operation was incident free and was an incredible experience for all of us. The wreck had been observed with noted features but not enough to say it was the *Waratah*. I was going to need far more tangible evidence to convince the world I had found the *Waratah*.

This second diving operation was financed by a British company chairman from Surrey. Adrian White's grandfather had been a general servant on the *Waratah* so he had more than just a passing interest in the ship. I was to meet

Diver in decompression stage. (Courtesy of Emlyn Brown)

this fine gentleman after I had met with Geoffrey Jenkins in Pretoria. Adrian White loved the novel *Scend of the Sea* and Jenkins made mention of me and my attempts to find the ship. Adrian and I were to meet several times and discuss plans.

Although this second dive expedition was incident free, I was stunned to learn that Patrick Wagner, the photo journalist on my expedition, had been killed when his PC 12 jet slammed into a mountain near Nairobi, Kenya. South Africa lost a stable of highly respected cameramen, photographers and photo journalists.

Equally distressing, Rehan Bouwer had a malfunction while doing a deep Trimix dive in Wright Canyon off the Natal coast. He surfaced and signalled for attention then went back down again with the deep cover diver to urgently complete his decompression. But Rehan was out of gas and the deep cover diver was not able to descend any longer with Rehan to rectify the problem and Rehan went back to the surface. A serious free flow prevented Rehan from maintaining or attaining neutral buoyancy and he eventually went to sleep and drifted into the Big Blue. Technical divers fully understand that the consequences can be fatal on deep dives with mix gas. Many highly experienced and well-known divers have lost their lives. I then learned that the medical officer on the 1997 dive expedition, Professor Johnny Van Der Walt, had also died in an unrelated diving accident. Johnny was also a deep cover diver for Rehan on the Wright Canyon dive.

Having read the report of enquiry into this accident and having been close to Rehan, I can only conclude that the circumstances of this event must have been terrifying and a terrible loss to fellow divers and family. His young son was utterly devastated.

Adrian White remained in the picture and continued his support. I had to do some very serious considerations now in my attempt to gather some positive identification of that wreck. I had always liked the idea of towed video surveillance or towed array as it is known in the marine industry. Bob Ballard used one to discover the *Titanic* and obtained amazing images of the wreck I teamed up with Dr Peter Ramsay. This time we were going to go back to the wreck site with the latest digital side scan sonar and conduct very high-resolution images of the wreck off the Xora River. Klein side scan is the most advanced in high-resolution digital sonar imagery. A shipwreck can be revealed in the most astonishing detail.

This June 1999 expedition was kept secret from the media. The crew were given strict instruction not to speak to the press. The *Ocean Stroom* was placed under charter and we operated out of Durban. Peter Ramsay and his Marine Geoscience team and some crew from Propshine Diving were to accompany this secret operation. The ship was again crammed with electronic equipment and an electric winch for the towfish secured to the deck. Sleeping accommodation was less than fabulous and earplugs drowned out the whine of the propeller shaft running through our stern section sleeping quarters. It was by no means a room with a view but a room for twelve *Waratah* search crew members and flight cases.

Mitty Chelin gave the order to 'let go' and the *Ocean Stroom* slipped out of Durban harbour towards the bluff. Once across the breakwater, Mitty did a slow turn and pointed the bow in a southerly direction headed for the Xora and Bashee rivers. On 27 July 1909, the luxury liner *Waratah* had sailed the same course. This particular expedition made me really seasick. I simply hate being seasick and lose interest in everything. I don't eat and generally cover my head in my bunk. Many crew got seasick and my poor brother, who was the cameraman and had to film the event, just wanted to die a quiet

The team preparing. (Courtesy of Emlyn Brown)

death. Not to mention the galley above our quarters wafting the smell of chips evenly blended with diesel fumes coming from the stack. Just writing this part has made me leave the room for a while – I hope you are still there!

The towfish was deployed very early in the morning as we were going to search the entire 80-square-mile grid to eliminate any other possibility of a wreck within that area. I had no knowledge until this expedition that another wreck over and above the one we already knew about might have existed. That would have increased the odds, but with only one wreck, the odds were narrowed. I would only know much later if any other options were open to me.

It was hot in the control room, all the electronic equipment was generating heat and there was no air conditioning. Mowing the lawn is a tiresome and laborious process. You are only sailing at 3 knots with the fish scanning the sea bed in search of a promise of a wreck. Tell-tale signs of debris or unusual features show up now and again but you never stop to investigate. You carry on until the grid is cleared out, going back to the anomaly by doing a series of passes to build the image. This alone can take all day.

Peter wanted to start the survey on the outer fringes of the grid in deep water and work towards the shore and the 1977 wreck and then continue going closer to the shoreline. It was the logical method of approach as we needed to know what else was out there over and above the 1977 wreck.

Contact was made. The fish had clipped the edge of the wreck and it was the beginning phase of a very revealing sonar image. More passes over the wreck were made and Peter started to build the images. It was astonishing to see this shipwreck slowly coming to life on a screen from 177m below all by the process of complex digital signalling. It was a moment that only very few people in the world are able to share and witness as this process is a specialised process involving only the scientists and people within the marine industry.

I was seated next to Peter. His highly trained eye scanned the instrument while I tried to think of something to say that would be intelligent. Slowly the image continued to build with Peter performing minor adjustments here and there. I looked at Peter and asked the question: 'Do you think it is what it is?' Peter nodded without saying a word. The image on the screen was the wreck of the *Waratah*. I was looking at the ship that Edward Joe Conquer had witnessed roll over and sink. The superstructure had collapsed while the bow and stern were perfectly visible, although somewhat crushed. There was minimal debris around the wreck except for what resembled ladders. The length and beam of the ship along with the tonnage tallied up with that of the *Waratah*.

An attempt to lower a video camera system to obtain video images was going nowhere in that current. I knew that hanging anything over the side of a ship was not going to work no matter how fancy and elaborate that technical masterpiece was. The current was like a very fast-flowing river at the best of times. I believed that we needed to tow a camera into the current and over the wreck. In a return voyage to the wreck site, I had a camera bracket machined and fitted to an unused side scan sonar towfish. The video signal was fed topside and we deployed the fish over the stern of *Ocean Mariner*. It was like flying a kite with the danger of it crashing into the wreck. I decided to image at a safe height, keeping clear of the wreck. Once I obtained good images I would go in closer and closer, risking the loss of the fish. As long as I had sufficient images to grab in the post production to compare with a model and photographs, I was happy.

This is where the previous navigation log and the excellent seamanship of the master, Mitty Chelin, is of immense importance when returning to a wreck site for further survey investigation. The low-light black and white camera began sending acceptable images to the surface. The ship's masts and a propeller could be seen. The twin screws of the *Waratah* were an identifiable feature to look for. Nevertheless the champagne stern matched that of the *Waratah*. It gave the vintage of the wreck and we thought maybe the other screw was buried in mud. In the post analysis specific video images were grabbed and matched with close-up photographs of a model and the ship's plans. A final post analysis was held at the Marine Geoscience offices in Cape Town with the impressive large-scale motorised model of the *Waratah*.

Everything matched. All the King's horses and all the King's men agreed that what I was looking at was the *Waratah*. I could now do a press release that the *Waratah* had been located and identified supported by impressive images to prove it beyond all reasonable doubt. The press went to town on the news and sonar images of the shipwreck flashed around the world. Television and radio interviews followed both locally and overseas, especially in the United Kingdom and Australia. It was truly a brilliant story, and the facts were not going to spoil it. I was besieged with reporters to such an extent that Peter Ramsay and I booked into a hotel to escape the attention. It was truly extraordinary. Now that we were all convinced that the *Waratah* had been located and identified I wanted an expedition befitting such an accomplishment to film dramatic images of the *Waratah*. I had read a book on the *Lusitania* with interest, of how the wreck was explored with a submarine – a yellow submarine at that. I read how fishing nets had wrapped around the propeller while the sub was exploring the wreck. Submarine diving accidents are not unusual and if no rescue plan is in place, or if the submarine is not prepared for any eventuality, the crew may as well be on the moon.

Delta submarine crew. Back row, left to right: Joe Lilly (technician), Richard Slater (pilot); front row, left to right: Chris I. James (pilot), Kendal Brown (cameraman), Emlyn Brown (self-time photographer). (Courtesy of Emlyn Brown)

The Delta submarine was prepared for such an eventuality and the propeller was dismantled from within the sub and dropped free from the shaft. It was a versatile little sub, self-contained in a fully equipped container with back up spares and electronic gear. After much negotiation and budget considerations Richard Slater and I blocked in a window of operation for a dive mission for January 2001. This was followed by months of planning entirely via the internet and telephonic conference calling.

The submarine dive support ship *Toto* was placed under charter operating out of Durban. The arrival of the four submarine pilots and the submarine by sea went like clockwork. After a hive of activity preparing the sub and the support ship, *Toto* sailed for the wreck site in perfect weather conditions. The ROV system ordered from Australia did not arrive due to technical problems. This was a disappointment as I wanted to emulate what Bob Ballard did on the *Alvin* sub. The ROV Jason was mounted in a garage on the bow of *Alvin* and operated from within. *Alvin* landed on the *Titanic* while the ROV camera was propelled into the interior of the ship. I had to settle for using internal and external cameras to record the wreck instead.

There were many doubts about the submarine operating in the strong current. I considered that the Delta crew had operated in the Gulf Stream and were experienced with strong currents. I also hedged my bets on the fact that the sub was an untethered vehicle and free to use the current to its advantage with sufficient ballast to drop down and punch through the current which is only about 15-20m deep. The Delta submarine was to operate flawlessly on every dive mission. The Delta crew hardly mentioned the current. I entered the hatch with pilot Chris Ijames in command. I had to lie on my stomach facing a large double-thick acrylic view port that filled rapidly with sea water to create ballast for sinking the submarine. I remember making a wry remark to Chris trusting that what was happening before my very eyes was supposed to happen and that all systems were performing as they should. knowing some of the principles of buoyancy afforded me to make such a sardonic remark. For the ill-informed it would have been alarming.

With the Delta conning tower awash with sea water, the sub turned away from *Toto* with a burst of thrust placing it a safe distance from the side of the ship. Permission to dive was confirmed from the bridge with Dave Slater tracking the sub in real time underwater. We sank fast and soon we were on the floor of the Indian Ocean. I was about to see what Joe Conquer had witnessed ninety-two years earlier; a ship roll over and disappear beneath a tempestuous sea.

Over the years I had pursued the film based on Geoffrey Jenkins' novel. Various producers showed interest in the proposal but either did not have the means to breathe life into a production or had little idea where to start. I had many television programmes made on me and the *Waratah* both locally and overseas, including a Granada Television series called *Savage Seas* hosted by Stacy Keach. So I have had my own personal fill of television exposure. I was also under no illusion about making a feature film and its complexity, which requires a hide like a rhino and the durability of Teflon if one is going to see it through. I have long gotten over the emotional veneer of filmmaking. It's a business, and a tough one at that. It can even be a waste of time and money.

A vector was requested and relayed to the sub pilot. Chris gently positioned the sub and aimed for the wreck. We skimmed the ocean floor for a while and in that remarkable clear deep indigo blue ocean I could soon see a massive dark shape looming in the distance. All the years of research and surveying and wondering what it would be like to one day see the wreck of the *Waratah* filled my mind with anticipation.

'There she is,' I remember saying to Chris.

The wreck was truly massive. She was just sitting there, resting quietly on the sea floor, the odd fish darting about as the sub glided towards her. The cameras were rolling and Chris commenced blowing the tanks slightly just enough to raise the sub to give an aerial point of view of the wreck before going in for closer inspection. We were now flying over the wreck.

Suddenly I felt the blood drain from my face. My heart started to knock in its casing. I chose to ignore two military tanks, one with its cannon pointing at the sub and the next with its cannon pointing to the surface. I looked away at the sight of the stacks of truck tyres still in the hold of the ship and turned away at the sight of an upturned tank. I was in denial.

Besides this *was* the *Waratah*. We all knew that. Theory and practice had been tried and tested. Science backed me up here. Maybe I had slipped up with the manifest and not accounted for the tanks. What was happening? What had gone wrong? The modern tanks did not match the vintage of the *Waratah*. I was profoundly confused. Looking on in disbelief, I thought had I come this far to end up in a submarine on some other ship?

No other wreck ever showed up within the search grid in the extensive side scan sonar surveys. So how did we miss the *Waratah* and dive on this unknown wreck? The bridge requested a status update and the reply was heard loud and clear by all the crew on the bridge. 'This is not the *Waratah*. This is a transport ship of sorts.' What were thought to be ladders on the sonar image, were in fact the tracks of that upturned tank.

This wreck just resembled the *Waratah* in both size and design. I was in shock, and baffled as to how it could have all gone so wrong. To have come this close and it was a ship of the wrong vintage. I felt like a donkey with a carrot dangling in front of me.

I thought the media were going to go to town on me this time. Instead they were entirely sympathetic, as was Adrian White, who had bankrolled this submarine mission. I was extremely upset when I got a call from Adrian in Mauritius at the hotel and told him it was not the *Waratah*. In a calm, reserved, plummy British voice, he simply asked if I had any other ideas as to where the ship could be, brushing aside the massive amount this mission had cost.

I signalled the captain of *Toto* to head for the wreck site of the *Oceanos* which was on our return voyage back to the Port of Durban. We spent the day conducting a series of mind-blowing dives on the ill-fated passenger ship. I explored the wreck as much as possible, shooting dramatic video footage.

It was the strangest feeling to be exploring an ocean liner that was once destined to take passengers on a cruise had they won in the *Waratah* competition of 1998. The *Oceanos* was a few hours' steaming from the dive site and now it was at the bottom of the Indian Ocean – the irony of it all.

With research we discovered that the wreck thought to be that of the ill-fated *Waratah* was actually the *Nailsea Meadow*, a 4,926-ton ship transporting a cargo of tanks and military hardware for General Montgomery's Eighth Army on a voyage north towards Egypt via the Suez Canal and torpedoed by U-196 in 1942. According to records,

Wreck of the *Oceanos*.
(Courtesy of Emlyn Brown)

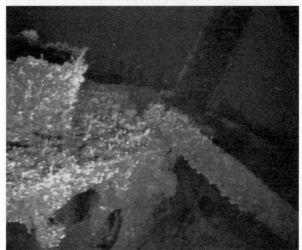

Nailsea Meadow mast.
(Courtesy of Emlyn Brown)

Nailsea Meadow tank tracks
displayed as the tank rests on
its canon. (Courtesy of Emlyn
Brown)

Fig. 31.—The Cargo Steamship "Nailsea Meadow," of 4,926 tons gross. (W. Parry & Son, Ltd., So. (Built by Messrs. Bartram & Sons, Ltd., and engined by White's Marine Engineering Co., Ltd.)

The *Nailsea Meadow.* (Courtesy of Emlyn Brown)

U-196 torpedoed the ship off Port St Johns. But this is not where the ship eventually sunk. She had drifted south with the current to a point just off the Xora River mouth where she finally settled on the ocean floor. That was the wreck the sonar picked up in all the previous surveys. Nobody expected this!

It was not the ship Edward Joe Conquer had witnessed roll over and sink, as the *Nailsea Meadow* sank some thirty-three years later. Neither was it the ship that Lieutenant Roos had apparently seen from the air. His dates do not match up because the *Nailsea Meadow* had not sunk yet. The 1977 side scan sonar survey report indeed confirmed a wreck off the Xora River supporting both eyewitness accounts of Joe Conquer and Lieutenant Roos.

My own collective surveys, and the 1999 high-resolution survey with Dr Ramsay, seemed to prove beyond doubt that the wreck, with assistance of an independent opinion in post-survey analysis, confirmed the unshakable belief that this was the *Waratah.*

Besides, historical research and gathered information over the years had always favoured the Xora and Bashee river vicinity. And still this ship eluded me right at the very end. A further aerial investigation with Bill Elston, who had seen a ship from the air just north of the Xora River in the 1960s, also showed nothing for our subsequent survey efforts. So what did all these observers see and witness over a period of half a century between 1909 and the 1960s? I believe that Edward Joe Conquer had witnessed this troubled ship become a *Poseidon* adventure through the eyepiece of his telescope off the Xora River in 1909.

Like the *Nailsea Meadow*, this was not where the *Waratah* finally came to rest. She must have been taken by the current further south down the coast, but by no means to where Peter Humphries expected her to sink. The weather conditions at the time and the ship's instability would have sent her to the bottom long before the 1983 search area. It is feasible that the *Waratah* finally came to rest in very deep water off the continental shelf and beyond reach. With regards to what Lieutenant Roos had seen, that is as deep as the mystery itself. The search for the *Waratah* had always been by way of design, but not an impossibility to locate a shipwreck by chance. Perhaps someday a survey will

2003 deck-work:
assembling technology.
Back row: Dough
Slogrove (technician);
crew member, *Ocean
Stroom*; Mitty Chelin
(master, *Ocean Stroom*);
Front row: John
Costello (author and
photographer); Warwick
Miller (geophysicist);
Emlyn Brown
(expedition leader);
Dr Peter Ramsay
(geologist/chief
surveyor). (Courtesy of
Emlyn Brown)

take place off the east coast and an anomaly will display itself on the screen and, with a casual or inquisitive closer look, may reveal itself as the *Waratah*.

I continue to review my research and survey reports with the feeling that something will attract my attention enough to set off once more and find the *Waratah* – she is not going anywhere, she will be found.

E.R. Brown,
2009

Should you wish to contact Emlyn or find out more about his work and how you might become involved, then please visit him at <u>emlynbrown@gmail.com</u>

In Conclusion

Now that we reach the end of the book, having shared experiences with men a century ago searching islands and oceans for a disabled ship, as well as Emlyn Brown's more recent quest beneath the waves, it is up to you to reach your own conclusions about the *Waratah*'s secret. Throughout the theories, hoaxes and premonitions she has stubbornly remained shrouded in mystery. Never has a ship been so hunted and puzzled over. This modern age, with the innovations and techniques now available, should be the perfect time to focus our attention back to the mission and finally locate the forgotten ship. One hundred years ago it was a challenge beyond imagination; now we have the technology.

Amongst the many possible hoaxes are the words of a man who claimed he had been part of the crew on the stricken vessel. He said that he had been on deck when he spotted a girl of about ten hiding and in a state of fear – presumably due to the weather. The man was Mr John Noble, and he described the ship suddenly lurching heavily, throwing both of them to starboard and into the water. He said he managed to get the girl safely to shore off East London. This remarkable story was told on his deathbed by Mr Noble, a Canadian seaman, to a nurse who transcribed his words as a statement sworn in the Oshawa Hospital, Canada, in 1932. Although no John Noble from Canada was listed among the *Waratah*'s crew, it is not impossible that he joined at the last minute. In his statement he produced a copy of Lloyd's listing for the *Waratah* and recounted talk of mutiny among the crew, to which he said he was not a party. He said they fell overboard at around 4.00 a.m. on 23 July, which does not tie in with the date the *Waratah* went missing, but it is possible this date should have read 28 July.

Whilst it would be easy to dismiss this story, the South African police did in fact report a man and child seen wandering in East London in early August 1909. They vanished before the police were able to make further enquiries but this story illustrates perfectly the many questions hanging over the disappearance of the *Waratah*. As seems inevitable with this mystery, each new piece of information seems to complicate the story further, merely raising more questions than it answers. The *Waratah* may take some coaxing yet before she will reveal her story to a fascinated world.

I feel enormous pity for those close to the people lost on board; to never be able to draw a line under a situation such as this would have been a horrific burden. More dives are needed, as is an ongoing project for gathering and checking out information which may have been kept out of the public arena, much as these journals have been. They reveal a huge amount and there may be more accounts by interested parties tucked away in a dusty corner somewhere.

The southern seas are treacherous and many ships had their final voyages within the search areas. When one considers all the evidence, including the size of the search ships

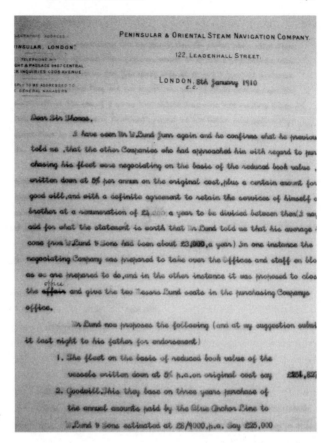

P&O letter in Blue Anchor
takeover.

and the weather they successfully endured, it does seem remarkable that the *Waratah* would have sunk – and yet everything ultimately points to that conclusion. Perhaps at some point a completely new field of thought will emerge. I hope that this book awakens interest in the tale; that it may inspire someone to write the rest of the story, to uncover what really did happen that night.

I have come across some remarkable people and stories in writing this book and have enjoyed it all; it confirms that people really do have an interest in past events and moreover that they are willing to help, as the many offers of pictures and information have been most appreciated. It is my belief that in time more information will become available. Walter's journal was filed in an old case in my attic for many, many years and I have been privileged to have had access to other such exceptional journals. People around the world may have their own pieces of information, or have heard stories handed down through their families, all of which might be able shed a little ray of light on the mystery and enable us to say one day, 'So that is what happened, how extraordinary!'

A website is to be set up to share information which is not in the book and for ideas to be discussed and debated. It would be marvellous to be able to finish the story.

P.J. Smith

BIBLIOGRAPHY

There are no definitive books upon the *Waratah* and the journals are the main essence of the book but many sources were of course used for other sections including the genealogy section for passengers and crew.

General

State Library of South Australia
State Library of Victoria
Flinders Ranges Research, South Australia
National Archives, Kew, England
National Archives, South Africa
National Archives, Australia
Australian dictionary of biography
Australian historical newspapers
Department of Justice births marriages and wills, Victoria, Australia
Irish Times; Scotsman; The Times; Toronto Daily Star

South Africa magazine
New Zealand historical papers
Hansard
Wreck site
Scots End genealogy South Africa
UK census and Scotland census
UK passenger lists
Ships' Nostalgia (www.shipsnostalgia.com)
rapidtp.co.za/museum/research
www.theshipslist.com including Ted Finch
Wikipedia

Books and Articles

Basil Greenhill, *Merhant Schooners* (Conway Maritime Press, 1988)
Peter Kemp (Ed.), *The Oxford Companion to Ships and the Sea*
David Reynolds, *A Century of South African Tugs* (Downstairs Graphics and Publications, 1981)
Clarence Winchester (Ed.), *Shipping Wonders of the World* Vols I and II (The Fleetway House, London)

Peter Ilbery, 'The Loss of the *Waratah*', 1909, Courtesy of the British Library QLF11451

Other Sources

Many genealogy sites were looked at and of special note is the site by Mike Scott-Williams and his special interest in *Waratah*.
Material supplied by Greenwich Maritime Museum
Material supplied by Archives of the United Kingdom Hydrographic Office
Material supplied by P&O Dubai

Visit our website and discover thousands of other History Press books.
www.thehistorypress.co.uk